COMMUNITY DEVELOPMENT ON THE NORTH ATLANTIC MARGIN

Community Development on the North Atlantic Margin

Selected contributions to the fifteenth international seminar on marginal regions

Edited by
REGINALD BYRON and JOHN HUTSON
University of Wales, Swansea

Routledge
Taylor & Francis Group

LONDON AND NEW YORK

First published 2001 by Ashgate Publishing

Reissued 2018 by Routledge
2 Park Square, Milton Park, Abingdon, Oxon OX14 4RN
711 Third Avenue, New York, NY 10017, USA

Routledge is an imprint of the Taylor & Francis Group, an informa business

Publisher's Note
The publisher has gone to great lengths to ensure the quality of this reprint but points out that some imperfections in the original copies may be apparent.

Disclaimer
The publisher has made every effort to trace copyright holders and welcomes correspondence from those they have been unable to contact.

A Library of Congress record exists under LC control number: 2001090207

ISBN 13: 978-1-138-73259-9 (hbk)
ISBN 13: 978-1-138-73255-1 (pbk)
ISBN 13: 978-1-315-18836-2 (ebk)

Contents

List of Contributors

Jørgen Amdam is Professor in the Department of Commune Planning and Administration at Volda University College, Norway.

Richard Apostle is Professor in the Department of Sociology and Social Anthropology at Dalhousie University, Halifax, Nova Scotia, Canada.

Paul Olav Berg is Professor at Nordland University College, Bødo, Norway.

Reginald Byron is Professor of Sociology and Anthropology at the University of Wales, Swansea, Wales.

Michael Christie is a Lecturer in the Welsh Institute of Rural Studies, University of Wales, Aberystwyth, Wales.

Jens Christian Hansen is Professor of Geography at the University of Bergen, Norway.

John Hutson is Lecturer in Social Anthropology at the University of Wales, Swansea.

Susan Hutson is Senior Lecturer in the Department of Sociology at the University of Glamorgan, Pontypridd, Wales.

Tim Jenkins is Senior Research Fellow in the Welsh Institute of Rural Studies, University of Wales, Aberystwyth, Wales.

Stuart Jones is a graduate student in Sociology, School of Humanities and Social Sciences, University of Glamorgan, Pontypridd, Wales.

Alison McCleery is Professor in the Faculty of Arts and Social Science, Napier University, Edinburgh, Scotland.

Diarmuid Ó Cearbhaill is Statutory Lecturer in Economics at the International Centre for Development Studies, National University of Ireland, Galway, Ireland.

Nicholas Parrott is a member of the Welsh Institute of Rural Studies, University of Wales, Aberystwyth, Wales.

Anne-Marie Sherwood is a Research Officer in the Rural Economy Research Group at the Welsh Institute of Rural Studies, University of Wales, Aberystwyth, Wales.

Peter Sjøholt is Professor of Geography in the Norwegian School of Economics and Business Administration, Bergen, Norway.

Håvard Teigen is Senior Lecturer at Lillehammer University College, Lillehammer, Norway.

Tony Varley is a member of the Department of Political Science and Sociology, National University of Ireland, Galway, Ireland.

Foreword

This volume brings together a selection of papers which address the theme of the Fifteenth International Seminar on Marginal Regions held in Newfoundland, Canada, in the summer of 1999. As has become customary, the seminar was held in two centres where participants were able to visit local development organisations and enterprise sites. The seminar began in St John's, from where we visited a number of local communities on the southern shore and studied their problems and opportunities. We then transferred to Terra Nova, where we saw more local economic development problems and projects on the Bonavista Peninsula.

Our hosts for the Seminar were Peter Sinclair, of the Memorial University of Newfoundland, and Richard Apostle of Dalhousie University in Halifax, Nova Scotia. The Atlantic Canada Opportunities Agency gave generous support to the seminar, for which we are most grateful. Our thanks must also go to Sean Cadigan of Dalhousie University, whose knowledge of the history of the communities we visited added a great deal to our appreciation of community development efforts in the region.

The editors have endeavoured to do justice to the wide range of papers given at the Seminar. We hope that the selection chosen will interest a wide variety of specialists and practitioners with interests in the economic and social welfare of communities on the North Atlantic margin.

PART I
NEW PERSPECTIVES ON COMMUNITY DEVELOPMENT

1 Looking to the Land: Regional Imagery, Quality Products and Development Strategy in Marginal Rural Regions

TIM JENKINS AND NICHOLAS PARROTT

Introduction

The "Rural" in Society

Rural areas in the Europe of today are characterised by three key features. Firstly, they are subject to processes which originate beyond the immediate locale (Lowe, 1996), and they respond in contrasting ways to the demands and opportunities facing them. Marginal rural areas, usually characterised by unfavourable farm structures and relative economic isolation, are likely to respond less positively than more favoured areas, thereby becoming even more marginal. Inter-linkage between the global and the local is particularly evident in the agricultural sector where local production of foods may be directly affected by global agreements and by global supply and demand trends (Marsden et al., 1990). Secondly, rural areas are increasingly characterized by diversity---in populations, economies and lifestyles. Rural areas are increasingly sites of new economic activities (e.g. tourism and recreation) as well as agricultural production, a "post-productivist" diversity which is the result of the in-migration of new people (Murdoch and Marsden, 1994) and policy encouragement. Thirdly, and most importantly in the context of this paper, rural areas are increasingly seen as both sites of consumption and as commodities in themselves. An increasingly key aim of rural policy is to satisfy public demand for high quality rural environments. The establishment of regional imagery and the production and consumption of quality products are both integral ingredients in such development.

Endogenous Rural Development

In general terms, rural development thinking has shifted its focus in recent years from narrow economics (e.g. job creation or raising regional income) to

3

more holistic concerns which see development as a process of improving the "total human condition" (Keane, 1990). One characteristic of this shift is the replacement of exogenous development dependent on external influence and investment by the encouragement of endogenous development strategies which emphasise the role of local people and institutions in the planning, implementation and evaluation of development programmes. Endogenous development has not proceeded without difficulty. Concentration on "the local" as a mobilising force brings the danger of ignoring wider structural issues such as the global processes mentioned above. Further, power over the definition and control of development may remain largely in the hands of authorities, and UK experience suggests that moves towards "partnership" approaches to rural development are often ad hoc, co-existent with more traditional models of local action, and conditioned by the particular economic, institutional and socio-political context of localities. Development in Wales, for example, has been dominated by the actions of an array of quasi-autonomous agencies whose perceived lack of accountability has been the source of much political ill-feeling.

Rural Development Policy and Performance

Traditional policy and organisational responses to rural development problems have generally concentrated on improvements to physical infrastructure in rural areas, stimulation of business development and growth, diversification of the economic base, and attraction of inward investment. Even where such policies are construed as effective within an administrative region (e.g. in Wales), they may have the effect of further marginalising outlying and less favoured areas within that region (e.g. in west Wales). Concentrating development projects in and around large settlements, for example, is often incompatible with traditional patterns of dispersed settlement and may pull real or potential jobs away from peripheral areas.

Two fundamental issues can be identified with respect to rural development performance. Firstly, policy has traditionally been sectorally-driven and hence dominated by agricultural considerations. Despite initiatives stressing diversification and the production of environmental goods (Jenkins, 1990), and despite the apparent shift from productivist logic towards a "logic of quality" (Allaire and Sylvander, 1997), agricultural support has been overwhelmingly oriented towards productivism. This has resulted in intensification of production, specialisation at both regional and farm level in a diminished range of activity, growth in average farm size, reduction in the number of farms and farmers (Hughes et al., 1996), and inflated land prices. Together with a restrictive planning policy, this process has reduced the scope and motivation for diversification into non-agricultural activities. Pressure for reform of the sectoral approach to policy is often relatively recent: the 1996 White Paper on the Welsh Countryside stresses the need for more integrative policies and the development of partnerships; and increasingly important EU funding is beginning to encourage integrated and locally-led approaches to rural development. In contrast, development activities in Scotland have long been characterised by a mix of spatial and sectoral policy, the implementation of a mix of bottom-up and top-down development policies (Hughes, 1992), and an increased awareness of the importance of integrated development.

The second issue in rural development performance is that of where resources should be focused---on problems or on opportunities. Arguably, the focus in Wales has consistently been on problems---of peripherality, poor infrastructure, agricultural decline, and the lack of an enterprise culture. In contrast, a focus on opportunities may mean more interest in the links between economic development on the one hand and the environment, cultural identity and language on the other; and heightened awareness of the globalization of markets and increased market competition, and hence of the importance of marketing as a development tool. Again, the Scottish contrast is instructive--- even the names of "Scottish Enterprise" and "Highlands and Islands Enterprise" seem ideologically linked to the exploitation of opportunities.

At EU level, the need for CAP spending reductions means strong policy support for productive diversification and away from productivism. Quality farm food marketing schemes have been suggested as instruments for long-term economic and environmental sustainability (Gilg and Battershill, 1998; Ilbery and Kneafsey, 1998) and for the protection of local farming systems by developing consumer demand for regionally identifiable and quality-assured foods (Marsden, 1998). New directions for policy include measures which build on the existing skills and resources locally available in rural areas and which encourage the development of markets based on demand for those resources.

Overview

Against this background, the remainder of this chapter is in five sections. Section 2 conceptualises the issue of regional imagery and quality production in rural development, drawing on a variety of sources. Sections 3 and 4 discuss the concepts of quality products and regional imagery which are then linked in section 5. Section 6 offers some conclusions for rural development strategy. The chapter is based on findings from a multi-disciplinary project entitled "Regional Imagery and the Promotion of Quality Products and Services in the Lagging Regions of the EU" (RIPPLE)[1] (Ilbery et al., 1999; Ilbery and Kneafsey, 1999b). The project focussed on 12 marginal regions in six countries and on a limited number of quality products and services (QPS) in each region. Interview surveys were conducted of producers, consumers and institutions relating to the chosen QPS within each study region.

Conceptual Perspectives

The analysis of regional imagery and quality product promotion requires an appropriate underlying conceptualisation relevant to marginal regions. The following draws on four main bodies of literature: marketing theory, regulation theory, actor network theory and consumption geographies.

Marketing

Marketing has long been a weakness in the rural development process, particularly in marginal regions, because of the small scale of many individual producers and the undifferentiated nature of their products. Lack of concern with demand factors, lack of skills in product presentation, and limited development of marketing networks have all led to dependence by agriculturally-based marginal rural areas on guaranteed markets and outside intermediaries. Yet, lagging regions have resources of potential market value in a climate of rising incomes, nostalgia for rurality, and homogenisation of production, as food markets become more differentiated on the basis of a range of socially constructed quality criteria. Certain aspects of marketing are, therefore, potentially important in rural development. These include the marketing competence and strategies of producers; the market awareness and decisions of consumers; market structures and the marketing environment; and the role of institutions and policy in facilitating competitiveness (Jenkins and Parrott, 1997).

From a marketing perspective, "quality" refers to the totality of features and characteristics of a product or service that bear on its ability to satisfy needs (Kotler, 1997). It is a key to the creation of value and customer satisfaction, although the concept can vary between consumers, products and markets. Quality-specific product differentiation can result from four processes (Jenkins and Parrott, 1997):

- certification by professional organisations, government, or other external bodies---e.g. appellations d'origine contrôlée certifications and organic symbols

- association---geographically with a region or locality (e.g. Scottish salmon or Welsh lamb), historically with a tradition or culture (e.g. crafts using Welsh slate or whisky using traditional Scottish production methods), or

6

through product traceabilty (e.g. cheese from a particular farmhouse dairy)

- specification---of production method (e.g. small-scale workshops or "authentic" recipes), or of raw materials (e.g. local wool or water from a particular spring)

- the generation of attraction by tapping into the subliminal wants of consumers---e.g. fashionable designs or attractive flavours.

Whatever the method used, the marketing objective is to generate a perception of quality which results in commercially significant differentiation in the eyes of consumers and commercially significant value-extraction on the part of producers.

An "image" in marketing terms refers to the set of beliefs, ideas and impressions held by a person about a product, and it comprises both rational and emotional elements (Graby, 1993). An effective image can benefit a product by defining its character and differentiating it from competitors, by delivering "emotional power" within potential buyers, and by establishing its value. Imagery concerns how reality is perceived rather than how it intrinsically is, and images have marketing consequences for market analysis (particularly with regard to consumer behaviour), marketing strategy (particularly with regard to product differentiation and positioning) and marketing programmes (particularly with regard to the appropriate marketing mix).

Quality and image are closely linked concepts in marketing. An image of product quality, or of a producer's concern for quality, can be created through the subtle use of the physical cues identified as relevant to consumers' judgement of quality. Quality can also be communicated through marketing elements such as premium pricing, packaging and the marketing channels used. Many speciality cheesemakers in Wales, for example, prefer delicatessen-type outlets over supermarkets because of the aura of quality which they bring.

Regulation Theory

Regulation theory allows theorisation of the broad institutional and economic processes which influence rural development. Its starting point is an analysis of how fundamental social relations are maintained in the face of the antagonisms that they produce. It is constructed around two key concepts: the régime of accumulation (the organisation of production, income distribution, exchange and consumption), and the mode of regulation (the institutional forms, procedures and habits which ensure that agents conform to its demands) (Murdoch, 1995; Ilbery and Kneafsey, 1999b). In relation to rural development, regulation theory views changes in global food systems in terms of progression through a series of food régimes (Fine, 1994; Goodman and Redclift, 1994). The current régime is characterised by the growth of trans-national food companies, reductions in government support for agriculture, and moves towards the liberalisation of agricultural trade; but it is also associated with increased flexibility in production, and increasingly discerning consumers concerned about production methods, variety and food quality. These latter characteristics provide the impetus for the development of new activities in rural areas, such as farmhouse processing (e.g. the recent growth of speciality cheesemaking in Wales), an interest in filling market niches (e.g. those for organic products), and growth in the speciality food sector.

Regulation theory has been criticised for its structuralist and economistic approach which ignores aspects such as cultural practices, social norms and non-dominant forms of accumulation, especially in peripheral regions (Flynn and Marsden, 1995). Responses to this critique have involved the adoption of a multi-layered concept of regulation (the "local modes of social regulation" ---Clark et al., 1997) which focuses on the complex social relations between actors who operate at a variety of spatial scales with a variety of motives and values. Local places do not simply react to global forces, but are part of an "interactive" process in which local actions can have consequences at a wider scale. In this way, policies are influenced by local specificities which feed back into national and international regulation.

Actor-network Theory

Whereas regulationist approaches adopt a structuralist framework by explaining new economic forms in terms of external economic, societal or structural pressures, network analysis adopts a more internalised approach, viewing the economy as a "grid" of inter-relations between actors who define themselves and their interests in the context of relationships with others. Networks can be defined as consciously created and structured relationships with specific economic, social or political purposes; and actor-network theory seeks to understand economic structures as the outcomes of active attempts to construct, impose and maintain such networks. An analysis of power, seen as the outcome of social processes and of collective action, is central to such analysis.

Actor-network theory has been applied to the analysis of change in the British countryside (Marsden et al., 1993). Actors are defined as the loci of decision and action, and distinctions are made between the market arena where actors as producers (e.g. producers of quality products) represent themselves economically, the social arena where actors as consumers (e.g. actual and potential consumers of quality products) represent themselves socially, and the regulation arena where institutional actors (e.g. organisations charged with promoting quality products) represent themselves politically. These processes of representation lead to various types of rurality being promoted, and the strength of representations depends on the power of the networks through which they are established. In turn, this depends on the economic, social and political positions of the actors involved and the nature of the relationships that they build. Institutional, regional and self-regulatory quality marks for food products are thereby seen as representations through which producers attempt to build networks with consumers and institutions with producers. The RIPPLE surveys showed that, within and between the relevant groups of actors involved with quality products, there exists a variety of actor networks ---formal or informal, horizontal or vertical, ideological or commercial, and voluntary or enforced.

Consumption Geographies

Consumption geographies explore the role of consumption in the construction, representation and experience of place. Consumption, particularly of food, is an important factor in the construction of place identity (Crang, 1996), and has been interpreted as a place-creating act (Sack, 1992) with social and cultural meanings (Marsden, 1996; Bell and Valentine, 1997). Consumer behaviour is of particular interest: with regard to food, many consumers are increasingly interested in, and knowledgeable about, its origins, the farming practices involved, the processes through which food is transformed into consumer products, and food safety.

Consumption is increasingly conceptualised as a process intimately bound up with the construction of consumers' personal identities in terms of status and belonging (Giddens, 1991; Jackson and Thrift, 1995). Two main interpretations of the relationship between consumption practices and individual identity can be distinguished (Glennie and Thrift, 1996). The first stresses the process of cultural fragmentation, whose features include the disappearance of stable social markers (e.g. class or traditional gender roles), the challenge to tradition and ritual, and the disappearance of place-specificity in everyday life. Cultural fragmentation tends to empty objects of wider cultural meanings, suggesting that consumption is simply a utility-based process centred on individual identity. The second interpretation is that, through a process of reflexive modernisation, the human sense of self is deepening, and this opens up many positive as well as negative possibilities for social relations which can be reinforced by consumption. In place of earlier homogeneous class-centred constellations of consumers, the process produces social and market segmentation and many consumer sub-groups, features integral to increasingly reflexive contemporary societies. As a result of growing cognitive reflexivity, social relationships and consumption decisions rely less on the traditional social structures of class, family and mass production, and more on the increasing amounts of knowledge generated by a growing number of political, scientific and marketing institutions.[2] Equally importantly, reflexivity is aesthetic and "aesthetic cultural capital" (Ilbery and Kneafsey, 1999b) is attached to consumption goods, especially food which is central to the construction of "lifestyles" (Bell and Valentine, 1997).

Hence, taste, aesthetics, sensibility, personalisation of demand, and quality are increasingly important to consumers at the expense of traditional features such as price and convenience. Such trends indicate a growing potential market for regional QPS which can be produced and marketed in a way which exploits the "cultural meanings" attached to their locations of origin.

Conceptual Issues and the RIPPLE Surveys

This conceptual framework was used for the RIPPLE surveys of producers, consumers and institutions (Jenkins et al., 1998; Parrott et al., 1999a; Parrott et al., 1999b). Ideas from the four areas outlined above were used to ensure theoretically-informed questioning aimed at a better understanding of crucial themes. These include the marketing of QPS specifically from marginal regions; the links between national/international and local/regional modes of regulation and accumulation; the links between geographies of production and consumption; the significance of "the rural" as a site of consumption; the ways in which meanings are constructed around particular products and places; and the extent to which regional QPS contribute to endogenous development through the configuration of networks at local and extra-local levels.

Traditional marketing theory suggests that producers treat demand as "given", identify it through market research, and seek to satisfy it through appropriate production and marketing. Small QPS producers in marginal regions, however, often lack local markets, are short of the resources and skills required to enter more distant markets, and have little flexibility in production. They therefore need alternative ways of representing themselves and their products in the market arena, and may use less formal methods to build networks based on trust, traceability and product quality. In fact, such network characteristics often offer a potential competitive advantage: the BSE affair, for example, damaged trust in conventional production and marketing patterns to the benefit of many traditional extensive livestock producers. The RIPPLE producer survey showed that alliances with other actors are largely through personalised relationships characterised by trust and traceability; and that product quality is defined in terms of production method, raw materials and personal involvement rather than in terms of consumer perception or product promotion.

10

Consumer behaviour theory stresses the importance of the social arena and the construction of personal identities in terms of status and belonging, suggesting that consumer perspectives on QPS are not necessarily regionally-focussed. Ethical demand in the form of organic or animal-friendly products, for example, are not territorially-delimited. However, a sizeable minority of consumers are interested in the processes involved in the food production and marketing chain, and the RIPPLE consumer survey showed that for many consumers traceability and freshness are of primary importance, as is support for the local economy: this effectively leads to demand for food with clear local or regional origins. Trends within the social arena, therefore, suggest a strengthening of markets for regional QPS produced by identifiable small producers using traditional methods and inputs. In contrast, wider awareness of regional products appears strongly related to tourism and travel, suggesting that current developments in the leisure sector also contribute to a general strengthening of markets for regional QPS.

Institutions operate largely in the regulation arena, seeking to help producers in product marketing and to guarantee product quality to consumers. Institutional actors thus build networks by enrolling producers and consumers in the process of constructing quality and exploiting regional imagery. By involving geographical origin in product identity, they transform local knowledge into property that is exploitable by localities and their producers (Ray, 1998). However, the RIPPLE institutional survey showed this regulatory pattern to be characterised by conflict between institutions operating at different geographical scales. The EU's PDO/PGI regulations, for example, often conflict with national views which see national images as more powerful means to product differentiation than regional ones, and with local views which see individual producers' brands as more marketable than regional designations. The survey also confirmed the tendency for institutions to compete to enrol producers and consumers into networks, and it showed that close formal co-operation between producers and institutions is rare, largely due to the wide range of institutional objectives and functions found within any single study region.

Quality Products and Services

Definitions of Quality

Quality can be both an objective attribute which can be externally verified, measured, controlled and replicated; and a subjective experiential phenomenon which varies between individuals, regions and countries. Useful definitions of quality products must implicitly accept this potentially conflicting ambivalence (Sylvander, 1993). More precise definitions of quality vary by product: organic product quality, for example, is defined in terms of authenticity (guaranteed by the production processes), ethics (the result of environmentally-friendly production methods), and biological, sensorial and nutritional aspects (Vastoia, 1997). Quality of other food products is often associated with "traceability" which provides consumers with (often vague) guarantees of quality. An essential feature of quality, whether it is communicated through a focus on management processes (e.g. through ISO standards), the products themselves (e.g. through eco-labelling), or marketing devices (e.g. high prices, attractive packaging or advertising), is that it is a "positional" characteristic. It positively differentiates products above norms or minimum standards in ways recognised by consumers, and is therefore able to command a market benefit, normally in the form of a price premium (anon., 1993). Quality, therefore, can give competitive advantage to products, processes, producers or regions.

Going beyond a marketing perspective, the conceptualisation of food quality involves a number of considerations (Ilbery and Kneafsey, 1999a). Firstly, a product's quality is determined by the many-faceted interactions of all those involved in its realisation and appreciation---i.e. all the actors in the marketing chain from initial producer to final consumer, each of whom may entertain different perceptions of quality. Secondly, constructions of quality are dependent on the social, cultural, economic and political context in which they are determined. Thirdly, the concept of quality is dynamically (re-) negotiated among the actors involved. Powerful actors can potentially appropriate the concept for their own products to enhance their own market position: most quality assurance schemes, for example, are initiated and controlled by large corporate retailers (Fearne and Kuznetsof, 1994), and their terms (e.g. high levels of product hygiene and consistency) may be beyond the means of many small producers.

Perceptions of Quality

Although quality is constructed by numerous different actors, there has been little research into how it is perceived by these actors. Actor-network approaches suggest the inherently political nature of quality construction in a competitive market place, as with the French appellation d'origine contrôlée laws under which prestigious wine-making regions establish a monopoly rent (Moran, 1993). The concept of quality can also be theorised as a representation through which producers, consumers and institutions attempt to establish and maintain stable alliances. The most stable alliances are likely when the concepts of quality held by each of these groups are in broad alignment. Successful marketing of QPS requires producer and institutional actors to align their representations as closely as possible with those of consumers, suggesting the importance of market research, demand-led production, and targetted marketing.

The analysis of quality perception by consumers is rooted in psychology and psychometrics (Vastoia, 1997). The RIPPLE consumer survey showed that few consumers deny buying what they regard to be quality items, at least occasionally---an unsurprising finding, given that quality product consumption contributes to construction of personal identities. Manufacturers' brands and named retailers are the most important indicators of quality; whereas appearance, presentation, and specific regional provenance are less important. Clearly, trust is important to consumers---specifically, trust in major manufacturers and retailers: such trust is presumably based on the assumption that quality control is more effectively enforced within a hierarchical company than within a region of disparate and independent actors, and suggests the importance of traceability and official quality marks as quality indicators for regional products. However, a significant proportion of food consumers are less concerned with the most easily definable aspects of quality (such as official certification, geographical or cultural association, or specification of production method or raw materials) than with features such as freshness. Freshness in turn is often associated with local provenance, suggesting the importance of clearly defined networks involving local producers, intermediaries and consumers, possibly in the form of direct selling which recognises the importance of the social context of purchasing decisions.

The RIPPLE producer survey showed that producers' constructions of quality vary widely according to product. Many producers prefer objective notions of quality, related to animal husbandry (e.g. specific cattle breeds), production method (e.g. the use of raw milk for cheesemaking), or official certification (e.g. organic certification); while others stress subjective elements such as flavour (e.g. in speciality cheeses), product differentiation (e.g. niche marketing of small lambs), or product originality (e.g. in craft production). The extent to which such quality constructions align with those of consumers also varies widely. Objective constructions may align closely with the requirements of the major multiple retailers (e.g. for meat) and for some committed final consumers (e.g. those concerned with animal or environmental welfare); while the alignment of subjective constructions may be less easily ensured (e.g. the flavour of cheese or the attractiveness of crafts may depend on the assumption that discerning consumers will have similar standards). However, product differentiation often entails the risks of promoting subjective constructions of quality.

Quality constructions among institutions surveyed under RIPPLE include objective, subjective, relative and absolute definitions, with most respondents hesitant to define quality in terms of one particular factor, tangible or intangible. However, a stress on consumer perception, presentation and promotion suggest a strong marketing approach to quality, as does a strong institutional awareness that perceptions of quality differ significantly between customers, market segments, products and stages of the marketing chain. The more formalised constructs of quality popular with consumers, such as certification and traceability, are less valued among institutions, although their importance is more noticeable in sectors which have well-established, widely recognised, independently verified, premia-generating quality assurance schemes. There is growing emphasis within institutional circles on developing and communicating concepts of quality. Often, this is part of a strategy to create market niches and differentiate products, but in some cases it is with the aim of achieving a price premium, and in others it is seen as necessary purely to maintain market share. Many multi-sectoral agencies also undertake activities (e.g. product development and training programmes) in which quality promotion is integral but not explicit.

Regional Imagery

Regional Images and their Promotion

Regional images are representations of place involving meanings which may vary spatially between individuals and change over time. Place promotion is the conscious use of publicity and marketing to communicate selective images of specific geographical localities (Gold and Ward, 1994), or the selling of a selected package of facilities or of a whole place through images composed of associated attributes (Ashworth and Vogt, 1994). Although place promotion has a long history, the conscious application of marketing techniques to places as a solution to planning problems, and increasingly as a philosophy of place management, is relatively new. An even more recent focus has been on the promotion of rural places, especially in the tourism literature: of particular relevance here are trends in cultural, heritage or green tourism in which tourists seek experiences specifically associated with rural areas. European policies (e.g. LEADER) have also fostered the promotion of rural places, not only as the basis for tourism but also as an aid to the development of the strong sense of community regarded as a necessary pre-requisite for successful endogenous development (Ray, 1996).

Commodification of Regional Images

Different aspects of regional image can be "commodified" for promotional purposes by a variety of actors, including local authorities, tourist boards, producer groups and private sector companies. "Commodification" suggests that certain ingredients of images (such as local cultures) can become products with exchange value. The Scottish Tourist Board, for example, describes Scotland's tourism "product" as its landscape, culture and people; and the commercialisation of Scottish culture has meant that certain artefacts (e.g. tartan) have become emblematic of Scotland and its products. The linking of specific products to the "cultural markers" of regional image can, in principle, enhance the value of those products, and rural areas can re-valorise themselves through their cultural identity (Ray, 1998), thereby retaining more of the value-added accruing to products produced within them and taking more control over their economic activity.

In general, links between products and their region of production are not well-developed in the UK, in contrast to some other EU countries, notably France. To an extent, this is associated with the difficulties of creating effective place images: in marketing terms, it is a problem of defining the "product" and the target market within which it will be "consumed" (Gold and Ward, 1994). Regional images operate at a variety of levels; they can be promoted differently for different purposes to different consumers; and assessing the effectiveness of promotional campaigns is complex, given that perceptions are moulded by many different influences and that stereotypes are resilient and long-lasting. There is also no necessary coincidence between the jurisdictional boundaries of a promotional authority and the spatial units "consumed" by visitors, residents or product buyers. Thus, for example, although it may make developmental sense to regard west Wales as a unitary region because it faces common problems of peripherality and underdevelopment, it is far from unitary in terms of landscape, culture and administration.

Like constructions of quality, regional imagery is assembled, or created, from a combination of many sources. Also, as with quality, regional images can be understood as representations which actors use to try and establish stable networks. For instance, institutions may construct a particular regional image and make use of regional imagery to complement incentive packages such as duty-free industrial zones, food centres and national technology parks in order to attract inward investment. Producers, however, may have a narrower view of regional image shaped by their own experiences of living and running a business within the region: they are, therefore, often aware of negative aspects of regional imagery, such as economic problems, geographic peripherality or certain stereotypes, and it may be difficult for them to regard it as a useful form of product differentiation which can relate to both tangible and intangible aspects of their products and help them to establish networks with consumers. Consumers' perceptions of regional imagery may be shaped by their own experiences as tourists, residents or onlookers; and by the constructions of others, such as film and television programmes, newspaper and magazine articles, music, novels, and hearsay, as well as formal sources such as public authority promotional schemes and travel literature.

As with quality constructions, the most stable networks and alliances are created when the regional images held by producers, consumers and institutions are in broad alignment. It follows that for regional imagery to be successfully used in the marketing of QPS, producer and institutional actors should seek to align their representations with those of consumers. The RIPPLE surveys in west Wales showed a strong convergence between producer and consumer perceptions of the Welsh regional image, with both sets of actors referring to rurality and high environmental quality, and with an awareness of negative aspects to the image, such as lack of enterprise and inward-lookingness. Yet, the extent to which producers make use of positive imagery depends on the type of products and how they are marketed, and there is accordingly wide divergence in the use of regional imagery in product marketing. Some producers (notably in cheese and craft sectors) see severe drawbacks in using regional imagery, both in terms of differentiating their own products and in terms of overall maintenance of Welsh product quality. Such differing perceptions lead to fragmented networks being developed, making it difficult, for example, to envisage an institutionally-led common approach to the marketing of Welsh products.

In fact, in seeking to identify the most powerful producers of regional images, the scope for institutional involvement often seems marginal. A popular TV programme or novel can influence public perceptions of a region more substantially and directly than an institutional promotion campaign. Knowledge about where consumers get their information also suggests that consumer perceptions of regional imagery and quality exist in spite of, or independently of, marketing strategies. There are also clear conflicts between actors as to the type of image to be promoted, most notably as between a traditional image (stressing culture and heritage) and a modern one (stressing progressiveness and dynamism). Again, this suggests that actor networks are likely to be fragmented as different groups of actors operationalise their different views.

Regional Images and QPS

Regional Images and the Promotion of QPS

In policy terms, the construction of quality is increasingly related to products invested with the "cultural capital" of specified regions. EU legislation (Council Regulation 2081/92) protects food products which are produced in defined geographic areas and which possess characteristics either essentially due to their geographic environment (Protected Designation of Origin---PDO), or attributable to their geographical origin (Protected Geographical Indication---PGI). However, such protective devices rest on the assumption that location of production defines and guarantees quality (an assumption which may not always accord with consumers' perceptions); and that configurations of actors involved in niche markets for regional QPS are able to resist the encroachment of more powerful networks, such as multiple retailers' own brands of "traditional" products.

With the exception of Moran's study of the French and American wine appellation systems, there is a paucity of research on the use of regional images to promote QPS. Moran cites the case of the French region of Châteauneuf-du-Pape, which historically did not have a reputation for premium wine and which could not be strongly distinguished environmentally from other parts of the Rhône valley. The establishment of a strong regional identity was, therefore, essential if the wines were to sell at high prices on the international market, and this was achieved through the appellation laws (Moran, 1993). The Châteauneuf-du-Pape name is now internationally recognised---a successful example of the linking of product quality and regional image.

Discourse analysis suggests that QPS producers encode meanings into the communications surrounding their products, but also that producers can never be sure how the encoded meanings will be understood since, whether visual, written or verbal, they are dependent on context (Burgess, 1989). The success of the imaginary geographies constructed in Scottish tourism, for example, lies in their resonance with perceptions and experiences already embedded in people's "commonsense understandings" of Scottish geography (Hughes, 1992). Similarly, the perceived "authenticity" of regional food in Northern England is based on personal factors, such as knowledge and experience, as well as on product-related factors (Tregear et al., 1997).

Linking Quality to Region of Origin in West Wales

The RIPPLE surveys in west Wales encompassed four sectors: lamb and beef, organic products, speciality cheese, and crafts. In most cases, producers do not always link quality to region of origin. Organic producers consider quality to lie in attributes and criteria directly related to raw materials and production methods---region of origin is, at best, irrelevant and, at worst, misleading since it deflects attention from true quality promotion. Speciality cheesemakers tend to see quality in terms of their own performance as producers rather than of region of origin, and consider that regional branding and promotion would reduce product differentiation rather than increase it.

Craftspeople may sometimes use regional labels and symbols to increase turnover and appeal to profitable market segments (principally tourists), but this is often done cynically in the belief that such consumers have a low conception of quality. For many craftspeople, quality is emphatically not linked in marketing terms[3] to region of origin since such linkage can act as a cover for poor quality crafts from free-riding producers.

A straightforward link between quality and region of origin is also difficult to discern among consumers. Unprompted, consumers tend to associate quality with particular manufacturers or retailers and with production method rather than with regional origin. Deeper probing, however, shows that quality is a subjective notion perceived differently by different actors with a variety of differing motives and values. Consumer perceptions of quality, for instance, are influenced by a range of factors (e.g. age, socio-economic status, education, gender, residence and lifestyle), which in turn help to shape consumers' responses to the use of regional images as an indicator of quality. Furthermore, studies of consumption geographies show that purchase decisions are also affected by the socio-economic context: products bought directly from (or which are directly traceable to) producers, for example, are potentially invested with greater degrees of "authenticity".

Institutions fall into two groups---those directly representing particular producer interests, and those with a more general developmental viewpoint. The extent to which the former link quality to region of origin largely matches that of the producers they represent: hence, lamb/beef is promoted in a way that makes an explicit quality-region link; organic produce is largely promoted independently of region; and crafts institutions generally make little use of overt regional imagery. The general developmental institutions, while appreciating the necessity to link quality with regional origin in consumers' minds, show little agreement over how such association can be implemented in practice. Not only do views differ over what constitutes quality, there is also divergence on the image which Welsh regional origin should convey. Should Wales be promoted as backwards-oriented, steeped in history and heritage, and noted for its traditional quality processes and products? Or should its forward-lookingness be stressed, with its potential for high-technology and contributions to a vibrant modern British and European culture? The problem is exacerbated since Wales has not hitherto been a high-profile region (in contrast to Scotland) either overseas or within Britain, suggesting the need to "re-brand" it.

Among the study sectors, lamb/beef is the most successful in achieving a clear link between quality and region of origin. Welsh lamb and beef promotional campaigns make specific reference to their Welsh origin; build upon the positive associations of Wales with livestock-rearing on traditional farms, green valleys and good stockmanship; and link such associations with

18

quality assurance. Lamb production in particular is seen by consumers as an extensive form of agriculture which makes use of environmentally attractive hill land and which is conducted by farmers continuing a traditional way of life. Such perceptions mean that it is relatively easy to link lamb with an attractive image of Wales in times of increasing environmental stress and quality of life concerns. In contrast, it is more difficult to envisage an effective association between product and place where products are not obviously land-based, where production methods are intensive, and where producers are more obviously business-oriented.

A persuasive alternative view of the link between quality and regional image is found in the organics and crafts sectors. Producers and institutions in both considered that product quality is the primary foundation upon which a regional image should be based. The implications of this insight---that products create the images---are that developmental effort is best expended on improving product and process quality, and that an appropriate image will naturally follow. Promoting a regional image in the hope that product quality will follow brings the danger that consumers feel cynically manipulated, and that unscrupulous free-riding is encouraged by producers of low quality products.

Conclusions

Niche Markets and Regional Development

Key policy-forming institutions suggest that the demand for regional QPS is strong. "Consumers are tending to attach greater importance to the quality of foodstuffs" and there is "a growing demand for agricultural products or foodstuffs with an identifiable geographic origin" (EU Regulation 2081/92). People are increasingly seeking "quality, scarcity and novelty of products" (OECD, 1995: 19), and the OECD advocates a strategy for rural development based on the development of "niche products" which target defined and un-exploited market segments in order to reduce the need for competition solely on the basis of price. Future directions for many rural areas, therefore, may include product differentiation strategies (e.g. quality marks) which help to create niche markets for QPS, and marginal regions may have particular opportunities in terms of their imagery and popular perceptions surrounding the traditionality and authenticity of their products. It is likely that many rural areas are not achieving their full potential in terms of marketing products which offer authenticity of place of origin to consumers with a growing interest in QPS.

Niche markets can bring together regional imagery and QPS, and can be conceptualised as the outcomes of the intersecting networks of particular producers, institutions and consumers. Actor-network theory suggests that all three sets of actors are engaged in a constant process of alliance-building in attempts to enrol allies into their networks through a process of representation of their own perceptions, needs or wants in relation to QPS. This conceptualisation is particularly applicable to producers and institutions, but it is also relevant to consumers since they increasingly seek to redefine rurality and authenticity. For example, the speciality cheese-making sector in west Wales is of comparatively recent origin, but consumer demand for its products has made it an integral part of the region's rural image.

The Extra-local Context of Regional Development

The "actor-oriented approach" to rural development (FitzSimmons and Goodman, 1998) emphasises Ray's insight that local development action is only fully understandable when juxtaposed with enabling extra-local forces (Ray, 1998) and a wider structural environment (Jenkins and Parrott, 1998). Producers operate within global production/consumption relationships; consumers' enthusiasm for regional QPS is informed by wider social movements such as environmentalism; and institutional conflicts arise at all geographical scales from the local to the global. Local and regional actors, therefore, build networks within a context of extra-local regulation and change; local networks are linked to extra-local ones through key agencies such as LEADER; and local processes are affected by extra-local interventions such as tourist flows. In short, local processes are embedded in, and feed back into, global processes in a continual cycle of interaction.

The precise configuration of a particular regional QPS network and its relations with extra-local networks contribute to its effectiveness in promoting rural development. Endogenous and exogenous processes in rural development are in dynamic tension, as each set of actors represents its own conceptions and demands; and the representations which dominate are those flowing through the most powerful networks. Nevertheless, representations are in social and regulatory, as well as economic arenas, such that power relations are not always obvious. Three examples can be cited. First, the policy goal of promoting and protecting regional QPS often conflicts with increasingly stringent requirements in response to wider food hygiene concerns. These impose intolerable costs on some small QPS producers, suggesting that events (or the media's interpretation of them) can undermine policy intentions and introduce subtle empowering and dis-empowering effects. Second, economic logic suggests that multiple retailers will increasingly dominate supply chains and force traditional producers into compromise with consumer demands (Marsden, 1998). The RIPPLE producer survey, however, showed that significant numbers of consumers and small producers refuse to accept large retailers' conceptions of quality on ideological as well as practical grounds. Third, many QPS consumers and producers are motivated as much by lifestyle and ethics as by conventional economic concerns, suggesting that many local networks are sufficiently robust to withstand the encroachment of multiple retail capital into traditional QPS markets based on existing artisanal circuits.

Actor-networks, then, are affected by broad processes operating at different geographical scales. Their intersection takes place within international and national regulatory contexts which facilitate the current regime of accumulation, but with potential for niche markets to emerge to meet the demands of increasingly disanchored, segmented and knowledgeable consumers. The macro-processes of regulation and accumulation are mediated at the local level through the local mode of social regulation, which consists not only of institutional, political and economic structures, but also of culture, traditions and place history. It seems probable that such processes will become increasingly important features in the future development of marginal rural regions.

Notes

[1] FAIR3-CT96-1827. RIPPLE is a collaborative research programme funded under the EU's FAIR programme and involving the Departments of Geography at the Universities of Coventry, Lancaster, Leicester, Caen, Valencia, Galway and Trinity College Dublin; the Scottish Agricultural College (Aberdeen), the Institute of Rural Studies (University of Wales, Aberystwyth), Cemagref (Clermont-Ferrand), Teagasc (Dublin), Department of Economics (University of Patras), and the Institute for Rural Research and Training (University of Helsinki).

[2] However, the validity of such knowledge is increasingly questioned as shown, for example, in the BSE and GMO affairs in the UK, and this results in continual revisions of self-identity in the light of new information, knowledge and persuasion.

[3] In production terms, however, the use of some distinctively local materials, such as slate or Welsh gold, provides an important link between local provenance and quality.

References

Allaire, G. and Sylvander, B. 1997. Qualité Spécifique et Système d'Innovation Territoriale. *Cahiers d'Économie et Sociologie Rurales* 4, 30-59.

Anon. 1993. *Scotland Means Quality: A Single Quality Mark for Scottish Food and Drink Products.* Edinburgh: Scottish Food Strategy Group.

Ashworth, G. and H. Vogt. 1994. Marketing and Place Promotion. In J. Gold and S. Ward (eds.), *Place Promotion: The Use of Publicity and Marketing to Sell Towns and Regions.* Chichester: Wiley.

Bell, D. and G. Valentine. 1997. *Consuming Geographies: We Are Where We Eat.* London: Routledge.

Burgess, J. 1989. The Production and Consumption of Environmental Meanings in the Mass Media: a Research Agenda for the 1990s. *Transactions of the Institute of British Geographers* (NS) 15, 139-161.

Clark, G., I. Bowler, A. Crockett, B. Ilbery and A. Shaw. 1997. Institutions, Alternative Farming Systems and Local Re-regulation. *Environment and Planning* A, 29, 731-745.

Crang, P. 1996. Displacement, Consumption and Identity. *Environment and Planning* A, 28, 47-67.

Fearne, A. and S. Kuznetsof. 1994. Northumberland Lamb: a Case Study of Consumer Attitudes towards Branded Fresh Meat Products. *Farm Management* 8, 502-512.

Fine, B. 1994. Towards a Political Economy of Food. *Review of International Political Economy* 1 (3), 519-545.

FitzSimmons, M. and D. Goodman. 1998. Incorporating Nature: Environmental Narratives and the Reproduction of Food. In B. Braun and N. Castree (eds.), *Remaking Reality: Nature at the Millennium.* London: Routledge.

Flynn, A. and T. Marsden. 1995. Rural Change, Regulation and Sustainability. *Environment and Planning* A, 27, 1180-1192.

Giddens, A. 1991. *Modernity and Self-identity: Self and Society in the Late Modern Age.* Cambridge: Polity Press.

Gilg, A. and M. Battershill. Quality Farm Food in Europe. A Possible Alternative to the Industrialised Food Market and to Current Agri-environmental Policies: Lessons from France. *Food Policy* 23, 25-40.

Glennie, P. and N. Thrift. 1996. Consumption, Shopping and Gender. In M. Lowe and N. Wrigley (eds.), *Retailing, Consumption and Capital.* Harlow: Longman.

Gold, J. and S. Ward (eds.). 1994. *Place Promotion: the Use of Publicity and Marketing to Sell Towns and Regions.* Chichester: Wiley.

Goodman, D. and M. Redclift. 1994. Constructing a Political Economy of Food.

Review of International Political Economy 1 (3), 547-552.

Graby, F. 1993. Countries as Corporate Entities in International Markets. In N. Papadopoulos and L. A. Heslop (eds.), *Product-Country Images*. New York: International Business Press.

Hughes, G. 1992. Tourism and the Geographical Imagination. *Leisure Studies* 11, 31-42.

Hughes, G., A.-M. Sherwood and P. Midmore. 1996. *Welsh Agriculture into the New Millennium: CAP Prospects and Farming Trends in Rural Wales. A Report to the Development Board for Rural Wales and the Welsh Development Agency.* Aberystwyth: Welsh Institute for Rural Studies.

Ilbery, B. and M. Kneafsey. 1998. Product and Place: Promoting Quality Products and Services in the Lagging Rural Regions of the European Union. *European Urban and Regional Studies* 5, 329-341.

Ilbery, B. and M. Kneafsey. 1999a. Niche Markets and Speciality Food Products in Europe: towards a Research Agenda. *Environment and Planning* A, 31.

Ilbery, B. and M. Kneafsey (eds.). 1999b. *Regional Images and the Promotion of Quality Products and Services in the Lagging Regions of the European Union: Final Report to the European Commission (FAIR3 CT96 1827).* Coventry: Coventry University Department of Geography.

Ilbery, B., M. Kneafsey, T. Jenkins, P. Leat, N. Parrott, J. Brannigan, F. Williams, G. Clark and I. Bowler. 1999. *RIPPLE Final Regional Report: UK.* Aberystwyth: Welsh Institute for Rural Studies.

Jackson, P. and N. Thrift. 1995. Geographies of Consumption. In D. Miller (e.), *Acknowledging Consumption: a Review of New Studies.* London: Routledge.

Jenkins, T. 1990. Future Harvests. *The Economics of Farming and the Environment: Proposals for Action.* Godalming: Council for the Protection of Rural England and World Wide Fund for Nature.

Jenkins, T. and N. Parrott. 1997. Marketing in the Context of Quality Products and Services in the Lagging Regions of the European Union (RIPPLE Working Paper 4). Aberystwyth: Welsh Institute of Rural Studies.

Jenkins, T. and N. Parrott. 1998. Marketing Structures in the Study Regions: An Overview (RIPPLE Working Paper 6). Aberystwyth: Welsh Institute of Rural Studies.

Jenkins, T., N. Parrott, G. Hughes, H. Lloyd, A.-M. Sherwood, P. Leat, J. Brannigan, F. Williams and S. Petrie. 1998. Producer Survey Results and Analysis: UK

(RIPPLE Working Paper 8). Aberystwyth: Welsh Institute for Rural Studies.

Keane, M. 1990. Economic Capacity amongst Small Rural Communities. *Journal of Rural Studies* 6 (3), 291-301.

Kotler, P. 1997. *Marketing Management.* 9th ed. Englewood Cliffs, N. J.: Prentice Hall.

Lowe, P. 1996. Blueprint for a Rural Economy. In P. Allanson and M. Whitby (eds.), *The Rural Economy and the British Countryside.* London: Earthscan.

Marsden, T. 1996. Rural Geography Trend Report: the Social and Political Bases of Rural Restructuring. *Progress in Human Geography* 20, 246-258.

Marsden, T. 1998. New Rural Territories: Regulating the Differentiated Rural Space. *Journal of Rural Studies* 14, 107-117.

Marsden, T., P. Lowe and S. Whatmore, S. (eds.). 1990. *Rural Restructuring: Global Processes and their Responses.* London: David Fulton.

Marsden, T., J. Murdoch, P. Lowe, R. Munton and A. Flynn. 1993. *Constructing the Countryside.* London: UCL Press.

Moran, W. 1993. The Wine Appellation as Territory in France and California. *Annals of the Association of American Geographers* 83, 694-717.

Murdoch, J. 1995. Actor-Networks and the Evolution of Economic Forms. *Environment and Planning* A, 27, 731-757.

Murdoch, J. and T. Marsden. 1994. *Reconstituting Rurality.* London: UCL Press.

OECD. 1995. *Niche Markets as a Rural Development Strategy.* Paris: OECD.

Parrott, N., T. Jenkins, J. Lampard, P. Leat, F. Williams and J. Brannigan. 1999a. *Consumer Survey Results and Analysis: UK* (RIPPLE Working Paper 9). Aberystwyth: Welsh Institute for Rural Studies.

Parrott, N., T. Jenkins, F. Williams, P. Leat and J. Brannigan. 1999b. *Institutional Survey Results and Analysis: UK* (RIPPLE Working Paper 10). Aberystwyth: Welsh Institute for Rural Studies.

Ray, C. 1998. Culture, Intellectual Property and Territorial Rural Development. *Sociologia Ruralis* 38 (1), 3-20.

Sack, R. 1992. *Place, Modernity and the Consumer's World.* Baltimore: Johns Hopkins.

Sylvander, B. 1993. Quality Products: An Opportunity for Rural Areas. *LEADER Magazine* 3, 8-21.

Tregear, A., A. Moxey and S. Kuznesof. 1997. Marketing of Regional Foods: A Policy Perspective. Paper presented at the Agricultural Economics Society Annual Conference, Edinburgh.

Vastoia, A. 1997. Perceived Quality and Certification: the Case of Organic Fruit. Paper presented at the 49th Seminar of the European Association of Agricultural Economists, Bonn.

2 New Public Management and Peripheral Regions

PAUL OLAV BERG

Introduction

This paper represents a tentative and preliminary attempt to discuss a group of problems that has thus far attracted little attention in the literature concerning local and regional development. So far there has been little empirical documentation on which to build. The aim of this paper is to present background material for further analysis of local and regional consequences of the reorganisation of the public sector that is currently taking place in Norway, as well as in the other OECD countries. Briefly these consequences relate to:

- Changes in the geographical distribution of employment and population;
- Changes in the delivery of public services;
- Changes in price policy and differentiation of prices for public services;
- Competition as opposed to monopoly in the services' market.

Approach

In the course of the last 10 to 15 years, many of the central government administrative bodies responsible for public administration, infrastructure and the supply of public services have been given a freer position in relation to central government. This implies that they have been transformed from central government agencies to more autonomous state-owned bodies like public companies and state-owned joint-stock companies. In Norway, reorganisation has been implemented against a background of changed domestic political conditions, while also being inspired by recent international administrative policy trends ("New Public Management" (MPN) dogmas).

It is too early to form a clear picture of how successful this reorganisation has been, judged on the basis of the arguments that were put forward to justify the changes. Research that has been conducted at the LOS Centre at the University in Bergen suggests, however, that at the same time as the "corporatised" and more autonomous bodies and institutions face increasing

27

pressure to improve their efficiency, this may at the same time undermine political control. Among the unforeseen consequences may also be that the scope for the public to influence the supply of public services through their own democratic bodies may have been impaired (Grønlie and Selle, 1998; Christensen and Lægreid 1998, 1999). More local autonomy thus seems to imply less democracy! To the extent that this has happened, what are the consequences---also along a centre-peripheral dimension? Do the consequences differ between centrally and peripherally located areas and regions? To what extent have the new autonomous bodies and institutions been instructed to take into account societal and social as well as regional policy considerations?

These questions may be illustrated through an example. It would probably be generally agreed upon that the postal services should perform to standards required, before and after having been given a more autonomous status. Furthermore, this should also apply in areas where the population base is so small that the income from postal traffic does not fully cover its costs. To what extent has the recent transformation of the postal services from a government agency into an autonomous state-owned company changed this institution's scope for observing societal or regional considerations?

Background

Internationally, Norway has, together with other Scandinavian countries, over the years gone relatively far in defining the provision of infrastructure and welfare services as public responsibilities. There are several causes for this. One obvious cause is that geographical and distance-related characteristics, together with an earlier shortage of private funding alternatives, have made an extensive governmental commitment necessary. Another reason is that a public commitment has been seen as a necessary condition for securing the provision of a basic supply of infrastructure and welfare services in all parts of the country. In addition to social and regional policy concerns like this, nation-building and military concerns have also brought about a state engagement, especially within the communications sectors (Hallin, 1999).

The way the public sector has been organised has gradually changed over time. At the very beginning, the various public services were an integrated part of central government administration. Over time, the administrative and operational responsibility were transferred to more free-standing agencies like directorates. At the same time there has been a decentralisation of tasks, partly to central government agencies at regional and local levels, and partly to county and local municipalities. The central government's provision of services has increased over the last 50 years, during a period in which the public sector has gone through continuing expansion, parallel to the development of the welfare state.

Within central government administration, directorates and central government agencies and institutions have long since sought a position that is as free as possible from the state as owner. This matter came initially up for discussion in the 1950s. At that time the discussion focused on the degree of independence for the main state-owned communication companies; the postal services, telephone and telegraph services and the state railway. The government, however, at that time wanted to retain control over their operations, as these institutions were considered to play an important role as instruments in welfare policies and in regional equalisation policies. A unanimous Norwegian Parliament (Stortinget) wished in the 1960s to go no further than to grant these bodies status as autonomous directorates with special responsibilities (Grønlie, 1998).

After a while in which the debate was absent from the political agenda, it reappeared in the 1980s. This time it was inspired by the new climate for administrative policies which was developing. An ideological shift took place, internationally as well as nationally, characterised by a scepticism of the growth of the public sector, and by the desire for a slimmer and more efficient state. These market-liberalistic trends gave less legitimacy to the idea of a continued expansion within the public sector. At the same time they promoted and facilitated endeavour for structural devolution through "corporatisation". After years marked by optimism in public planning, a reaction set in. At the same time the efficiency of the performance of the public sector came to be questioned. It was alleged that the organisation of central government service suppliers were not sufficiently adapted to new competitive conditions. One topical catchword was "the competitive state". It was claimed that the public sector was both too extended and too costly.

OECD as Trend-setter Promoting New Public Management Dogmas

From the 1980s and onwards, a series of doctrines and dogmas under the collective label of "New Public Management" arose. The basic ideas are that the public sector may be made more efficient by adopting organisational structures, originally developed in the private sector. Greater efficiency may furthermore be obtained by exposing the public sector to more competition.

The main feature of NPM is an emphasis on economic norms and values. This implies that many traditional norms and values of the public sector are seen as subordinate to economic norms. This dominance is also connected to strong opinions about how economic norms and values have certain effects on other considerations. Emphasising efficiency implies changes in the formal organisation of the public sector, in procedures, in expertise needed and in relation to the private sector (Christiansen and Lægreid, 1999). The main components of NPM are "hands-on" professional management which allows for active, visible, discretionary control of an organisation by persons who are "free to manage". Furthermore they include explicit standards of performance, greater emphasis on output control, increased competition, contracts, devolution, disaggregation of units and private sector management techniques (ibid.). Through devolution and contracting, policy-making is sought, separated more clearly from policy administration and implementation. Policymakers make policy, and then delegate the implementation to managers, and hold them accountable through contracts.

These NPM dogmas imply that traditional public administration through laws, administrative rules and negotiations should be replaced by "target-to-effects" incentive systems. "Management-by-objective-and-result" (MBO) is also a concept used in this context. More emphasis is to be put on results than on the ways by which results are achieved. There should be a clearer division between politics and administration. Political decision-making authorities should concentrate on policy-making and strategic planning, whereas it should be left to the operational units to run their activities as efficiently as possible within the political frames that have been set. The "New Public Management" doctrines seem to have made a considerable impact in Western industrialised countries. These countries' own interest organisation, OECD, has to a considerable extent acted as a trend-setter through its comprehensive "PUMA" programme, by actively influencing its member countries (OECD, 1995).

What Impact Have the "New Public Management" Dogmas had in Norway?

Recent research shows that the impact of the NPM dogmas on Norwegian public administration has thus far been generally limited. Norway has been a reluctant reformer in this area. This applies generally to the main features of the NPM dogmas, like the introduction and implementation of "target-to-effects" incentive systems, to outsourcing and above all to privatisation, in which Norway has shown more restraint than most other OECD countries.

In one field, however, the NPM dogmas may seem to have had a breakthrough in Norway. This is the phenomenon of structural devolution or "corporatisation" within central government. Former directorates, government services and other administrative bodies have on a large scale been converted into state-owned enterprises, public corporations and state-owned joint-stock companies and to some extent also into foundations. The number of former central government bodies that have undergone such a process since 1980 is about 50 (Statskonsult, 1998). What is the background for this phenomenon of granting greater decision-making authority and autonomy to independent subordinate bodies?

It appears that the Norwegian parliament and the Cabinet have had a rather low-level role in this process, whereas the administrative bodies themselves have by far dominated the process (Lægreid and Roness, 1998). In particular the leaders of the various administrative bodies have led the way, in order to maximize the freedom of their positions in behalf of their respective government services. These endeavours have regularly been supported by the trade unions, as more autonomy would carry the prospects of a freer wage structure.

As stated before, this situation may be compared to a similar discussion that took place in the 1950s and 1960s. At that time, the government wanted to retain political direction and control, in order to ensure an equalisation of the social and geographic distribution of infrastructure and government welfare services. Under the new political conditions of the 1980s and 1990s, the Storting (parliament) and the Cabinet have not apparently to the same degree been preoccupied with such objections. In addition, the efforts to gain a more independent status could this time draw support from the winds of change that were blowing the "New Public Management" dogmas along.

Among the various political parties, it has been the Conservative Party (Høyre) in particular, which has for a long time been a strong advocate of a "smaller and more retracted state", and has supported these efforts for autonomy. The Labour Party has also, perhaps a little more hesitatingly, supported these efforts, to some extent governed by a different set of motives. In a period in which the public sector has faced a pressure for down-sizing, "corporatisation" has been seen as a more favourable alternative (Grønlie, 1998). However, these questions have been only marginal on the political agenda. The reform work that has taken place, has through the NPM dogmas been introduced as a universal, non-political technique---as a method of obtaining better efficiency and a better service supply for the general public. Recognition of the political implications and consequences connected to the corporatisation process, for instance related to democratic values or to regional development considerations, have largely been absent.

Inadvertent Consequences of the Corporatisation Process?

The corporatisation process was based on arguments that more local autonomy would at the same time ensure more efficient overall political direction. When political decision-making units are relieved of having to deal with detailed matters related to running operations, they should allegedly be more able to deal with more strategically important matters. It has thus been a clear condition that more local operational autonomy should be combined with necessary strategic political steering and control. In such a process, goals were to be determined and external conditions were to be defined in accordance with societal and social considerations that the government as owner wanted to prioritize.

The extent to which this has happened so far is debatable. So far, knowledge of the consequences of the application of NPM dogmas, and especially of the devolution of commercial activities by way of "corporisation", is rather limited. Recent research, however, suggests as already mentioned that democratic direction and control of the new autonomous bodies may have been weakened. In a recent report (Christensen and Lægreid, 1999) NPM-related reforms are seen generally to undermine political control. The structural devolution of commercial units and activities implies more fragmentation and less political control generally, and over commercial activities more specifically. Competition and the use of contracts has generally increased, thereby changing the relationship between political leaders and subordinate institutions and individual actors. The relationship seems to place more emphasis on the individual, short-term and strategic aspects, potentially undermining the traditional profile of institutional, collective commitment and ethos.

It is warned that the "target-to-effect" incentive systems that have been introduced, as well as the NPM related reforms themselves, may impair political-democratic leadership, in spite of the fact that this process was introduced as a means of strengthening democratic control (Lægreid and Roness, 1998). To the extent that this is the case, it will also include "user democratic" aspects. One consequence may be that consumers and the general public will lose opportunities to influence the decision-making processes that decide the supply of public services in their local areas.

Regional and Local Consequences of the "Corporatisation" Process?

The opponents of NPM-related reforms, and especially of the corporatisation process, have feared that it would result in changes in the social and geographical distribution of public services that would be unacceptable. The most sceptical feared that this process, in addition to leading to reductions of government employment in peripheral regions, would also result in a down-sizing of welfare services, gained previously through regional policy efforts (Grønlie, 1998).

The reason why the counter-arguments from the 1950s and 1960s did not appear in the 1980s and 1990s may be that there had simply been a change of policy. Paradoxically, this new policy seems to have manifested itself through a lack of political attention to these questions. On the basis of a White Paper from 1991-1992 (St. meld. nr. 35 (1991-92)), the Storting maintained that the primary rule should be that government activities should be run by administrative bodies that were part of the central government (directorates etc.). The process of "corporatisation", which at that time had already been going on for several years, is evidently not in accordance with this position stated by the Storting. As mentioned, this process had come into being as a result of the government bodies' own desire for more autonomy, assisted by the international "management winds" which had had an effect throughout this period. Apparently there has been limited attention paid to possible social and geographic inequalities which might arise as a result of this process. As observed by Grønlie, politicians favouring structural devolution ("corporatisation") are generally less preoccupied with the problems created by this process, than are politicians who are against it or sceptical of it. If the object itself (a slimmer state) is perceived as good, the propensity to disregard negative implications and consequences will be correspondingly greater (Grønlie, 1998).

Great Challenges

The prospect of NPM-related reforms that have been implemented so far being reversed in the foreseeable future is not very realistic. This implies that one will have to live with the implications and consequences that may appear. Some of these consequences, which have so far have been little foreseen may be increasing geographical and social inequalities throughout the country. This is of course not acceptable from a regional policy point of view. The rhetorical arguments for "corporatisation" included, as previously mentioned, more efficient strategic political direction and more local autonomy on the part of the new institutions. Making this political direction more explicit and concrete is a political challenge today. It is important that built-in societal and social, as well as regional policy considerations, be observed by the new autonomous governmental bodies. The point is how to ensure continued democratic control of a part of the public administration that has now obtained more autonomy in relation to political direction (Lægreid and Roness, 1998).

A further challenge is to develop methods that can give a better basis for calculating the costs of observing the societal and social considerations in question. The example of the mail service can again be given. Previously, the costs of offering a minimally-acceptable service level in parts of the postal market that are unprofitable on strictly commercial terms would be covered by cross-subsidisation. This has been practised throughout the 350-year-long history of the Norwegian postal services. According to the new NPM dogmas, such cross-subsidisation should no longer take place. Costs related to taking political or societal considerations should now be made explicitly visible, and they should subsequently be covered by explicit grants over the government's budget. The question then arises: how can such costs be estimated? Grant estimates of this type were made for the mail service for 1998, which was the first year of this new practice. These estimates are, however, said to be subject to considerable uncertainty (St. prp. nr. 1 [1997-98] Ministry of Transportation). Practice so far also indicates that such grants are vulnerable to cuts when the price of taking societal or social considerations becomes visible.

More Research is Needed

In Norway, little attention has been paid to the local and regional consequences of this restructuring of the public sector. Such consequences will, however, be of importance to anyone who wishes to study how central government authorities influence conditions for local and regional development. The State is an important regional policy actor! It should, however, be possible to formulate some hypotheses about such consequences, based on a general knowledge of the functioning of markets. An institution that no longer has its income (or the coverage of its deficit) granted through government budgets is supposed to fund its activities through selling its services in the market. There is little doubt that such an organisation will be subject to pressure to improve its efficiency. This has been part of the objective of the restructuring. In order to be able to compete with private market participants, in cases where markets and real competition exist, it is important that the new autonomous bodies are granted the same conditions of competition as private market participants.

To the extent that societal or social considerations imply that "unprofitable" parts of the activities should be subsidised by the government, such costs are, according to the NPM dogmas, supposed to be made explicitly visible, and to be explicitly granted over government's budget. Profitable parts of activities subject to competition should not pay for this subsidisation. The income resulting from certain activities that stem from monopolised markets could, however, be used partly to pay for unprofitable activities, as is the case with the postal services. Theoretically, this looks plausible enough. The new autonomous state-owned bodies are supposed to gain not only an ordinary return but a maximum dividend on the capital employed, similarly to enterprises in the private sector. In accordance with ordinary market conditions, they are further supposed to ensure incomes that fund their operations, and to ensure a financial basis for further expansion.

Societal Considerations and the Logic of Markets

However, when societal considerations are to be observed by state-owned bodies that are supposed to operate under market conditions, several dilemmas naturally arise. In markets where the new autonomous bodies meet competition, for instance in the telephone market, an ordinary competition strategy will imply that the competition is met first and foremost in market segments and in geographical areas where the competition is keenest. A natural consequence of this is to lower prices in central parts of the markets, whereas prices are maintained in peripheral regions where there is less competition. There are examples, for instance from the petrol market, that show that prices are kept high in parts of the market with little competition, to compensate for the losses inflicted by price wars waged in central parts of the country. To the extent that new autonomous state-owned bodies are not directed to observe defined societal or social considerations, it should be expected that they will act according to a corresponding "market logic" (as practised by the state-owned oil company STATOIL).

Another matter is that state-owned enterprises will often have a strong market position as they often are monopolies. In some instances they have also carried with them the responsibility for public administrative tasks that they formerly used to be responsible for. For instance, the telecommunication service that was converted into the state-owned joint stock company TELENOR in 1994, carried with it the responsibility for the administration of the telecommunication network as such. To the extent that this market position is actively or passively used to further the commercial ends of the enterprise, creating a super-profit, the question of misuse of market power may arise. The extent to which this actually takes place may be an open question and should be an object of research. There are indications, however, that the suspicion that misuse of market power actually takes place is not entirely hypothetical. TELENOR has already several times been indicted by its new competitors for taking advantage of its administrative authority over the telecommunication network, and has been ordered to change its practices.

Negative Consequences for Peripheral Regions

There are strong indications that the restructuring of the public sector that has taken place according to the NPM dogmas may have serious negative consequences especially for peripheral regions and peripheral local communities; consequences that to some extent may seem to have been foreseen. It is a serious challenge for the political authorities to ensure necessary political direction through drawing up directions and contractual conditions for concessions, in order to ensure that social and societal, as well as regional policy considerations are observed. Gaining the necessary knowledge through research, in order to focus on the consequences of this process, is a further challenge. This will contribute to more accurate political direction and action.

References

Christensen, T. and Lægreid, P. 1996. "Administrative Policy in Norway: Towards New Public Management", LOS-senter notat 9647. Bergen.

Christensen, T. and Lægreid. P. 1998. "Den moderne forvaltning", TANO Aschehoug.

Christensen, T. and Lægreid, P. 1999. "New Public Management: The trade-off between political governance and administrative autonomy". Unpublished paper.

Grønlie, T. 1998. "Drømmen om en konkurransetilpasset stat. Ytre fristilling som styringspolitisk redskap 1945-1995", in T. Grønlie and P. Selle (eds.), *Ein stat? Fristillingas fire ansikt*. Det Norske Samlaget.

Grønlie, T. and Selle P. (eds.). 1998. "Ein stat? Fristillingas fire ansikt". Det Norske Samlaget.

Hallin, G. 1999. *Avreglering och regional utveckling. Regionala konsekvenser av institutionella ändringar i Nordens kommunikationstjänster*. Nordregio R 1999:1.

Lægreid, P. and Roness, P. 1998. "Frå einskap til mangfald: Eit perspektiv på indre fristilling i statsforvaltninga", in T. Grønlie, and P. Selle (eds.), *Ein stat? Fristillingas fire ansikt*. Det Norske Samlaget.

OECD. 1995. "Governance in Transition: Public Management Reforms in OECD Countries".

St. meld. nr. 35. 1991-92. "Om statens forvaltnings---og personalpolitikk".

St. prp. nr. 1. 1997-98. Ministry of Transportation, Program category 22.1 "Mail", page 138.

Statskonsult. 1998. "Fakta, former og fristilling: Statlige virksomheter med ulike tilknytningsformer". Rapport 1998: 18.

PART II
THE CHANGING FORTUNES OF FARMING AND FISHING IN THE ECONOMIES OF MARGINAL REGIONS

3 Reflections on the Swedish Policy Responses to the Fisheries Crash of 1967

REGINALD BYRON

What Happened, and Why

The disastrous crash in the herring fishery in the summer and autumn of 1967 was without warning. The previous ten years had been very good ones, and over this period something like a thousand Swedish fishermen had taken out bank loans to buy new boats. That year, the fish stocks collapsed. We are now in a better position to appreciate why this happened than people were at the time: it was largely the consequence of the extension of the commercial capital market into fish-catching, especially in the decade from 1957 to 1966, which provoked an enormous expansion of the Swedish fleet and, in turn, a huge increase in its catching-power. This catching-power put such great pressure on the herring stocks that the resource was bound to decline sooner or later. At that time, no one could have predicted when this might occur, or that, when it did, it would not be a gradual diminution in landings which would give the industry time to re-adjust, but rather would be a dramatic collapse which saw the catches of individual boats drop by half, two-thirds, or three-quarters from one season to the next.

The consequences were far-reaching. Nearly half of Sweden's west coast fishing fleet had been replaced with new boats built since 1960; this included two-thirds of the boats in the six main herring-fishing communities; and in a couple of these places, 75 or 80 per cent of the boats were practically brand-new. Most of the men who owned these boats had bought them with bank loans, and were still making mortgage repayments. The custom was that these loans were secured by co-signatories who were normally fishermen in other boats; these men, in turn, had loans which were secured by still other fishermen.

When the herring fishery collapsed, some of these fishermen could not meet their loan repayments. The banks foreclosed, reassigning the debts to those who had signed sureties. Widespread panic was triggered as these men were forced to sell their boats at great losses in order to pay off other fishermen's debts (as well as their own), and in doing so exposed still others in the complex networks of co-signatories which in many small fishing communities tied nearly all the adult men together. Before the cumbersome machinery of parliamentary government could react with a recognition of the problem and appropriate measures to counteract it, two-thirds of the Swedish North Sea fleet had disappeared, and the industry was in ruins.

How could this have happened in a well-regulated country like Sweden, whose economic and social welfare institutions were, at the time, regarded by many as a model of modernity? Ironically, it is likely that it was at least partly *because* of Sweden's modernity that things happened the way they did.

Modernity and the Social Organisation of Fishing

It has been argued (most persuasively by A. F. Robertson, in his book, *Beyond the Family* [1991]), that many of the institutions of modernity that we now take for granted have been shaped by the necessity to accommodate or to support "the family", or the particular ideal form of it that is defined by national policy. Individual, independent nuclear families have been enabled ---with the development of these supporting institutions---to escape the full impact of the strains and scarcities which routinely beset them over their developmental cycles, so protecting the nuclear family as itself the institution which provides the modern nation-state with the stable, controlled population growth that is a fundamental prerequisite of economic growth and rational planning. While most western European countries, including Sweden, have an wide range of social institutions (including banks) and social welfare programmes designed to support the family and mesh with its needs, these institutions and programmes are largely geared to the needs an industrial worker with a spouse and one or two dependent children: a nuclear family defined by exclusive co-residence and consumption, supported by means of waged or salaried employment that is dispensed by, or under the surveillance of, the state.

These institutions of modernity are not, however, very well suited to maritime households, which are often extended or joint in form, in which kin and in-laws collaborate in production and consumption, but typically are not co-resident; nor (until recently) was their mode of livelihood under the close surveillance of the state or readily reconcilable with its standard ideological models. In Sweden, as in many other Western countries, government officials have difficulty in coping bureaucratically with the concept of a joint patrimony held by a father and sons or a set of brothers-in-law, none of whom is its executor or is able to put an exact value on his own share. Officials also have difficulty in assessing fishermen for pay-as-you-earn taxation, since they do not have wages or salaries, but take a percentage of the catch as their reward. Largely because they are not wage-earners, strictly speaking, and they are the holders of capital---often quite large amounts---that is not tied up mainly in a house or land, fishermen are classified not as normal workers or even within the same category as farmers. They are classified as employers or entrepreneurial capitalists, despite the fact that they have no employees, and are taxed accordingly; moreover, fishermen and their families do not qualify for some of the benefits that are taken for granted by waged or salaried employees.

During the boom years of the postwar herring fishery, and most particularly during the 1960s, Swedish fishermen had allowed themselves to be persuaded that commercial banks and state loan agencies extended and accelerated the capacity of their own forms of local-level social organisation to accumulate capital. Their own, vernacular institutions that had developed in fishing communities over the preceding two centuries had relied on pooled savings and gradual capital accumulation in the form of family patrimonies: sons' and nephews' shares in boat ownership were financed by their fathers and uncles, and capital was continuously and incrementally reinvested in boats and equipment over the generations. The pace of expansion in catching-power was thus limited by the rates of growth in capital that were endogenous to each community; generally this rate was fairly moderate, or low. The extension of bank lending in a big way into the capitalisation of fish-catching changed this calculus.

By the 1960s, the increasing willingness of banks to loan large amounts of money to fishermen had created a vast increase in the fleet's catching power, but the fishermen later found themselves hostage to the inflexible contracts that they had signed, which demanded regular repayments predicated upon regular incomes. When the crash came, not only did the banks recall their loans, but hundreds of family patrimonies carefully accumulated and nurtured over the generations were lost in the process, destroying the prospect of sons succeeding their fathers, and bringing fishing, as a mode of livelihood, as a means of supporting a family, and as a way of life, to an abrupt end in many small communities, perhaps forever.

By 1970, seven out of every ten men who in 1965 had been a fisherman--- and whose income had supported a family---were no longer fishermen. In Sweden, the scale of the problem was perhaps small by comparison with the current situation in Canada that has been brought about by the closure of the Northern Cod fishery, which has displaced tens of thousands of fishers: in Sweden, the number of men who lost their livelihoods as fishermen following the crash of 1967 was a little over 3,000.

Coincidences and Intentions

The effects of the crash were mitigated by a regional industrial infrastructure that, from the mid-1960s, had been expanding rapidly. and could absorb nearly everyone who wanted a job. There were two industries in particular which were adjacent to a number of fishing communities along the west coast and, by coincidence, were starting up or significantly expanding their operations and hiring large numbers of workers just as the fishery went into steep decline: the Esso petrochemical works at Stenungsund; and the Volvo car factory at Torslanda, which was built on a green-field site to manufacture the 140 series, scheduled to begin production in 1966. One or the other of these industrial employers was within 30 km of the great majority of the west coast communities which were worst affected by the loss of fishing employment.

That commuting on a daily basis was possible from the many of these places was due to another coincidence that began to occur in the early 1960s, which involved a series of decisions about the improvement of the transport infrastructure on the west coast. The result was the construction of new roads, bridges, and the introduction of regular RO-RO ferry services operated by the Highways Department, which could carry private cars, trucks and buses, for the first time linking previously isolated communities into the public road network.

Nonetheless, in the years following the crash, up to the mid-1970s, there was a gradual leaching away of the former fishing populations in the places most distant from these industrial centres. Daily commuting to industrial jobs was not possible from all of these places, and even where it was possible, the journeys might involve more than one ferry crossing, or took a couple of hours in each direction, or were sometimes uncomfortable or impossible in bad weather or during the winter. As the former fishers moved to the mainland to be nearer their places of work, their houses were kept as second, summer homes if they could afford to do this; or they were sold, most often to people from the city, again for use as second, summer homes. The local population left behind were mostly in the older age-cohorts.

By the mid-1970s, it was becoming apparent that a considerable number of former fishing villages were losing most of their year-round populations of people of working age, or were in danger of doing so, thus jeopardising the continued viability of local schools, post offices, shops, and other community-based institutions, services, and businesses. A spiral of decline was already in train; in some places, 50 per cent of the population was over 65 years of age; in others the last food shop, serving only a few year-round customers, was in danger of going out of business.

In March 1978, the county authority, whose jurisdiction extends over the whole of the west coast from Gothenburg north to the Norwegian border, and includes nearly all of the communities that were most affected by the fisheries crash of 1967, took the decision to define the maritime fringe of the county as a development region, whose economy and population characteristics needed at least to be stabilised, if not restored where this was feasible.

With characteristic Swedish thoroughness, the first thing they did was to commission a major research programme to establish exactly what the situation was in each of the communes in the designated development region. Detailed statistics were collected on the structures of the populations and the dynamics of the local economy; exhaustive inventories were made of every job that was sustained locally, and of every service that was provided or could potentially be developed; studies were made of the existing transport and communications infrastructure and use-patterns; and investigations were undertaken on potential land-uses, tourism, and recreation in each area.

Since public and parliamentary opinion strongly favoured the maintenance of these places as living communities, the idea of relocating their remaining year-round populations nearer to growth centres was not, apparently, a serious policy option. Further, given the small scattered populations and difficulties of transport, especially in the winter, the likelihood of persuading any major industrial employers to locate in these places was remote. The county authorities, constrained by circumstance, were forced to take a "small is beautiful" and low-growth or no-growth approach, aiming to prevent things from deteriorating any further if, say, relatively small amounts of money could keep a food shop open from one year to the next, or a little start-up money could generate a job or two here and there. This contrasted to their policies in the rest of the county, which was geared toward attracting high-growth business and industry to replace the jobs lost in ship-building and the other traditional industries then in decline; this was, of course, the prevailing ethos at the time.

Regeneration: At a Price

Meanwhile, the rationalisation of the fishing industry was taken in hand. The state Fisheries Board was given the task of scaling down the size of Sweden's fleet to match the resources available in national waters through a series of five-year plans, based on estimates of fish population trends supplied by its marine research office, and following government guidelines that fishing should provide a stable and adequate livelihood for those in the industry.

In implementing these goals, the Fisheries Board has employed a stick-and-carrot approach. The stick is the licensing system: each commercial vessel must have a licence in order to qualify for state supports and benefits;

the number of licences is controlled by the Board of Fisheries, and it is intended that their number should gradually decline. New applications for licences are rigorously scrutinized as to the personal and financial backgrounds of the applicants and the economic viability of the proposed venture: the procedures are lengthy and highly formalised. Another means of control is through the imposition of quotas and closed seasons on certain fish stocks and the requirement that fishermen keep log-book accounts of the origin and quantities of all the fish they catch, or risk losing their licences. While fishing firms which are regarded as inefficient or redundant are encouraged to go out of business through financial incentives to give up their licences and scrap their boats, others are given grants and loans to improve profitability and to provide more employment in places where it is needed.

The bias is toward smaller enterprises: cheap state loans are not available in amounts that would be of much help in financing the construction of a large, new herring trawler at, say, 30 to 50 million kronor. The policy is that large, highly-mechanised and capital-intensive boats do not employ any more men than smaller, less-sophisticated boats, but consume much more fish, so causing a decline in the scope for employment in the industry and the relative competitiveness of smaller fish-catching firms.

Compared with the view from the top, the view from below is not as easily located, because there are a number of views that vary with the placement and perceptions of fishermen in different sectors of the industry. Some of the regional fishermen's associations are much more able to present a united expression of their members' views than others. The West Coast Fishermen's Association is the biggest, but perhaps the least homogeneous regional association. It has over 2,000 members, ranging from week-end rowboat fishermen to those involved in hundred-million-kronor businesses. If fishermen at these extremes have anything in common, it is a deep distrust of the Fisheries Board's five-year plans and the idea that fishing can be planned and rationalised like agriculture. Any fisherman will point out that fishing is not husbandry but hunting, and the wild and mobile resources upon which they depend cannot be made to conform to bureaucratic estimates and projections, like cows or potatoes.

Among the west coast fishermen, there is a clear division between the big herring fishermen and the rest; often the former are referred to as "Fiskebäckers" although by no means all of them are from the village of Fiskebäck. These men and their crews own and operate about 100 of the newest and largest herring trawlers in Sweden. Interestingly, there was a handful of communities on the west coast which survived the crash of 1967 almost intact; the best-known of these places was Fiskebäck, and one of the main reasons why they did not lose their boats is that most of these men were adherents of churches which discouraged borrowing, and so these men were not beholden to banks in the way that many other fishermen were (see Byron, 1993a, 1993b, 1994a). Nowadays, the Fiskebäckers raise the very large amounts of money they need for their businesses though a combination of family networks and (sometimes) the international finance markets, using the trifling sums of money offered by the Fisheries Board, if at all, only for minor improvements to their boats. Their economic power underwrites their political influence. When they want to say something, they ring up the Director-General of the National Board of Fisheries or the Minister of Agriculture at their homes in the evening, and their influence is sufficient to ensure that they, or their spokesmen, are always included in negotiations at the highest levels. Privately, over a glass or two of beer, Swedish fisheries officials will tell you that it is not the government who call the tune in fisheries policy, but the Fiskebäckers. The ability of these fishermen to influence affairs does indeed rival that of the Fisheries Board itself, yet is entirely informal and lies completely outside the neat flow-charts and organisational diagrams of the industry that the Board of Fisheries depicts in their publicity material.

The Fiskebäckers will survive come what may. What is more worrying is the fate of the smaller-scale fishermen. Not so long ago, fishing was one of the least-regulated economic activities in Sweden; now it is one of the most-regulated. There are pages and pages of regulations for everything. The skippers are accountable for every last kilo of fish they catch. The have to fill in complicated forms to say how much of what species they caught where, at what time of day. If the bureaucrats suspect that the information is not accurate, they can reprimand the skipper, arrest the boat, haul him off to court and fine him or take away his licence.

Skippers say that the Fisheries Board seems to think that they have nothing to do except read their bulletins and regulations and fill out their forms. When all these rules were brought in about reporting catches and getting licences and subsidies and quotas, it was too much for some of the fishermen. The older, smaller-scale fishermen did not have much formal education. Many of them had left school at fourteen or fifteen. They could not understand the bureaucratic jargon, or what they were supposed to do, or why. Their families had been fishing people for generations; centuries, perhaps. They were independent and hard-working people who had never made any demands on the state, but some of them would now say that the state forced them out of their livelihoods just as surely as if it had set fire to their boats.

Concluding Remarks

By the middle of the nineties, the state's attempts to manage the fishery had largely succeeded, at least according to their own figures: the number of fishing units within the official sector was more or less in balance with the scientific estimates of sustainability, and the incomes of these fishermen were comparable with those in other sectors of the economy. In this sense, the fishing industry could be said to have been stabilised---even, perhaps, regenerated. But it could be argued, firstly, that much of this might well have occurred had the market been left to its own devices; and secondly, that there was a great deal of shutting of barn doors after the horses had already bolted.

That the crash occurred in the first place was at least partly the consequence of the failure of the state's agencies to appreciate the possibility that the extension of unregulated bank lending in fishing would lead to an enormous increase in catching-power, or to react with appropriate regulatory measures when this first became apparent (by 1963, total landings in Swedish ports had doubled since 1960, and by 1964 landings had tripled). Institutional inertia, later followed by a violent lurch in the opposite direction, managed both to allow the economic base of dozens of communities to be wiped out in the crash, and then, as an unintended consequence of over-regulation and excessive bureaucratisation, to destroy the livelihoods of substantial numbers of those smaller-scale fishers who had survived the crash.

Did it, or does it really matter? Unlike the people who live in remote communities in Newfoundland where alternatives to the fishery are scarce or nonexistent, those who lost their livelihoods in the Swedish fisheries crash or as the unintended consequence of subsequent state policies managed to find other jobs, many of them without having to move away from the places in which they and their families were settled. Viewed unsentimentally from a strictly utilitarian point of view, perhaps it does not matter very much what these people and their communities have become.

But we might regret that something, or rather, many things of value have been lost to us. Fishing in Sweden, as elsewhere, was a contest of human cunning and courage pitted against the unpredictable caprices of nature and the elements. It was a test of the strength and effectiveness of family ties and inter-household cooperation, a demonstration of the utility of vernacular modes of organising and managing capital and labour which were developed over the centuries for the express purpose of providing for their children and to re-create and maintain the economic conditions which could underwrite social reproduction and the livelihoods of the generations of families to follow (Byron, 1994b). Now, all these vernacular institutions, borne of necessity, which gave real, muscular work to the idea of "community", of interdependence between neighbours and of the interdependence of adjacent generations in staking out a more-or-less self-sufficient way of life that long antedated the modern industrial state's planning and social welfare institutions, have disappeared. All those who have left fishing, as well as nearly all those who have remained, have become clients of the state, under the direct

46

surveillance and discipline of its agencies, dependent upon their largesse. This is, evidently, what the Swedish model of modernity demands. And so it could be said that the fisheries crash of 1967 completed the process of national modernisation, bringing the last of Sweden's citizenry firmly within the all-encompassing orbit of its planning and social welfare institutions.

References

Byron, R. 1993a. Öckerö: Domestic Organisation and Social Change in a Swedish Maritime Community. *Ethnologia Scandinavica* 23: 58-72.

_____ . 1993b. Fishermen's Organisations and the Assertion of Local Interests in Western Sweden. *North Atlantic Studies* 3 (2): 32-37.

_____ . 1994a. *Portraits of the Past: Bohuslän Society in the Twentieth Century.* Göteborg: Ethnologiska föreningen i Västsverige.

_____ . 1994b. The Maritime Household in Northern Europe. *Comparative Studies in Society and History* 36 (2): 271-292.

Robertson, A. F. 1991. *Beyond the Family.* Cambridge: Polity Press.

4 How are Young People Coping with Economic Restructuring?

JENS CHRISTIAN HANSEN

Introduction

The answers to the question raised in the title of this paper can be sought at many levels of analysis. I consider the local community level the most relevant one, and this level is analysed in the third part of the paper, but case studies must be situated in a wider context. I have chosen demographic indicators for this contextualisation, as indicators of structural changes. They are presented in the first part of the paper.

Structural changes in the communities involved do not just happen in a vacuum. They involve institutional and individual actors (Hansen and Selstad 1999). Two sets of actors are involved: those who actively take part in the restructuring process, and those who have to evaluate the consequences of the process for their individual life projects. The first set of actors could be called *actors with power,* the second are *powerless actors.* Actors with power get their power through political mandate, administrative position and economic resources. Powerless actors are not directly involved in the politico-administrative system, and they do not play important roles in the local economic system.

This dichotomy is just about as risky as most dichotomies. Many actors with power would tell you, if asked, that they feel powerless. On the other hand, if powerless actors do not like what they see when their local community is being restructured, they may choose to leave, and if many of the powerless actors make this choice, their decisions may have important consequences for the future of their communities. The *actors with power* will be discussed in the second part of the paper. The objective is to identify important actors who take part in the restructuring of resource-based communities. This part of the paper is concluded with a brief discussion of the relationships between the two actor categories. The *powerless actors* are studied in their local contexts, in the third part of the paper.

49

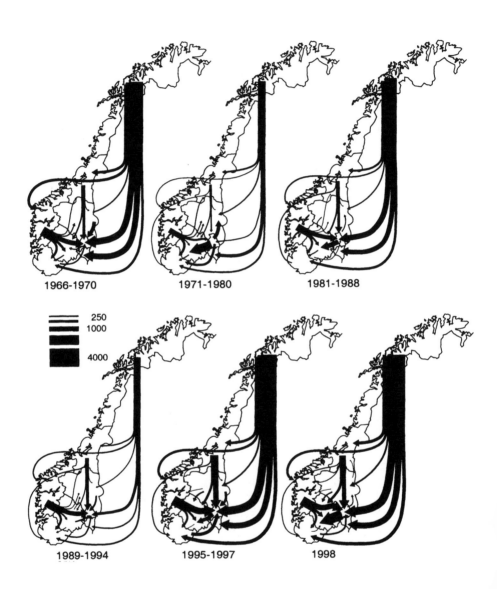

Figure 4.1   Net migration streams between the major regions in Norway between 1966 and 1999 (after Høydahl, Skiri and Østby, 2000)

Demographic Effects of Structural Change

Net migration is used as a simple indicator of restructuring. Roughly speaking, net in-migration means growth, net out-migration decline. Figure 4.1 shows net migration streams between major regions in Norway between 1966 and 1999 (see Figure 4.2 for the delimitation of regions). Figure 4.1 simplifies space and time, because both regions and time periods are aggregates. Still, some major features emerge which indicate a relatively permanent centre-periphery system, although migration streams from periphery to centres vary over time. Arrows go from the north to all other regions, and also Trøndelag and the west are out-migration areas, mainly to the capital region and the coastal parts of the southeast. The south is also on the receiving end. One effect of in-migration to the capital region is a spill-over from this region to the neighbouring parts of the southeast.

The heavy net out-migration from the national peripheries in the second half of the sixties reflects the restructuring of primary activities (push factors), as well as the concentration of new service jobs (pull factors) in the south-eastern part of Norway. The 1970s seemed to introduce a more balanced migration pattern, and the terms "consolidation" and "turnaround" have been used to describe this new trend. The driving force behind this process was the general increase of local public service jobs made possible because of increasing oil revenues. New public jobs have been created also in the eighties and nineties, although population decline in many peripheral areas has reduced the number of customers for many of these services. With increased prosperity private services expanded, but they were more centrally located than public services (this process has been described in Hansen 1997b).

Industrial restructuring was delayed in Norway, as compared to most other Western European countries, because the government had money to subsidise ailing manufacturing firms after the slump in the world economy triggered of by the 1972-73 oil crisis. It was assumed that this crisis was a temporal, conjunctural phenomenon, not a serious long-term structural problem. It gradually became clear that this assumption was wrong, and although support has been given to companies in trouble---particularly in less urbanised parts of Norway---far into the nineties, an industrial restructuring process accelerated from the late seventies into the eighties. This process is reflected in net migration streams during the eighties (Figure 4.1), where net out-migration increased, not only from the north, but also from the west, where resource-based export industries were important (this process has been described in Hansen 1995). The crisis in the North Atlantic fisheries, which hit north Norway very hard, is analysed in Hansen (1999).

In the late eighties, much of the restructuring of manufacturing industries had been completed, and the gradual entry of Russian cod into Norwegian fish

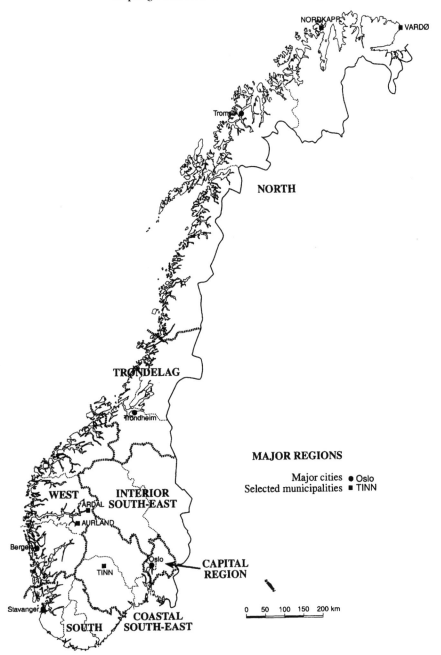

Figure 4.2   The major regions of Norway

processing since 1990 improved the situation in many fishing communities. At the same time, an overheated national economy had to be cooled down, resulting in job losses in consumer-oriented industries (building and construction, retail trade, financial services). National unemployment rates increased from under 2 per cent in 1987 to almost 6 per cent in 1993. Since many of the consumer-oriented industries were concentrated in major urban regions, unemployment rates increased in urban areas as well as in the periphery. As a consequence, unemployed people in the periphery stayed where they were because the pull factor of central areas had been strongly reduced. Vocational education systems for unemployed, combined with unemployment benefits, made it possible to remain in the periphery instead of moving to central areas in the hope of getting a job there. This trend is demonstrated in the interregional migration map 1989-1994 (Figure 4.1)

The two last maps in Figure 4.1, depicting average net migration streams of the 1990s, look very much like the map of the late sixties. Net migration streams increased from west Norway and Trøndelag around 1994. Net in-migration to the Oslofjord region and to the south (where Stavanger, the oil capital, was the magnet) persisted throughout the nineties. Since 1995, the situation has become worse, seen from the periphery. National unemployment rates were declining from around 6 per cent in 1993 to less than 4 per cent in 1998. Demand for labour increased in the major urban regions, and unemployed or underemployed people from the periphery again started to move to more central areas. The situation in the north is particularly worrying, but also in Trøndelag and the west net out-migration has increased in recent years. The great winner has been the coastal southeast, where medium-sized towns have become attractive alternatives to a more and more congested capital region, with rapidly increasing housing costs. The last years of the century has been a period of rapid regional polarisation. If this polarisation continues into the next century, the result may be a critical thinning-out of peripheral regions, with serious economic and social effects for the people involved. Is this process inevitable? If not, who are the actors who can find new directions for regional development? This is the question which will be discussed briefly in the next section.

Actors with Power

The historical overview of regional demographic change, related to structural labour market changes and general economic structural changes, leads us to think of regional restructuring as an effect of national restructuring, which again is an effect of global restructuring. In such a perspective, the roles of global institutional actors, transnational companies, national political institutions and leaders seem overwhelming.

This paper, however, focuses on national and local actors, and the interrelations between them. Their importance varies over time and in space. Regional and local development in Norway after the Second World War was organised centrally. Scarce resources had to be directed to places and regions where war damage had been extensive, such as in north Norway. Industrial projects undertaken, but not completed by the Germans during the war were taken over by government agencies, such as the case of the aluminium smelter in Årdal in Sogn. The fishing industry and other natural resource-based industries were developed as part of a national economic policy. The socialist government believed in central planning.

An understanding of the need for a regional policy gradually emerged after 1960, when a Regional Development Fund was set up to encourage development in regions which had not fully profited from the economic boom of the 1950s. This boom continued into the 1960s and the early 1970s. Regional policy implied directing new growth to peripheral areas, as well as transfers of industrial activities from central areas. These policies were defined on a national level. The main role of local actors was to convince central actors that their localities needed new development. They were lobbyists, not entrepreneurs. The entrepreneurs were imported, attracted by generous economic incentives. Many of these entrepreneurs were soon exposed as opportunists rather than innovators, and their enterprises floundered. Major national industrial companies, state-owned or private, also located new factories in areas covered by the Regional Development Fund. But strategic functions remained near the head offices. The local plant managers took orders from above, and there was little room for local innovation.

The post-war industrial boom in Western countries came to an end during the early seventies. In Norway it was prolonged, through economic support systems, until the late seventies. Public money went into ailing firms in order to keep up employment. But this counter-conjunctural policy had to come to an end. New models were needed. Central government did not have the courage to formulate an alternative restructuring policy which accepted that jobs would have to be lost in order to improve the economic performance of the enterprises. Such an alternative policy would be particularly problematic for peripheral regions. On the grassroots level, disillusionment with national policies became widespread. The alternative was to give more power to local actors. New jobs could be created through local mobilisation. The municipality already organised the production of most local public services, and it also had the responsibility for physical planning. Why could the municipalities not also become arenas for local economic development? Government money paid the salaries for new economic planners in peripheral municipalities. Instead of spending money to attract businesses from the outside, resources were now oriented towards small local entrepreneurs. In some cases, the local mobilisation process went even deeper---young people, women, and voluntary organisations were brought into the process. Powerless local actors were to become local actors with power. Cynical observers have suggested that central government actors supported the bottom-up approach because they realised that their own top-down strategies had failed.

What about the effects of this bottom-up approach? There are success stories---mainly from communities with strong, innovative political leaders. But generally speaking, the results were disappointing. Most municipalities were too small to be able to set up a competent and efficient restructuring administrations. The turnover of administrative officers as well as of locally-elected politicians created discontinuity problems. The mobilisation efforts to convert powerless local actors into actors with power gave disappointing results. Many of the small, local enterprises which were set up either failed or remained very small, with negligible employment effects. In all fairness, it should also be made clear that the general conditions for new economic growth in the late seventies and early eighties were not favourable. These were the years of drastic restructuring of resource-based industries following the period of counter-conjunctural policies. Local authorities therefore often found themselves more occupied with saving what could be saved in ailing enterprises than developing new alternatives.

In the second half of the eighties, national actors in a way took over the bottom-up policy. It was still considered right to encourage small, local initiatives, but the rules of the game were set from above. Municipalities had to make strategic plans of action in order to get state money for local restructuring funds. The bottom-up dynamics were defined from the top. Local actors went through the motions, but often became disillusioned with their own roles.

In a recent book on regional economy and politics, Håvard Teigen (1999) makes a point of showing how the role of the state in economic planning and in particular in regional development planning has been reduced since the late eighties. Norway is still probably one of the most planned societies in Western Europe, but more and more restructuring actors have realised that this kind of planning cannot solve all the problems related to economic and regional development. Teigen also notices that the role of the Ministry of Municipal and Regional Affairs has been reduced during the nineties, and that of sectorial ministries has increased. Regional development is not well co-ordinated on the national level, and local restructuring actors do not quite know whom to address. Local political actors also discover that they can do little without the active involvement of local, private enterprises. But most of these local business actors tend to shun the local political networks. The assumption that they co-operate in dynamic local business networks is not often validated in research. The local business actors participate in local social networks, but choose their business partners without necessarily giving priority to other local business actors. Many local communities in peripheral Norway have been dominated by a single factory, often part of a national or international company. Most of them have shed labour through restructuring, thereby losing local goodwill. It is therefore worth noting that some of these companies have been active in successful local restructuring processes in recent years, as in the case of Rjukan presented in the next part of the paper.

Most of the local political actors mentioned in this overview have had stronger links with national political actors than with local actors without power. Despite a continued and extensive effort to restructure marginal areas in Norway, numerous local actors without power, and in particular the young generations, have decided to make their future elsewhere. On a macro level, this can be seen in the maps showing net migration flows. It is now time to discuss the local settings which young people growing up in the periphery have to relate to when they decide whether to stay or to go.

The Attitudes of Young People to Local Restructuring

Five municipalities have been selected to illustrate how local actors have tried to cope with restructuring (Figure 4.2). The first example, Aurland in west Norway, is a rural community which was dramatically changed as the result of hydroelectric power development, and the focus is on how this development influenced school leavers' attitudes to their local community. The second example, Rjukan in Tinn in Telemark county, is a one-company town which has lived through eighty years of restructuring, often dramatic for those involved. The case focuses on the decline of electro-chemical industry since the mid-sixties, and restructuring efforts made during the last twenty years, with a special attention to reactions of young people to changes in the community. The third example is that of the post-war aluminium one-company town of Årdal in west Norway. It illustrates how three generations have responded differently to life in the community. The two last examples are both from fishing communities in the far north, where the restructuring processes following the resource crisis in the second half of the eighties have had dramatic consequences for people living in there. The municipality of Nordkapp is presented as a "worst" case; that of Vardø to introduce problems related to immigrant workers in the fish processing industry.

All the five cases deal with natural-resource based communities in peripheral parts of Norway. The resource base varies from place to place, and restructuring has taken place at different times. The cases are unique

56

examples of local outcomes of restructuring processes related to global resource problems, outcomes which young people have to respond to. Although unique, the cases give empirical support to tentative general conclusions about young people's attitudes to local restructuring.

1.   *Why do Young People Leave a Prosperous Community, Enriched by Income from Hydro-electric Development? The Case of Aurland*

In June 1999 more than 80,000 passengers took the small train starting at 900 meters above sea level at Myrdal station on the Oslo-Bergen railway line and ending 20 kms later at the south-eastern extremity of the Sognefjord: the Aurlandsfjord. 1,800 people live in the municipality of Aurland. Tourism gives few permanent jobs, is highly seasonal, and most tourists pass rapidly through. Part-time sheep farms on steep slopes along the fjord dominate local agriculture. Most people living in Aurland have their income from service jobs---on the railway, in the hydro-electric station, in transport, and building and construction work, but most of them work in local public services; which are of a high standard, because the municipality has an important source of income in Oslo Energy, which has to pay for the right to use Aurland's natural resources. But Table 4.1a shows that during the period 1985-1999 there were more deaths than births in Aurland, and a net out-migration of more than 120. As a result, Aurland's population declined by 6 per cent during these 15 years. No exodus, no disaster, but nevertheless a persistent loss of population. An ageing population cannot reproduce itself. Around 50 per cent of school leavers also left Aurland.

Several studies have been made of education and job aspirations of elementary school   leavers in Aurland (Selvik, 1974; Solberg, 1980; Tønnessen, 1985; summarized and updated in Hansen, 1997a and Hansen and Grønlund, 1999). The restructuring of rural Aurland began in 1969, with construction work on a big hydro-electric development scheme, completed in 1984. In 1972, the 11- to 17-year-old boys were fascinated by what was happening around them, and wanted to become engineers or truck drivers. A follow-up study undertaken in 1978 found that most of the boys had chosen a secondary education preparing them for such jobs, but that they had not chosen to work on the local construction site. The study suggests that one reason for this was that most of the construction work was over in 1978, but it also suggests that the young people had listened to their parents, advising them to find work in service occupations. In a third study from 1984 (Tønnessen, 1985), the same persons were interviewed, now 22 to 28 years old. Most of them had completed their education. Generally speaking, their original education plans had been more ambitious than their final choice. The study explains this by referring to favourable local conditions. Aurland could

Table 4.1   Population change 1985-1991, case studies

a) Aurland

Period	Pop. 1.1	Nat. incr.	Net. migr.	Pop. change	Pop. 31.12
1985-89	1946	7	-118	-112	1834
1990-94	1834	8	52	62	1896
1995-99	1896	-17	-51	-65	1831
1985-99	1946	-2	-117	-115	1831

b) Tinn

Period	Pop. 1.1	Nat. incr.	Net. migr.	Pop. change	Pop. 31.12
1985-89	7270	-239	-150	-394	6876
1990-94	6876	-159	70	-95	6781
1995-99	6781	-158	-73	-234	6547
1985-99	7270	-556	-153	-723	6547

c) Årdal

Period	Pop. 1.1	Nat. incr.	Net. migr.	Pop. change	Pop. 31.12
1985-89	6370	97	-202	-113	6257
1990-94	6257	71	-397	-321	5936
1995-99	5936	93	-224	-130	5806
1985-99	6370	261	-823	-564	5806

d) Nordkapp

Period	Pop. 1.1	Nat. incr.	Net. migr.	Pop. change	Pop. 31.12
1985-89	4525	94	-645	-550	3975
1990-94	3975	84	-145	-57	3918
1995-99	3918	60	-452	-401	3517
1985-99	4525	238	-1242	-1008	3517

e) Vardø

Period	Pop. 1.1	Nat. incr.	Net. migr.	Pop. change	Pop. 31.12
1985-89	3365	-21	-329	-357	3008
1990-94	3008	45	-41	2	3010
1995-99	3010	28	-330	-292	2718
1985-99	3365	52	-690	-647	2718

Source: Statistics Norway. 1999 date are provisional.

Notes: Subtotals for natural increase and net migration do not always add up to the sum total, because the latter may have been adjusted, while the subtotals have not.

pay for numerous jobs in public services. The elementary school leavers therefore chose vocational studies relevant for the expanding local labour market. Young people from Aurland knew that higher education might lead to out-migration, partly because they had to take this education outside Aurland, partly because there were few local jobs for people with higher education. One-third of those interviewed in 1984 had already left Aurland, and one-fifth had temporarily left Aurland for higher education elsewhere, and probably only a few of these would return. The 1984 study assumed that one-half of those born in Aurland between 1956 and 1962 would leave Aurland for good before they were 30 years old.

Svein Tønnessen, himself from Aurland, in 1985 believed that the favourable local labour market situation could not last much longer. A high level of public services had been reached, and most of the jobs were held by young people. He assumed that the 16- and 17-year-olds who were finishing elementary school in 1985 would be aware of this, and therefore would proceed with secondary education. He interviewed 32 school leavers about their plans. To his surprise, he found that only one-fifth of them intended to continue their education. The great majority wanted to live and work in Aurland. Why shouldn't they find local jobs when school leavers before them had succeeded? Besides, they had observed that higher education easily led to out-migration. Tønnessen was worried on their behalf. They risked not getting local jobs, and they might also be losers on a national labour market which primarily needed people with secondary and higher education.

In 1996, two of the 1984 school leavers from Aurland---one of them a graduate student of geography in Bergen---tried to find what had happened to their school friends. Had they lost out in Aurland? Had they become losers in the national labour market? Almost one-half of the 1984 class lived in Aurland in 1996. Most of those who had not continued their education after elementary school remained in Aurland. The men had found jobs in small private firms, through kinship and friendship. The women initially worked in temporary jobs in playschools, old peoples' homes and in other public services, but soon found out that they needed more education to get a permanent job. The regional college in Sogndal offered teachers' and nurses' courses, and a new express boat service made it possible for Aurland students to live at home when studying there. Some of the male school leavers had gone to technical college, in the hope of finding local jobs with Oslo Energy and Norwegian Railways. Many of the women found relevant jobs in Aurland, as vacancies in existing public jobs gave them openings in the local labour market. There were fewer local openings for men with higher education. As a consequence, out-migration was more frequent among men than among women. This indicates that the modern service-producing society offers more local openings for women than the old, commodity-producing society. Young men, not young women, may be the first to leave peripheral communities in the future.

In some ways, things did not turn out as Tønnessen had believed in 1985. But there are similarities between the school leavers of the mid-seventies and of the mid-eighties. About one-half of them have left, and among them were people who had not expected to leave. Many other migration studies have come up with similar results. The Aurland case shows that different age cohorts meet varying opportunities when they leave school, but in the long run, the young tend to choose an education which is more related to national standards than to local needs. In many ways Aurland is a good place to live in, with adequate public services. It has gradually come out of its geographical isolation. Many of those growing up in Aurland prefer the local lifestyle. But for many of them, Aurland is too small, and the local labour market does not present them with jobs they have educated themselves for. The age group 20-29 is declining, the number of retired people increasing, and the local demography is not very dynamic (Table 4.1a).

Aurland is by no means in crisis, but the perceptions about the community held by those who grow up there, expressed through their choices of education, occupation and residence, slowly erode the part of Aurland's resources not related to natural, but to human capital. Through their actions, the "powerless" local actors have the power to change the community, slowly, but in a problematic direction.

2. Forty Years of Restructuring in Rjukan

Historical background The location of Rjukan in Tinn municipality (Figure 4.2) is both typical and atypical. The town lies along a narrow valley ending in a steep rock wall. A river draining an extensive mountain plateau falls over this rock wall. Similar locations have given rise to numerous one-company towns, where hydro-electric power is used in energy-intensive metallurgical and chemical industries. What makes Rjukan atypical is that is is situated far from the coast. Norsk Hydro initially produced fertiliser there, using a new, energy-intensive technology taking oxygen and nitrogen out of the air. The finished products were taken down to the coast on a single-track railway, including a ferry. The disadvantages of distance were countered by energy advantages. The first big hydro-electric power station in Rjukan was completed in 1911, at a time when there was no technology for transferring high tension electricity over long distances.

Before the arrival of Norsk Hydro, Tinn had been an overpopulated rural community, with a maximum population of 3,550 in 1855, and less than 3,300 in 1900. Emigration to the United States had been considerable since the 1870s. Between 1900 and 1910, during the construction period, the population almost doubled, to 5,500; 2,200 of them lived in Rjukan. In 1920, Tinn's population was 12,000, and 8,500 of them lived in Rjukan, the fastest growing one-company town in Norway between 1900 and 1920. At that time, the introduction of new technologies in the production of agricultural fertilisers had already reduced the competitive advantages of Rjukan, and Norsk Hydro would probably have left the town if it had been politically possible. An alternative location had already been selected near the coast, and new chemical complex was opened there in 1928. New transmission technology now made it economically possible to transfer hydro-electric power from Rjukan to the coast. As long as international markets for fertilisers expanded during the 1920s, Norsk Hydro could keep running both the inland plants as well as the new plants at the coast. But with declining export markets in the early thirties, Hydro had to reduce production. Notodden, an inland one-company town situated between Rjukan and the coast, suffered most. The Norwegian government intervened in the restructuring process, setting strict conditions for giving Norsk Hydro permission to transfer hydro-electric power from the inland power stations to the coast. This was the first important case where government intervened to save one-company towns in difficulty---a policy which became widespread in the 1970s. The Second World War "saved" Rjukan, and post-war economic growth made it possible to consolidate the production in Rjukan through the fifties. In 1960, 10,000 people lived in Tinn; two-thirds of them in Rjukan. Norsk Hydro employed 1,700 people. In 1963, Norsk Hydro reduced the production of fertiliser in Rjukan, and in 1965 the company presented a ten-year plan of factory closures. During the sixties, Norsk Hydro employment in Tinn was more than halved (to 700 people), and the municipality lost 1,500 inhabitants. Annual net out-migration between 1964 and 1970 fluctuated between 200 and 300 persons. The powerless local actors saw the writing on the wall and left. It was not hard to find new jobs elsewhere, since the restructuring of Rjukan started before industrial restructuring became widespread in Norway.

Regional policy measures were introduced, resulting in 500 new jobs in manufacturing industries in the sixties, not sufficient to compensate for the jobs lost. Most of the new jobs were in enterprises coming from the outside, and several of these enterprises went bankrupt after a few years. Local political authorities, backed by central authorities, also worked hard to persuade Norsk Hydro not to close its processing plants. The carrot was public funding for alternative jobs, the stick was to hold back permission for further transfer of hydro-electric power from the region.

Tinn was not a poor municipality. Like Aurland, it had considerable income in the form of company taxes. It therefore could afford to expand its public services, which meant new jobs, many of them filled by women. But male industrial workers made redundant often went into early retirement, and some of them left---perhaps as return migrants to their place of origin.

The 1970s and 1980s were characterised by continuous industrial restructuring, not so dramatic as that of the sixties, but population continued to decline, from 8,300 in 1970 to 6,500 by the end of 1999. The drainage of people through out-migration was less important than in the sixties. But one effect of many years of out-migration has been a gradual ageing of the population and an excess of deaths over births (Table 4.1b). Between 1985 and 1999 the population decrease was more than 700. Three-fourths of this was an effect of negative natural increase, one-fourth an effect of net out-migration. One cause of the reduction of net out-migration in recent years could be that a long blood-letting period was over, that there is at present an equilibrium between demand and supply of jobs. But it could also be an effect of the ageing of population; elderly people tend to stay, whereas young people leave. It should also be added that in recent years Tinn has received foreign immigrants, most of them political refugees.

Local actors with power tried hard to get new jobs to Tinn during the seventies and eighties. After the dramatic restructuring of Norsk Hydro, local actors tended to turn elsewhere for allies, but the results often were disappointing. Towards the end of the eighties, Norsk Hydro once more entered the stage, this time in a more positive role than during the sixties and seventies. Its electro-chemical production in Rjukan was very unprofitable, and Hydro did not want to modernise its plants since the new technologies involved the use of oil or gas in the production of fertilisers, and therefore transport costs would be prohibitive. In 1988, a deal was made between the government and Norsk Hydro. Hydro was permitted to close down the remaining processing industries and to transfer hydro-electric power out of the region. The condition was that Hydro replaced the lost jobs with new jobs. In 1988 less than 600 persons worked in various Hydro activities in Rjukan, 400 of them in electro-chemical manufacturing. In 1999, 710 people were at work in Norsk Hydro's industrial park, 500 of these in Hydro companies, 200 in other firms. Most of the jobs are in technological consulting services, in accounting and financial services, and in various commercial activities. Norsk Hydro employs 40,000 people world-wide, and the Rjukan enterprises have an important part of their markets within the company. At present, Norsk Hydro in Rjukan is a service industry with access to markets all over the world. People working within the old system have been retrained, and young people also profit from training-on-the-job offers. Co-operation between local political actors and Norsk Hydro has improved during recent years, and there is a guarded optimism among local restructuring actors. Is this optimism shared by actors without power?

Is Rjukan a liveable place for young people? Surveys have tried to answer this question. The first study (Førlandsås,1979) is based upon questionnaire interviews with five cohorts of elementary school leavers between 1954 and 1971, aged between 18 and 21 when interviewed in 1978. The first cohort left school before the restructuring process had begun, the last in the middle of it. It seemed reasonable to assume that local labour market conditions would influence migration; more people would leave when the local labour market was shrinking. But Kjell Førlandsås found that almost 60 per cent of the 1954 school leavers had left Tinn by 1978, the corresponding percentage for the 1971 cohort was 40. Whereas 60 per cent of those who had left, mentioned further education as an important reason for leaving, only 36 per cent mentioned work as a good reason to move. The majority educated itself out of the community. But would they come back? Forty-three per cent of those who had left said no. Most of these held highly qualified jobs, and they were embedded in their present communities. The 53 per cent who might consider going back were less integrated in their present places of residence, and many of them worked in secondary industries. Almost all the potential return migrants mentioned a safe job as an important condition for coming back, but only 17 per cent would accept a job in the existing manufacturing industries of Tinn. After so many years of negative trends in the local labour market, the out-migrants did not have confidence in it. Tinn was not able to make use of the valuable human capital it had exported.

The second study (Hendriks 1992) looked at Tinn in 1991, when, as a result of restructuring, there were more jobs in tertiary than in secondary activities. Coen Hendriks made the assumption that the local labour market in 1991 would be compatible with the work aspirations of the young. He found that most of the women worked in low-skilled jobs, either in the tertiary sector or in factories recently established in Rjukan. Many of the men tended to hold high- or medium-skill jobs. The local secondary education system was not specialised enough to offer courses leading towards high-skill jobs---there were simply not enough students. Most low-skilled workers were recruited locally, but managers in small and medium-sized enterprises complained about the shortage of qualified job applicants for skilled jobs. Hendriks points out that many of these managers had recently arrived in Rjukan, that they managed branch plants of national firms, and that they had little knowledge of the potential of return migrants.

Hendriks also interviewed three cohorts of school leavers, the oldest from 1980, the youngest from 1990. Compared to Førlandsås's study, many more of Hendriks's informants were still in secondary school or in higher education, both because they were younger and because a larger proportion of young people completed a higher education than was the case during the fifties and sixties. Hendriks divided his respondents in three groups; non-migrants, return migrants an out-migrants. As was the case in 1978, most of the out-migrants left to continue their education. But there was a difference. Almost 40 per cent of the out-migrants gave as the most important reason for leaving that they did not feel themselves at home in Tinn. They wanted to go elsewhere to continue their life projects.

Three-fourths of the non-migrants and return migrants did not intend to pursue higher education. The current restructuring had given them new and interesting openings in the local labour market, with opportunities for training on the job. Many of those who never left or who came back gave priority to family-related issues. They wanted jobs for both wife and husband, and nursery schools for their children, and Tinn had much to offer families with small children. Many of the return migrants did not want to live in Rjukan itself, but preferred to live downstream, near a big lake, less in the shadow than the valley, where it was easier to find a one-family house, and closer to urban centres farther south.

Whereas two-thirds of the population of Tinn lived in Rjukan in 1960, at present this is the case of only one-half. The urban centre carries less weight, and this is a drawback in the eyes of the single young people growing up in Rjukan, as it is for young people from rural areas and small towns all over Norway. Whereas young people in the 1950s usually went straight from elementary school to work, most young people at present live through a new intermediary phase of life, between elementary school and work. The young often leave home in this phase of life, primarily for higher education, but also for a different lifestyle. This intermediary phase of life is one of distancing from the parent generation, and from the place they come from. It is also one of new personal relationships, which easily could lead to permanent out-migration for many of those who originally might have thought that the intermediary phase only would be a spatial parenthesis in their lives. By changing their lives, the young actors without power also change the community they grew up in. It is to questions of changes in lifestyles from generation to generation, and consequences of these changes to the communities these generations pass through, that we turn in the next case.

3. Changing Attitudes to Life in a West Norwegian One Company Town: The Case of Årdal

The aluminium smelter town of Årdal As in the preceding cases, a description of the restructuring of the community is necessary in order to understand changing attitudes to daily life over time (detailed information about Årdal is available in Amdam, Gjestland and Hompland 1997). In 1898 local landowners in Årdal sold their waterfall rights to external investors. Årdal, like Tinn, was an isolated and overpopulated rural community with 1,800 inhabitants in 1865, but only 1,300 in 1900. Out-migration, in particular to the United States, had taken its toll. Plans for hydro-electric development were presented, but it took a long time to convert plans to reality. Construction work started in 1910, but the company, owned by Norsk Hydro since 1911, soon decided to keep Årdal waiting, and concentrated its efforts on Notodden and Rjukan. A certain amount of activity (dam building, tunnel drilling, road construction) went on in the inter-war years, but Norsk Hydro never got as far as to finish the power station. It sold out to German investors in 1941, and a frenetic and inefficient construction period started. Up to 5,000 people, many of them prisoners of war, worked in Årdal, but by 1944 the investors abandoned the almost-completed power station and aluminium smelter.

After the war, the property was confiscated by the Norwegian authorities, and work on the power station was taken up again. In July 1946 Parliament decided to set up a state-owned aluminium smelter company. Production of aluminium began in January 1948. A pig iron smelter started production in 1949, but closed after 10 years. The company employed 500 people in 1946, 1,400 in 1950. Three-fourths of the workers were recruited outside Årdal, mainly from neighbouring communities along the Sognefjord. The population of Årdal increased from 2,200 in 1946 to 7,500 in 1970. It took 20 years to convert the industrial community from a collection of temporary barracks to a modern, small town. Many of those living in barracks commuted between their small farms and Årdal. Production increased from 25,000 tons in the early fifties to almost 175,000 tons in the early seventies, when employment reached 2,000. The economic results were satisfactory during most of the fifties and sixties, but the company ran into difficulties in the early seventies, and the number of employed people was reduced for the first time. The company recovered later in the seventies, but in the early eighties it once more became unprofitable, and the State had to save its own company and write off the debts. Årdal and Sunndal Verk, as the company was called, was managed from Oslo. The first managing director, a strong and not very democratic leader, held the job from 1947 to 1964. He and his successor tried unsuccessfully to diversify the production, going as far as a partnership with Alcan between 1966 and 1974---an unhappy episode in the history of Årdal.

Årdal seemed doomed to remain a smelter town. Little was done to improve working conditions in the furnace halls and to clean up the local environment. Local actors in Årdal---politicians and labour unions---were loyal to the Labour Party, to government, and to the state-owned company. In the long run, this acceptance of the status quo by the local actors with power affected the lives of the powerless local actors. Before turning to them, the background history should be completed. The 1980s was a period when, even in Norway, the ideas of a planned economy lost some of their force. Non-socialist coalition governments between 1981 and 1986 raised the question whether government ownership in manufacturing industries could be reduced, if private capital was willing to take over. After the catastrophic results in Årdal in 1981 and 1982, the political leadership of the Ministry of Industry floated the idea that Årdal and Sunndal Verk might be organised differently. In 1984 it was asked to start talks with Norsk Hydro about further co-operation. In 1986 Parliament decided to sell the government's shares in Årdal og Sunndal Verk to Norsk Hydro, also an important producer of aluminium. The process was completed in 1987. As a result of the take-over, local leadership---and responsibilities---had become stronger, cost-consciousness more visible, the physical environment cleaned up, inside as well as outside the furnace halls. A protocol was signed between the company and local political actors about the need for a profitable company, even if that could mean employment reductions. New investment in the production process led to a decrease in employment from almost 2,000 in 1985 to 1,250 in 1997. Whereas only 5 per cent of the production workers in 1987 were certified skilled workers, the proportion in 1997 was 70 per cent. By the end of the nineties, the furnace work is highly mechanised, quite clean, and performed by skilled workers. In 1950, a week's training was considered a sufficient preparation for hard manual work. The first female worker entered the furnace hall in 1972; at present around one-quarter of the production workers are women.

A characteristic problem of isolated one-company towns without hinterlands is that they only serve very local markets. This meant few jobs for women. As the public service sector increased, new jobs for women were created. In Årdal in 1960, 9 out of 10 men held a job, but only 2 out of 10 women. In 1990, 62 per cent of the women had a job. The local multiplier of the aluminium smelter was not big enough to compensate for lost jobs in the smelter. As a result, population declined, after a 1970 maximum of 7,500, to 6,600 in 1980 and 5,800 in 1999, a reduction of almost one-quarter in 30 years. Table 4.1c shows a community where there still is a small surplus of births over deaths, but with a steady net out-migration.

Why do Young People Still Leave Årdal? The industrial restructuring process, as described above, has been relatively successful, but the community still loses people. Why? In an in-depth study, Eli Fosso (1997a, b and c) has investigated changing attitudes to work, education and daily life in Årdal. The first generation of industrial workers came to Årdal in the pioneering years around 1950. The work they were offered in the furnace halls was so hard that the majority quit during the first six months. When those who stayed on grew older, they found, in many cases, that they had lost their health to the company. When their children entered the labour market around 1970, they were advised, not least by their parents, not to work for the company. In a

66

study from the early seventies, more than 70 per cent of the adults questioned said that they would not recommend furnace hall work for young people. Before entering the labour market, most young men of Årdal had summer jobs in the furnace halls, and most of them did not like the heat, soot and dirt there. To them, the knowledge of the company stopped there. In fact, many other jobs in the company were less strenuous, but their existence were under-communicated by the hall workers and by the company itself. Young men who left school at the age of sixteen tended to find these jobs, in maintenance, repair and transport work. But jobs in the furnace halls were still filled by in-migrants.

When the secondary school system was developed in Årdal, priority was given to the gymnas, a general study qualifying for university studies. The engineers and those who held higher administrative jobs at the company and in the community claimed that key personnel would leave Årdal if their children were not offered this option. The company itself and the labour unions did not press for vocational training courses, and the industrial workers wanted their children to get an education which liberated them from industrial work. If priority had been given to vocational training, the part of the company which needed skilled workers might have become more visible for the local population, and the effect could have been that more of the young people in Årdal might have found local jobs.

As things were, social as well as geographical mobility became part of the lives of most children growing up in Årdal. More than one-half of the primary school leavers in 1972 left Årdal. Årdal was a good place for children to grow up in, but also a place young people tended to leave, either for work or for higher education. The dominant attitudes to education and work in Årdal might have been good for the life projects of those who grew up in Årdal, but they had negative effects for local industrial recruitment and for the demographic development of the community. As late as 1988, forty years after production had started, almost two-thirds of those who worked at the company, and only one-half of those under thirty, were not born in the community. The in-migrants filled the top and bottom jobs. 113 of 141 engineers and technicians in 1988 were in-migrants, and 73 per cent of those working in the furnace halls. The "natives" invaded the segments between the two extremes.

When Norsk Hydro took over in 1986, things changed rapidly. Recruitment was restricted to those who went into apprenticeships in order to get professional certificates. The furnace halls were modernised and renovated, and people in Årdal gradually discovered that work in the halls had changed for the better. Fosso (1997a) found that the young generations of the early nineties talked about the company in much more positive terms than the generations of the fifties and the seventies. Many boys entered vocational courses, but were sceptical of a certificate in electrochemistry which might well give them an entry to the company, but there was also a risk that it would bind them to it. They preferred courses in mechanics and machinery, which would give them openings outside the company and Årdal. Those who entered the company in the nineties were more professionally trained than previous generations, partly because most of them had understood that there were no openings for unskilled workers. Besides, the work in the furnace halls had changed. The hard physical work is done by robots.

Those who had opted for non-vocational, general studies of the secondary school were more sceptical about future work in the company. Their frame of reference was the national labour and housing market. The cities were magnets. Many of them entered higher education institutions. They still tend to talk about Årdal as a community with few job opportunities outside the furnace halls. Forty per cent of the out-migrants of the eighties held the view that they would never find a suitable job in Årdal. Perhaps they knew better, but preferred using this view as a justification for leaving a community they simply would not like to live in. Many return migrants found that their old friends were not there. The local social arenas were dominated by those who never had left, and the return migrants felt like outsiders among them. As a result, many of the return migrants left after a short while.

A study from the early seventies (Schiefloe 1975) used the term "one generation society" to characterise Årdal. Fosso (1997c) described three generations. The first generation looked at the jobs in the aluminium smelter as a means of liberating themselves from a stagnant rural life. Their children liberated themselves from Årdal by moving out. The third generation does not put a negative stamp on Årdal, but many of those belonging to this generation use secondary and higher education as a ladder out of the small community into a larger, urban world. Just like in Aurland and Tinn, many people leave despite the fact that the communities they are leaving can offer a wider spectrum of jobs than that available for previous generations. Without explicitly stating it, it is the community as such they want to leave, because they believe in other, more global lifestyles.

4. Coastal Finnmark: A Worst Case

Introductory remarks The economic crisis hitting fishing communities in Finnmark in the second half of the 1980s bears many resemblances to the cod crisis in Newfoundland. It was not only a crisis arising from over-exploitation of marine resources. International and national institutional conditions played their role, and many local actors with power got into trouble because their whole livelihood was threatened. An account of the crisis and the gradual recovery in the nineties is found in Hansen (1999), and from this study some

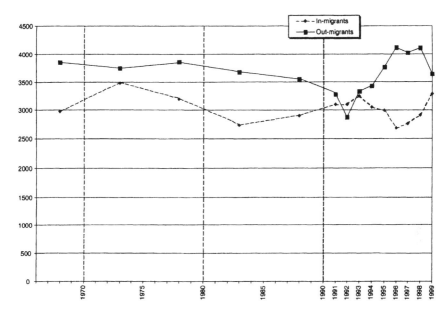

Figure 4.3   Migration to and from Finnmark, 1966-1999

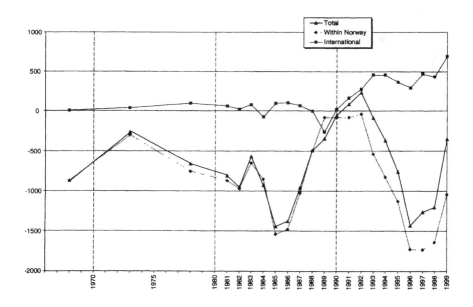

Figure 4.4   Net migration, 1966-1999

69

demographic indicators are presented, as a background for the local cases of Nordkapp and Vardø.

Figure 4.1 reminds us that the acute crisis of the late eighties was embedded in a persistent process of out-migration from north Norway for the last 40 years. Figure 4.3 gives information about migration streams to and from Finnmark since 1966. Only in 1992 did more people arrive than left, an effect of rising unemployment rates in Norway as a whole. If out-migrants from Finnmark lost their work elsewhere in Norway, and could not find new work there, they returned "home", where it was cheaper to live if you only had unemployment benefits to live on. As soon as the national labour market changed for the better in 1993-1994, the gap between out-migrants and in-migrants widened. Figure 4.4 points out the importance of immigration in Finnmark after 1990. Without the immigrants, the situation would have been even gloomier. The impact of immigrants will be discussed in the case of Vardø.

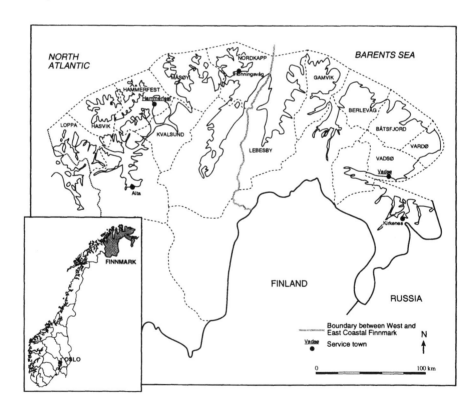

Figure 4.5   Map of Finnmark

Finnmark is divided in Inland and Coastal Finnmark (Figure 4.5). Coastal Finnmark is divided into a western and eastern part. The two service towns, Hammerfest in west Coastal Finnmark and Vadsø in the east, form a category of their own. Table 4.2 follows population development within Finnmark after 1980. There was population growth in Inland Finnmark, and the service towns experienced only a small negative change. But the rest of Coastal Finnmark lost 23 per cent of its population between 1980 and 1999. Coastal east fared better than the west, especially in the 1990s, because many Russian fishing boats landed their cod there. Table 4.3 focuses on the young. The 16 to 29 years cohort was reduced by 24 per cent between 1980 and 1997. In Coastal west the reduction was 39 per cent! The cohort increased in the service towns of Vadsø and Hammerfest between 1980 and 1990, but decline set in during the nineties, in particular in Hammerfest as the centre of Coastal west. Vadsø fared better, being the seat of the county administration.

The quantitative data presented here indicate that something is wrong in Coastal Finnmark, and that local actors without power, the young people, express their opinion of the situation by leaving the region. We now turn to the two cases, Nordkapp and Vardø, to investigate the causes of this desertion.

Table 4.2   Population development in Finnmark, 1980-1998

	Population			1980=100	
	01.11.80	03.11.90	01.01.99	1990	1999
Finnmark	78 692	74 148	74 061	94	94
Coastal Finnmark	40 006	35 220	33 421	88	84
Rest of Finnmark	38 686	38 928	40 640	101	105
Coastal Finnmark					
Service towns (Hammerfest, Vadsø)	15 710	15 241	15 333	97	98
Coastal West	12 609	10 180	8 819	81	70
Coastal East	11 687	9 799	9 271	84	79

Nordkapp and Vardø   You cannot get farther north in Norway than North Cape, and Vardø lies at the same longitude as Cairo. Parts of a 19th century pioneer fringe and an expanding fishing economy, the two communities attained their maximum population around 1968; 5,450 inhabitants in Nordkapp, 4,200 in Vardø. Since then, thirty years of decline: Nordkapp lost 35 per cent of its population and Vardø 34 per cent. The over-fishing of capelin during the seventies and early eighties, resulting in a ban on fishing in 1986, and the subsequent problems in the cod fisheries (capelin was the main

71

food of the cod) contributed to an acceleration of out-migration. In Nordkapp, every year after 1985 has been one of net out-migration, Vardø had only two years with net in-migration. A reduced out-migration during the first years of the 1990s was more an effect of an increase in unemployment rates all over Norway than of changes for the better in the local fishing economies. But the landings of Russian cod gradually brought new hope into the fishing industry, particularly in East Finnmark, where Vardø is situated. Tables 4.1d and 4.1e indicate, however, a turn for the worse in the second half of the 1990s, related to reduced fish quotas for arctic cod. The important point to be made is that fish stocks have always fluctuated. There has always been an inherent uncertainty about the future in communities such as Nordkapp and Vardø. Another point worth mentioning is that growth in services to some extent compensated for the loss of jobs in the fishing economy. But during recent years, growth has been replaced by decline also in service industries, and in public services in particular, as customers are getting thinner on the ground.

Table 4.3   The population of young persons in Finnmark, 1980-1997

	Number of persons			Change 1980 – 1997 (%)
	1980	1990	1997	
Coastal Finnmark	9628	8741	7312	-24
Service towns	3780	3932	3349	-11
Coastal West	3023	2484	1857	-39
Coastal East	2825	2325	2106	-26
Norway	864 205	916 170	912 916	+6

How are local actors coping with a long period of decline? Knut Bjørn Lindkvist (1997) interviewed local actors with power and powerless actors in Nordkapp and three neighbouring municipalities in the early 1990s. The actors with power held positions in the local political and economic systems. The powerless actors were unemployed adults following local vocational courses or being temporarily employed in public projects. Most of the local actors considered the economic situation critical, and that it involved them directly or indirectly. When asked about the future, their views diverged. Four-fifths of the actors with power held a positive view insofar as they believed that they would still live in their communities in the year 2000. This comes as no surprise. Most of them were elderly people who had always lived there; their power was locally embedded. Their boats caught the fish, or they were owners or managers of fish processing plants, or they took active part in the local political system. They had all to lose and everything to defend.

The powerless actors---mainly young people---had worked in the fish processing plants or in unskilled service jobs, but were unemployed when interviewed. A majority of them believed that they would have left their communities before 2000, and only one-third of those who intended to stay on, saw themselves as workers in the fishery system, offshore and onshore.

The actors with power wanted to defend the existing local production system, whereas most actors without power did not have confidence in it. The actors with power could not defend the existing system if the actors without power did not want to work in it. The dialogue between the two actor groups about a common ground should have been better. All the local actors overestimate the importance of the fishery system in the local employment system, and underestimate the importance of service jobs (in the four municipalities, 1,000 people worked in the fishery system in 1990, whereas 3,000 found work in services). Most attention was directed towards the fishery system. The actors with power had a point: without fundamental basic activities, non-basic activities would suffer. What is worrying was that the local actors with power did not come up with viable alternatives. If their assessment of the situation is realistic, then the Finnmark coast is doomed to be carried by, or alternatively to sink with the fishing activities. In Nordkapp, tourism has become very important, and many of the local actors without power see a potential here. But tourism is highly seasonal and does not provide many permanent jobs.

In 1991-1992, Gry Paulgaard conducted in-depth interviews among 15 to 20-year-olds in Honningsvåg, the centre of Nordkapp, in 1995 followed up by a questionnaire survey among primary school leavers (16-year-olds) in three Finnmark communities (among them Nordkapp and Vard˚) (Paulgaard 1996). The general view that work in the fish processing industry held low status, especially among women, was supported by her findings. Although one third of the 85 school leavers who were interviewed thought that the future of the fishing industry would become better, only 7 of the school leavers included the fishing industry in their future plans. They were all men, and most of them did so because they did not want to continue into secondary school. Daughters and sons of fishermen and workers in fish processing industries in coastal Finnmark around 1990 did not follow in their parents' footsteps. Paulgaard claimed that the young carried out-dated representations of these industries. Where they had got these out-dated views from is not clear. They may have got them from friends, from parents, or through the media. But at the same time, a more and more mediatised world gives the young potential alternative views of "the good life". These alternatives were perhaps not very realistic, but they made the old fishery system seem very out-dated. In her 1995 survey, Paulgaard found that school leavers' plans for the future were not influenced by their parents; that they chose independently of their parents' working background, and now we are talking of all parents. Apparently, there is a gap between the parental generation and their offspring. Part of this gap is created by outside influences which media bring into young people's minds in our globalised world.

When interviewed in November 1995 about their plans after elementary school, 89 per cent of those who were about to leave school in June 1996 had already made up plans for the future. Very few considered courses related to the fishing industry (only one of 23 in Nordkapp), and other vocational courses were not popular either. The great majority wanted to go into general courses in secondary school, in reality preparing them for higher education.

Many of the school leavers had already had summer jobs, some in fishing, and in Honningsvåg in tourism. North Cape held an attraction not only for tourists, but also for local youngsters wanting a summer job. Paulgaard notes that tourism comes in as an intervening opportunity, to the detriment of fishing industries. Summer jobs in tourism make fishing look even less attractive. The irony of it is that summer jobs in tourism do not often lead into permanent jobs, whereas summer jobs within the fishery system might have done so. The four major hotels in Nordkapp have altogether 1,100 beds, but almost 950 of them are available only from the end of May to the end of August.

Only a few male elementary school leavers have plans directed towards fisheries, and none of the female school leavers. Tourism provides summer jobs, but few of the young chose an education directed towards tourism. Most of the young go from primary to secondary school, and from there the road leads into higher education. Most of the human capital the students have acquired is then put to use outside Nordkapp. This process has gone on for more than 30 years, sometimes slowly, sometimes rapidly. The long-term effects are evident: the loss of human capital puts communities like Nordkapp in danger. By voting with their feet, the powerless local actors had shown that they after all had the power to change the community---unfortunately for the worse.

Many of those with summer jobs in tourism come from other parts of Norway or from abroad. The fish processing industry has also for many years attracted temporary migrants. Since the fisheries are seasonal and supply of fish varies throughout the year, the import of temporary workers had a rationale of its own, in particular as long as new arrivals were put to work after only a few days of rudimentary training. The fact that temporary workers were easily available, often coming from neighbouring parts of northern Sweden and Finland, may have retarded the modernisation of the processing plants. It was risky to spend a large amount of money in buying modern machinery in periods of fluctuating landings of fish. The owners or managers of processing plants appreciated the flexibility of the labour side of the production system.

In the late eighties, immigrants from distant countries, often arriving in Norway as political refugees, got jobs in the fish processing industry all along the coast of west and north Norway. Vardø is a case of a heavy concentration of such immigrants. Tamils from Sri Lanka arrived in Norway in the late eighties. Many of them had experience from fish processing industries at home. After the fall of the Soviet Union in 1989, Russian trawlers gradually began landing catches of arctic cod in Norwegian fishing ports, where they got much higher prices than in Russian Barents Sea ports. Finnmark, and especially east Finnmark, profited from this, and demand for labour in the processing industry increased. Since it was difficult to attract Norwegians to these jobs, the Tamils were welcomed. In Vardø, the easternmost fishing port of Norway, there were more than 300 in 1997, or around ten per cent of the total population. Table 4.1e shows a relative population consolidation in Vardø during the first half of the 1990s, and the Tamils should be thanked for that.

A recent study (Bersvendsen, 1998) shows that more than 100 of the 270 employed in the two most important fish processing plants were Tamils, and almost all of them worked where cod was filleted---104 out of a total of 134 filleting workers. This work was shunned by Norwegian men and by young Norwegian women, but both female and male Tamils filled the vacancies. Many of the Tamils bought houses in Vardø, and an Asian corner shop was opened. Hilde Skjerven Bersvendsen observed that many of them would have preferred other jobs in Vardø or elsewhere in Norway, but that their scant knowledge of Norwegian was an obstacle to such jobs.

A recent newspaper report from Vardø (*Dagens Næringsliv*, 1999) shows that many Tamils are now leaving Vardø. They started leaving during the summer of 1998, and in June 1999, there were less than 200 left. The Asian corner shop announced its closure sale on June 5th. Why do the Tamils in 1999 vote with their feet? One underlying cause is the reduction of arctic cod quotas, down to 500,000 tons in 1999 from 900,000 tons in 1997. This reduction has a stronger effect on a fishing port like Vadsø than on larger ports farther south where other species of fish to some extent could compensate for the loss. A Tamil foreman at the most important processing plant explains: "From the mid-nineties to 1997 we had good years with plenty of fish, always work to be had and a good income. Those of us who worked hardest could make 300,000 kroner a year (a little less than 40,000 Euros). Now we earn much less money, and many of the workers have experienced that six to eight years of hard work has not been good for their health". Those who first left have told those remaining that it is not difficult to find a job in one of the major cities. Norway is at present in a situation of almost full employment, and there are shortages of people for jobs that most Norwegians would not like to have, such as transport and storage work and cleaning jobs. The Tamil foreman says that Tamils in Vardø have sold houses for half the price they had bought them for, and that housing in Oslo is very expensive. But they feel that after all it is better to leave now, when there is still work to be had. Tamils who made their first acquaintance with Norway in Vardø are now prepared for the next step in a typical push-pull situation: deterioration in Vardø, and the world outside seems promising. To Tamils leaving the filleting tables in Vardø, driving a taxi or cleaning an old people's home in Oslo is seen as a better way of life. It does not come as a surprise that one of the local fish processing plant owners in Finnmark recently told an Oslo newspaper (*Aftenposten* 1999) that the Norwegian authorities should give Russian immigrants permission to work in the fish processing industry. And in 2000, the authorities opened up temporary migration from Russia.

Most people in coastal Finnmark get their incomes from work in services, but they live there because of the basic fishing economy. We have seen how imports of fish and labour have helped to keep this economy going. Finnmark will have to live with structural changes in the natural resource base and in commodity and labour markets in the years to come. But it does not look as if young people in the coastal communities have ambitions to reconquer the filleting tables or to man the fishing boats. Modernisation of the fishing system also leads to changes in working conditions. More specialised knowledge is required in production, marketing and administration, and some of the young people have acquired such knowledge, but most of them still carry with them out-dated views about work in the fishing system. Managers and other key personnel often come from other parts of the country to work in the Finnmark fish companies---which, by the way, often also have external owners. As long as this situation persists, local actors without power will go on leaving Finnmark. This is not a good omen for the future of fishing communities in Finmark.

Concluding Remarks

Economic restructuring is a continuous process taking place on and between different spatial levels. This paper has dealt mainly with the local level, through five case studies from natural resource-based communities in peripheral parts of Norway. The resources are either hydro-electric power (Aurland, Tinn and Årdal) or fish (Nordkapp and Vardø). Aurland exports its energy, whereas the other four communities have export-based processing industries. Aurland's market is protected in the sense that the energy is used mainly in Norway. The other four communities depend upon fluctuating export markets and are exposed to global competition. Their locations are historical---fish had to be processed near the fishing grounds, hydro-electric energy had to be used near the power station. Today, fish is often processed near the markets, the energy transmitted to more central locations. The communities survive because of inertia. The invested capital is the main justification for hanging on.

What was initially an advantageous location for utilisation of natural resources is now also a disadvantageous location for alternative economic activities. Two main strategies have been followed. One has been to extend downstream activities, for instance to make fish fingers instead of exporting frozen fillets, or to make aluminium profiles, tubes or rolled products instead of ingots. But such downstream activities tend now to be located near the markets. Most of the important enterprises in the localities studied are owned by big national companies who practice an internal division of labour, where the marginally located units are stuck with their traditional roles. Rjukan is an exception worth a closer look.

The second strategy is to establish new enterprises in these communities, as a counterweight to the dominant companies. But the remoteness and isolation of most of the communities work against this strategy. With regional policy support, some new firms have located production units in these communities, but the impact has been modest and often of a temporary nature. Local actors with power have often opted for a status quo strategy---let us go on doing what we already can do. Local entrepreneurship is encouraged, but is often relatively absent from communities which have been dominated by one single company or a cluster of production units within the same branch of industry. Local political actors are continuously lobbying the national decision level for decentralizations, but again with modest results.

The local actors with power often feel powerless. Their strategies are not necessarily appreciated by the young growing up in these communities. All the five cases demonstrate that young people vote with their feet, whatever strategies are being followed. The great mover is education, especially when the students have to leave their home places. They soon tend to root themselves in the centres where they study, and many young people who expressed their intention to come home after their education was completed do not return. The reason they often give is that there is no work for them. This is not necessarily true. Many young people carry with them representations of their communities which might have been valid when for instance their parents grew up. They undervalue the supply of skilled work in the processing industries, and they underestimate the number of jobs in local private and public services. This under-evaluation may be an effect of scant and haphazard information offered by the employers and other local actors with power. It may also be an effect of the reproduction of negative views of the employment situation, often transmitted by the parental generation. But behind these justifications for not coming home there are in many cases a lack of motivation for re-entering the social life of these small, isolated communities. The potential return migrants have experienced alternative lifestyles, and when they have to choose, they opt for these alternatives. But it is easier to complain about work opportunities than to state openly that they do not feel at home in the communities they grew up in. The case studies also demonstrate how out-migration gradually accelerates the ageing of the population of these communities, which again makes them less desirable for return migrants.

These final remarks are generalisations, and must be understood as such. No community is like any other community. The main objective of this paper has been to underline the word unique. When structural overviews and theoretical approaches to the concept of actors have been digested, time has come to tell the local narratives. A well-documented narrative, where the voices of local actors can be heard, is perhaps the best point of departure for the formulation of local and regional policies for marginal communities.

References

Aftenposten. 1999. Russisk fisk forer Bøtsfjord. 24 April.

Amdam, R. P., D. Gjestland and A. Hompland (eds.). 1997. *Årdal: Verket og bygda 1947-1997.* Oslo: Det Norske Samlaget.

Bersvendsen, H. S. 1998. Flerkulturelt arbeidsmiljø: Kem e det som skal telpasse sæ, vi eller dem? *Perspektiver på norsk fiskerinæring.* Rapport 1/98, Honningsvåg: Kystnæringssenteret.

Dagens Næringsliv. 1999. Vardø tømmes for torsk og tamiler. 22 June.

Fosso, E. J. 1997a. Vil ungdom bli boende på industristeder under omstilling. Arbeidsnotat 1997:7. Bergen: SNF.

Fosso, E. J. 1997b. Industristeders arbeidstilbud og generasjoners forhold til utdanning,arbeid og sted: eksempelet Årdal. Unpublished Ph.D. thesis, Department of Geography, University of Bergen.

Fosso, E. J. 1997c. Industriens barn. In Amdam, Gjestland and Hompland (q.v.).

Førlandsås, K. 1979. Tinn kommune i flytteperspektiv: en undersøkelse av utflytternes flyttemønstre og vilkår for tilbakeflytting. Unpublished M.A. thesis, Department of Geography, University of Bergen.

Hansen, J. C. 1995. The restructuring of one-company towns. In R. Byron (ed.),

Economic Futures on the North Atlantic Margin. Aldershot: Avebury.

Hansen, J. C. 1997a. Livsløp i tid og rom. In I. Frønes, K. Heggen and J. O. Myklebust (eds.), *Livsløp: Oppvekst, generasjon og sosial endring.* Oslo: Universitetsforlaget.

Hansen, J. C. 1997b. Municipal reform: A prerequisite for local development? In R. Byron, J. Walsh and P. Breathnach (eds.), *Sustainable Development on the North Atlantic Margin.* Aldershot: Ashgate.

Hansen, J. C. 1999. Why do young people leave fishing communities in coastal Finnmark, North Norway? In R. Byron and J. Hutson (eds.), *Local Enterprise on the North Atlantic Margin.* Aldershot: Ashgate.

Hansen, J. C. and I. L. Grønlund. 1999. De lokale omstillingsakt°rene: en komparativ stedsanalyse. Report 50/99. Bergen: SNF.

Hansen, J. C. and T. Selstad. 1999. *Regional omstilling: strukturbestemt eller styrbar?* Oslo: Universitetsforlaget.

Hendriks, C. 1992. Hvor blir det av Rjukan-ungdommen? Unpublished M.A. thesis, Department of Geography, University of Bergen.

Høydahl, E., H. Skiri and L. Østby. 2000. Sosialt utsyn 2000 (chapter on population). Oslo: Central Bureau of Statistics.

Lindkvist, K. B. 1997. Næringsomstilling i perifere fiskerisamfunn. Hvordan møter lokale aktører utfordringen? *Arbeidsnotat* 1997:6. Bergen: SNF.

Paulgaard, G. 1996. Ungdom i tre kystsamfunn: nye muligheter og tradisjonelle oppfatninger. SF 01/96. Tromsø: NORUT Samfunnsforskning.

Schiefloe, P. M. 1975. Engenerasjonssamfunnet: en sosiologisk studie i norsk distriktspolitikk. Årdalsprosjektet, rapport nr. 5. Oslo: Department of Sociology, University of Oslo and NIBR.

Selvik, A. 1974. Skolebarns aspirasjoner i marginale lokalsamfunn: sosiale indikatorer. Rapport nr. 12. Department of Sociology, University of Bergen.

Solberg, M. 1980. Utkantungdom, utdanning og yrke. Unpublished M.A. thesis, Department of Sociology, University of Bergen.

Teigen, H. 1999. *Regional økonomi og politikk.* Oslo: Universitetsforlaget.

Tønnessen, S. T. 1985. Arbeids- og utdanningsvandring: utdanningsnivo og arbeidsmarknad i Aurland, under og etter kraftutbygginga. Unpublished M.A. thesis, Department of Geography, University of Bergen.

5 Surviving the Farm Crisis: Ways Forward for Farmers in South West Wales

JOHN HUTSON

This paper opens with the background and findings of a research project which looked at fifty farm families in Pembrokeshire, south west Wales in 1980-81. It gives a brief account of the pattern of agricultural restructuring over the intervening period and the recent drop in farming returns which are down some 56 per cent from last year. It then goes on to report some of the findings from a re-study of these same farms some eighteen years on, giving an account of the way in which economic recession has an uneven impact on farm businesses according to the size of holding, type of farming, the stage of farm and family cycles as well as the life course.

Introduction

In this paper I look at farming. The conditions of farming production are generally taken to be more stable than fishing; however, farming can prove to be no less uncertain, and equally prone to unexpected crises created by technological pressure or policy change. In the autumn of 1980 I began on a research project to look at family farming in south west Wales. Some twelve years earlier I had done fieldwork in the southern French Alps where a peasant farming system was giving way to industrial work in an aluminium factory in the main valley and to work in tourism-related enterprises most of which were family run (Hutson, 1971). After some twenty years of outmigration, young people were now finding jobs locally and staying on in the village. From this earlier research, I became interested in the links between family and business as well as in how changing economic and social situations may influence family forms and strategies. Thus, the UK farming industry seemed a good place to pursue these ideas. Farming, as a major primary productive industry was unique in that 97.5 per cent of farms were family owned and run businesses (Harrison, 1975).

In south Wales, where I was working, Pembrokeshire had a diverse economy of farming, industry (the oil terminals and processing plants around

81

Milford Haven) and tourism. Eighteen years ago, I talked to fifty farm families as well as some estate agents, auctioneers, bank managers and agricultural merchants. The farm families came from 'snow ball' samples which rolled from three main sources, a local farmer contact, a lecturer on the agricultural training course in the local college and a list of county council owned farms. So it was not a formal random sample, but one which I think ended up with a reasonably representative variety of agricultural region, farm type and size.

Farm Families in Productionist Agriculture

In 1980 I had set out to compare family labour farms with ones which employed non-family labour. However, this did not turn out to be a very significant variable in the farms I looked at. More important than labour was the family aspect of farm management. The previous thirty years had been a very dynamic time in farming with rapid growth in both agricultural production and in farm businesses alongside fast moving changes in farming practice. In turn, all these aspects were supported and encouraged by the growing complexity of the farming context through the development and effects of new technology, markets, tax laws, tenancy laws, EEC and government policies and subsidies, in addition to the influence of the large commercial corporations which surround farming---the seed, feed, chemical and machinery companies, supermarkets and banks.

The early to mid 1980s was a time of some prosperity in farming. Maximisation of production was still the policy which drove farming and everything was geared to increasing output. One consequence of this emphasis on increasing production was a changed relationship between family, farm and business. There had been, what I called, a move from generational fragmentation to generational integration (Hutson, 1987, 1990).

Between the wars on small family farms in south west Wales, parents would aim to set up sons on farms of their own, usually as tenants, when they married---maybe also giving them some stock or machinery to start up with. After that, they were on their own to make their fortune, or not, by building on this foundation of occupational succession combined with pre-mortem inheritance. Daughters were expected to marry farmers. The youngest son would be expected to stay with his ageing parents working for his father on the farm and eventually inheriting either it or the tenancy.

From the 1950s, policies to increase production, new tax and tenancy laws and the rising cost of land all meant that the logical move was for children to remain on the family farm. With the pressure to increase production, farms were growing and needed not just children's labour but their management

82

skills for the farm business. Because these businesses were expanding, children had the opportunity to take on responsibility for running a new enterprise---such as building up the milking herd or improving lambing rates. The process of succession, bringing children into the management of the farm, thus became the critical process. Inheritance, the legal transfer of ownership, was put off into the future.

Of course, alongside the successes were the failures---those farms that went bankrupt or had no children to succeed. However, as these farms came on to the market, other farmers had the chance to buy more land and expand their businesses. Overall, the process was one resulting in fewer, larger farms---a process which has continued steadily with the "marginal" size of farms creeping ever upwards.

What impressed me at the time was the continuing importance of the relationship between family and farm. Farming was now fully commercial and big business, but it was still largely owned and run by families. Moreover, family needs still influenced business decisions. A child leaving school or university might precipitate a move to buy land, expand the herd or invest in a new parlour even if profit margins, interest rates or current grants might not make this the most commercially "efficient" time to begin such ventures.

Thus, how control was passed from one generation to another became a key process and succession was separated from inheritance. The contribution of family members went way beyond simply providing family labour. In the expanding businesses it was all about management. A family farm did not just mean a family-worked farm but a family-managed farm (Gasson et al., 1988).

This had a direct effect on family forms and the content of family relationships. There were new forms of extended family business partnerships as well as changes in what it actually meant to be a father, son, wife or daughter-in-law when people worked together in new ways. It was a clear example of the way the form and content of family relationships are linked to relations of production and market forces in particular cultural and social settings (Hutson, 1987).

The Beginning of the Farm Crisis

By the mid 1980s, only a few years after my first research ended, there was a major policy change away from a production-oriented agriculture to one which sought to be sustainable, extensive and environmentally concerned. This change was motivated by huge production surpluses and by a growing public perception of damage done to wildlife, the countryside and the landscape by the regime of intensive farming.

The changing direction of state support led to the introduction of quotas restricting production. In 1984, milk quotas, the first of the production quotas to be introduced, were imposed. Other quotas followed and both agricultural and non-agricultural diversification were encouraged---farmers were advised to consider rearing ostriches, running haulage firms or providing services for tourists.

Environmental and conservation programmes were also promoted. The concept of stewardship was introduced to replace that of production. Compensation was offered to farmers who took land out of production as "set-aside" and incentives were offered for the management of newly designated Environmentally-sensitive Areas (ESAs) or areas of Special Scientific Interest (SSIs). Additionally, in Wales, 80 per cent of agricultural land was classified as being of Less Favoured Area status and was thereby eligible for special subsidy support.

However, the loss of production oriented grants led to a general fall in farm incomes as production prices continued to rise and resulted in real hardship for those with debts to service. Children were no longer encouraged, nor were so keen, to join the family farm as agriculture seemed to offer an uncertain career and farms could not support two generations. Even if they wanted to farm later on when their parents retired, there was little other local employment around for them to do, while they put in some work on the farm or invested off-farm earnings in it.

There also began to be a change in the public's perception of farmers, who were now presented by the media as villains rather than as heroes. They were no longer seen as those who fed the nation but as polluters of nature and food; or as rural 'fat cats' being paid for letting wild geese graze their grass or orchids grow in undrained bogs.

Since farming makes and maintains the countryside, there were concerns on all sides about both the future of farming and the future of the countryside. In Wales, 82 per cent of the land area is under some form of agricultural use, and it is estimated that around 25 per cent of the working population of Wales is still directly or indirectly dependent on agriculture or associated businesses (Welsh Office, 1995, 1996).

The Current Situation

Through the media, everyone in the UK has heard about the crisis in agriculture, markets collapsing, input costs up, output prices down and farm incomes cut. Over the last three years, average UK farm profits are down by 82 per cent and that includes a drop of 56 per cent over the last twelve months to June 1999. Last year, milk prices to producers dropped by about 19 per cent and cattle prices fell by about 28 per cent. Lamb prices this year have fallen even more than that. Since 1996 the effects of the BSE crisis have really hit Welsh agriculture hard since it is based on livestock farming. All of which prompted me to go back and talk to the Pembrokeshire farmers I had seen back in 1980 to find out how they fared over the past 18 years. They also represented a reasonable sample to cope with in the three months research time available to me.

The Yellow Pages telephone directory lists farmers as an occupation and is an initial resource for contacting farmers. I wrote to farmers first and then followed the letter up with a telephone call to arrange an interview. Families were very welcoming, and I was often invited to stay for lunch. I read up my old notes before I telephoned so that I could re-establish my credentials by mentioning something from eighteen years back. The other side of the coin was that a number then asked me for articles written after the last research.

I managed to contact members of 35 of the original 50 farm families, including some who had moved farms. I failed to contact the other one-third, who were no longer living on, nor were their families still farming, the 1980 holding. Of those interviewed, 69 per cent were dairy farmers; 9 percent were arable vegetable farmers growing cauliflower, cabbage and new potatoes; and 6 per cent ran mixed enterprises. Most had experimented with some kind of agricultural diversification and 41 per cent of households had major pluriactive income from non-agricultural enterprises. Sixteen per cent were fully retired or no longer farming. Fifty-three per cent had children who were business partners who had fully or substantially taken over the running of the business. Only one farm was run by a woman, although most wives and daughters did work on the farm or ran farm enterprises unless they had another income producing job.

Most households said they had managed to survive the crisis so far although all had suffered loss of income. They tended to make jocular remarks such as, "Well, at least we won't being paying so much tax this year!". However, the actual example of one farm where the tax bill was down from £20,000 to only hundreds of pounds reveals only too clearly the real drop in income which such farm families have suffered. Nonetheless, and contrary to my expectations at this time of farm crisis, I did not find the level of desperation I had feared from reading the media reports. Why was this and what features could account for this contrast with the media image?

Findings

Those I revisited, by the very fact that they were still in business after 18 years, were self-selected as survivors. Just under two-thirds of my original sample were still in the phone book. The others might have had a very different story to tell. Although, it is probable that a majority of those whom I failed to contact are probably dead or retired from farming. In other words, they may have failed to hand their business on to the next generation rather than their business having failed. They may be failures of succession rather than business failures. However, the decision to sell up and retire may be linked to falling returns and market pressures. Thus, if those contacted who have left or retired from farming are added to those whom I failed to contact, the indication is that only 54 per cent of those families farming in 1980 were still farming in 1999. This would seem to confirm the severe pressure under which family farming has come during that period. Given that economic downturns do not hit everyone in the same way, why have these businesses survived? The type of production, locality, the stage in the farm cycle, and in the life course seem to be key elements in varying the impact of recession.

The type of agricultural production is certainly a significant factor. Sixty-nine per cent of my interview sample were made up of dairy farmers. No one was dependent solely on beef or sheep, although many had sheep flocks or suckler herds as well as large numbers of replacement stock. Dairy farmers were better off than livestock producers. The price of milk had fallen but not by the same proportion as livestock prices. However, even within my small sample, farmers varied from those who said they ". . . had no problems" to those who said they constantly thought, "Am I going to be here in 12 months' time?". There were those who confidently planned their next strategy to increase production or income as well as those who said, "We live day by day" or, "We just try to hang on and hope it gets better!". However, a common remark was that they were better off than "many of the upland livestock farmers".

Thus, the majority were dairy farmers and milk prices have not fallen as much as stock prices. Nonetheless, the dairy sector has not been without its problems and incomes are down by 20 per cent. A drop in milk price of 20 pence per litre represents a reduction of some £13,000 in the annual income of the average 70-cow herd. There has also been the introduction of £13 charge per collection of milk---insignificant to large producers but critical to small ones as it can amount to over £4,000 a year. BSE had been a devastating experience for most of them. They did not feel they deserved as much blame as they have had. Most could identify exactly which batch of feed caused their problem, but said they had had no idea what was in it at the time. And they talked of the cull of cattle as a terrible experience---seeing a generation of cows they had bred and reared from calves just going to slaughter---a further rejection of the work which gave them their livelihood and marked their identity. But dairy farmers did recognise that other sectors were worse off than themselves at the moment.

Thus, the Pembrokeshire region has the climate and geomorphology for dairy farming and some sheltered coastal areas have few frosts and are particularly suitable for vegetable crops such as winter cauliflowers or early potatoes. However, geographical remoteness from centres of population reduces marketing choices. For example, milk producers nearer to large centres of population have more choice of processor to sell their milk to.

The area is also one of great natural beauty so there is a tourist market for produce, accommodation and countryside activities. There are numerous current attempts to create and supply local niche markets. However, south Wales to the west of Cardiff is currently suffering an economic decline with less inward investment and the decline of traditional employment in military bases, oil refineries and even traditional forms of tourism such as bed and breakfast. However, the region is included within the area of west Wales which has recently been designated as qualifying for European Union Objective 1 funding of £1.6 billion for 2000-2006. Qualification is based on a GDP per capita for the area of less that 75 per cent of the EU average which is a further indicator of regional economic decline.

The point in business growth and in the life course of owners are other significant factors. Given the length of time they have been in business, my sample tended to be established farm businesses without recent heavy borrowings or large debts to service. More than half (53 per cent) already have successors who are well established in the farm business or who have taken over its running. Thus, succession and long-term survival are built into their business management strategies. Also, most farms were over two hundred and fifty acres which has now become the marginal size of viable, full-time agricultural holding.

Family Farms Today

A major interest of mine is in the links between business and family---how the one affects the form and organisation of the other---and the significance of this relationship came out strongly in both the earlier and the current research.

There appeared to be a strong link between expansion of the farm or of production and children coming into the business. All those who had expanded their agricultural businesses had children who had succeeded into the business. Where diversification or pluriactivity had taken place this was sometimes also a response to children joining the business. Margaret, with three sons, said: "We thought surely one of them will come into farming?". So she and her husband had borrowed money to buy a neighbouring farm which came up for sale while all the children were still at school. Half the current sample have children entirely or substantially involved in the farm enterprise.

However, most said they did not see themselves as a "family farm". One reason for this seemed to be that there was still a strong association of "family farm" with a small, inefficient and traditional holding. So for many it has strong negative connotations. Significantly, however, one of the very biggest commercial concerns did stress their family orientation as if, perhaps, to legitimise their commercial success. Nonetheless, it was interesting that among many of those denying their family farm status, there still seemed to be a clear involvement of family goals in the business. This might involve drawing money out of the farm for either retirement housing or for children's university education. Len gave free use of farm buildings to one son for his aroma therapy wholesale business and joined an ESA scheme, so that he could give his other son work laying all his hedges and give him a chance to set up his own business doing similar work on other farms. John and Nickie were in business with their son and with their daughter and son-in-law across a business partnership based on three holdings. There was also a consistent opinion that all children, regardless of gender or whether they came into the farm or not, should be provided for equally as far as possible from the farm. Paul had used capital from the farm business to put down a deposit on a school teacher daughter's house and this would count towards her inheritance. To me, these were all activities of enterprises where business decisions were clearly linked to family goals, yet all these farmers sought to avoid a "family farm" label.

There was a remarkable uniformity to replies about whether people would like their children to come into the business---"Only if that's what they want to do". Some expanded on this to explain that not only was farming going to be a hard living where commitment was vital, but that there were also considerable pressures to working with family members. Chris said, "My brother and I are very different people. We would never even socialise with one another if we were not brothers! We pull together when business is going well, but start to row as soon as the pressure is off!". Mike, who left the family farm when his farm enterprise went bankrupt in his late 30s, said of the period immediately after that, "It was the first time I had made an independent decision in my life!".

In the late 1990s, while farmers talked more of the downside and tensions of working with family, especially with falling markets and incomes, they still put great store on the security of a family business as "something you could always come back to", or as "a pool of financial and material assets that you knew you had access to". Today, many farmers regretted that their children would not be coming into the business, but fewer farms can now support two or more families as they did in the 1980s. The next generation will neither inherit an occupation nor the means to practice it. As Reg said to me "Thank God I haven't got a son coming in, and thank God I'm 50 and not 20!".

Illness and accident have always been linked to heavy manual labour and machinery or, more recently, to chemical hazards such as organo-phosphate poisoning. Accidental death or illness and a long tradition family obligation have meant that some sons and daughters have had to leave school early in order to come back onto the farm to replace their fathers or mothers. There is, however, an equally traditional reluctance of farmers to retire entirely. A determination to keep control of the cheque book can continue even when their successors are running the farm. Richard said, "I know it's an awful thing to say, but I am lucky my father is so ill. Here I am at 30-something running my own farm. All my peers round here are still working with their fathers!".

However, compared to 1980, fewer expected their children to come into farming and more considered retiring. These were both factors which directly affected the way farm business were currently run as well as how plans were made for the future. Several farms were being run down towards retirement by renting out land, leasing out quota, or going in for "set aside" schemes. For those with children taking over the farm, capital had to be invested in a retirement house. The size and luxury of this can cause considerable tensions to the successor who sees capital draining away or borrowings mount. Tenant farmers have particular problems since they have no house to retire to which means that during last ten years or so before retirement they must redirect capital from the farm business into a retirement house.

For those whose children do not want to continue the farm business, there may also be tensions. Parents might plan to sell up in order to realise their final retirement nest egg once they are too old or infirm to live in the country. However, Charlotte's children say, "Oh, don't sell the farm! We might want to keep it as a base to come back to eventually!".

Hilary's uncle told her that his neighbours, who had no children, had just sold up their farm and bought a nice bungalow with a good bit of capital left for their retirement. Whereas he, with three sons hoping to come into the business, was working as hard in his 60s as he had been in his 40s and had more debt than ever before. "Who has the better quality of life?", he asked.

Survival Strategies

Just as 18 years ago, farmers appeared well-informed and knowledgeable about both the national and international agricultural scenes. Many had travelled widely and had first-hand knowledge about both Canadian dairy herds that never went outside and New Zealand herds that never went inside as well as experience gained from their own visits on how their EU neighbours used and abused current regulations.

Such knowledge was used in the strategies farmers employed to maintain income in recession. While recognising that they were better off at the moment than some other sectors of the farming industry, a number of the farmers I talked to were actively pursuing various strategies to stay ahead of falling market prices by cutting production costs, producing more or by adding value to their produce. There were three main forms of such strategies.

Firstly, there were new production systems such as the so-called "New Zealand" system. By drying milk cows off and keeping them outside during the winter, savings could be made on buildings, labour and concentrates. However, this system needs well-drained land, hardy stock and seasonally-available skilled labour.

Another available strategy was going over to an "organic" production system. There is a premium on organic milk of about 10 pence per litre. One organic milk producer also made his own cheese and gained an even greater premium if cheese was taken into account (15 pence). Against conversion are factors such as the time and cost of converting, worries over animal welfare; and doubts that the current premium will hold up with increased production. Organic milk production had been begun by one farm six years ago and they reckoned the premium being paid for organic milk made a lot of difference to their survival.

New breeding strategies were also being used by several farmers to produce a more dual-purpose beef/milk breed to cope with problem of bull calves when breeding dairy replacements. They were trying to cross-breed their milkers to get more of a dual purpose animal whose male offspring will be good for beef and whose female offspring will be good for milk. No official advice was yet available from agricultural advisory services or breed societies. One farmer said his experiments hadn't worked up to now because while the bulls had good conformation for beef, the cows' udders were the wrong shape for current milking clusters---which shows the close development of breed characteristics with technology.

Others were considering making changes to their product. Options were fewer for dairy farmers---apart from going organic or making cheese. There were more options for arable farmers who tried to produce what suits their land and micro climate best. But it could also mean switching crops to maximise on the best subsidy available---growing flax or oil seed rape. What one farmer described to me as "ways of harvesting more subsidy off the land".

Secondly, there were new marketing strategies with some interesting changes in market involvement. Eighteen years ago milk producers did not get involved in selling their product, while vegetable growers used to be active market sellers in both wholesale and retail markets. Then, dairy farmers seemed the least involved in marketing. A tanker just came every day and took away the milk, and a cheque arrived once a month through the post. Today, dairy farmers agonised over price cuts, falling margins, and opportunities to gain a few more pence per litre from different processors. With privatisation of the Milk Marketing Board, they now have, at least in theory, a choice of companies to sell milk to. Although, in west Wales distance from large towns means that in practice they did not actually have much choice. However, there was a movement among some dairy farmers to set up regional co-operatives in order to be able to exert more leverage on processors and supermarkets.

Vegetable growers who 18 years ago would telephone around the markets looking for the best price, now used a local wholesale co-operative as intermediary for their sales to supermarket chains. This involved them in extra costs to pay for farm inspections to count their wildlife and inspect their buildings---how many blackbirds were on the farm and was their diesel tank properly protected---in order to join farm assured produce schemes run by supermarkets to attract customers concerned about food purity and environmental issues. Farmers found these payments frustrating because they might have to pay out to join several different schemes and they suspected that whenever the supermarkets were short of a product, they would buy in the cheapest produce from abroad regardless of its conditions of production.

Organic producers were able to sell to "box system" suppliers or specialist processors. Some also sold directly from the farm to summer visitors. A number of farms were adapting to find niche markets for their products such as local cheese, organic produce or Welsh Black Beef. Those who were successful did seem to have found a positive identity as producers of high quality food---adding value on the farm and retailing the product locally to minimise value leaking out of the local area (Parrott et al., 1999). Although, while this can foster an increasing regionalism, it can also create local competition within small and specialised markets which can serve to further divide rather than to reinforce the idea of a local farming community.

Thus, to some extent all farmers were realising the need to unite in resistance to powerful food wholesalers and retailers. The successful vegetable marketing group had been set up and there were also moves to form dairy co-operatives and other producer groups to counter falling market prices, but these ventures were struggling against a long-standing reluctance among farmers to co-operate as well as the differential effects of the farm crisis.

Today, unlike 18 years ago, 41 per cent of households gained major pluriactive income from enterprises other than agricultural production on the home farm. Such activities ranged from multi-million pound tourist theme parks to enterprises to marketing ear tags, bull semen or goat embryos. On-farm tourist ventures such as holiday accommodation were popular and many wives now had part- or full-time salaried jobs off the farm. In Pembrokeshire, tourism is the biggest regional income earner, although not all farms were well placed to benefit from this and fashions change. Felicia says she has given up doing Bed and Breakfast accommodation as "the younger generation want high class facilities". She now makes more money selling cakes at local Women's Institute markets.

Because of the cultural ideal in Wales that real farmers farm, those most likely to go into non-agricultural work on the farm or into off-farm work tended to be wives and children (Hutson & Keddie, 1993, 1995; Acheson et al., 1993; Bateman et al., 1993). Thus, farming still has very much a masculine culture, but there has also been a new dependency on farm women for financial viability. Before, women played a vital, but largely invisible, supportive role---looking after the calves, feeding the men or just being around to help when needed. Now, women were playing a very up-front role both as farmers in their own right and as wage earners bringing in an extra income not only to keep the family, but often to support the farm itself.

Thus, a number of farmers were surprisingly optimistic and entrepreneurial, actively seeking to reduce costs and combat falling prices by embarking on new systems of production such as organic farming, new types of production to add value such as cheese making, new schemes of co-operative marketing or new strategies for diversifying income.

Conclusions

There is a clear understanding that production subsidies will end. So farmers try to achieve a balance between continuing to harvest what subsidy they can in the short-term, while moving towards establishing a long-term niche in free markets through more effective co-operatives or local speciality outlets. The general feeling is one of fatalistic optimism. The dice seem to be loaded against them for the moment, but they are willing to try and adapt to meet the changing conditions. Marie said, "I bet you won't find many farms over three generations", (and indeed I did not) suggesting that to be the normal maximum life expectancy of a family business, and also as the result of the difficulties of the next generation continuing to farm in the current economic climate. On the other hand, it is probably even harder to start up farming from scratch than it was eighteen years ago, so the next generation of farmers must come from within farming.

In the boom time of the early 1980s, successful farms could only expand at the expense of the unsuccessful or unfortunate. In the late 1990s recession also hits unequally. Economic downturns do not hit everyone in the same way at the same time. Nor are farmers' reactions, or their scope for action in these circumstances, the same. The majority of the farmers I have seen have lost income but were in the type of farming, stage of business, and point in the life course where they could stand such losses---for a time at least. Others were not in this position, have left farming or will be forced to do so in the near future.

Remembering that just under half those families I talked to in 1980 are no longer in farming, I was struck by the resilience of those who remain. Luck has been with them as well as their structural position, but their ability to look on the bright side and the enormous energy and enthusiasm that still drives some of them in their 60s is remarkable.

References

Acheson, J., L. Davies and H. Edwards. 1993. *A Comparative Study of Pluriactivity in the Less-favoured Farming Areas of Wales: A Final Report to the ESRC.* Aberystwyth: University of Wales.

Bateman, D., G. Hughes, P. Midmore, N. Lampkin and C. Ray. 1993. *Pluriactivity and the Rural Economy in the Less-favoured Areas of Wales.* Aberystwyth: Department of Agricultural Economics, University of Wales.

Gasson, R., G. Crow, R. Errington, J. Hutson, T. Marsden and D. Winter. 1988. The Farm as a Family Business: A Review, *Journal of Agricultural Economics* 39 (1).

Hutson J. K. 1971. A politician in Valloire. In F. G. Bailey (ed.), *Gifts and Poison: The Politics of Reputation.* Oxford: Blackwell.

_____ . 1987. Fathers and Sons: Family Farms, Family Businesses and the Farming Industry. *Sociology* 21.

_____ . 1990. Family Relationships and Farm Businesses in South-west Wales. In C. C.Harris (ed.), *Family, Economy and Community.* Cardiff: University of Wales Press.

Hutson J. K. and Keddie D. 1993. *Household Work Strategies in the Brecon/Merthyr and Fishguard Regions: End of Project Report for the ESRC.* Swansea: Department of Sociology and Anthropology, University of Wales.

_____ . 1995. Pluriactivity as a Strategy for the Future of Family Farming in Wales. In R. Byron (ed.), *Economic Futures on the North Atlantic Margin,* Aldershot: Avebury.

Welsh Office. 1995. *Welsh Agricultural Statistics.* Cardiff.

_____ . 1996. *A Working Countryside for Wales.* London: HMSO.

6 Strategic Marginalisation and Coping Mechanisms: Farm Households in North West France

ALISON McCLEERY

The Policy Context

The Common Agricultural Policy (CAP) has arguably constituted the most contentious as well as the most expensive of the European Union's policies. Its objectives, as set out in Article 39 of the Treaty of Rome, were to stabilise volatile markets for agricultural produce, and may be paraphrased as follows:

- to increase agricultural productivity by the rational application of technology to the factors of production, including labour;

- to promote supply-side equilibrium, thereby ensuring a reasonable standard of living for the agricultural community; and

- to promote demand-side equilibrium, thereby guaranteeing food availability to consumers at reasonable prices.

That the CAP succeeded in achieving the first objective is not in doubt (Robinson, 1991); the second objective has been achieved superficially and at some social cost (Walsh, 1991); while the third objective cannot be said to have been achieved at all (Robinson, 1990). Furthermore, the issue of availability and cost of food is now wholly overshadowed by questions about quality, which at the time of introduction of the CAP was taken for granted. The existence of this gradient of successfulness, and even the advent of the various food scares of the 1990s, is hardly surprising, given that to both maximise farm incomes and minimise consumer prices might be seen as being mutually exclusive (Walsh, 1991). Yet it was probably never seriously in doubt that, as Pearce (1983) has emphasised, the policy's chief objective would be to maintain farm income and that its principal instrument would be price support. The outcome more than met the expectation; Ritson (1997) notes that what was unusual about the CAP was the severity with which that one objective came to dominate the way in which the policy was implemented.

Problems of the CAP

The huge expense of achieving such indifferent results has consistently undermined the public perception of "Europe". The perceived lack of benefits has been reinforced by a tripartite awareness, by farmers, by consumers and by environmental pressure groups, of specific and wide-ranging disbenefits. Few remained untouched by negative aspects of the CAP: it was responsible for stress in smaller and more marginal farm households; it raised the cost of living for millions of ordinary households in housing estates the length and breadth of Europe; and, finally, it left its mark on the environment of the countryside. Precisely because for too long it remained "obstinately production-orientated" (Gilg, 1991: 75), it encouraged agriculture to shift from a system based at farm and local community level to one dominated by agribusiness, with its unswerving focus on input supply, output processing and distribution: in other words, industrial-type production based upon economic efficiency, profit maximisation and maximum use of technological inputs (Robinson, 1991).

Inevitably, numerous commentators have noted the connection with environment destruction. Lowe and Whitby (1997: 290) pointed to "a series of environmental problems which have arisen in relation to European agriculture, problems which can broadly be ascribed to the intensification and concentration of production". Similarly, Robinson (1991) observed of the situation in the UK, that "such an agriculture is, inevitably, antithetical to widespread sustained functioning in ecological terms and . . . the environmental consequences of expansionist agriculture have been particularly severe", while O'Riordan (1987) produced some plain-speaking calculations of destroyed habitats. The UK response to this environmental stress was the well-timed pre-1987 General Election ALURE (Alternative Land Use and Rural Economy) package. Five million of the £25 million scheme was earmarked for the encouragement of diversification of farm businesses. These were followed a year later by the EC-wide McSharry reforms, much more clearly aimed at reducing surplus production (McCleery, 1992).

France and Rural Society

Less engaged than the British by environmental issues, France nevertheless constitutes "a country particularly bound by agricultural tradition" (Fearne, 1997: 22). France's family-farming agricultural economy represented not only an effective development model, but also a key embodiment of national identity (Hoggart et al., 1995). Against this background, the dominant position of France at the heart of the European movement, and of French agriculture in the EC during the policy-forming years, ensured that the original CAP was widely seen as a French victory. It would also be the main force behind the impetus which improvements in the agricultural sector gave to the impressive overall performance of the French economy during the 1960s. Without any revolutionary change in farm size and despite a reduction in the total cultivated area, yet output increased by over 50 per cent (Fearne, 1997). In other words, the pattern of farm structure largely stagnated, while France squeezed the CAP for all it was worth. Hence the contradiction, pointed up by Winchester (1993), between the outsider's image of France as a rural romantic idyll as distinct from the highly successful economic power which she is in reality. As Kay (1998) observes, the EU had committed itself to bearing the cost of an outmoded farm structure through the price supports of the CAP; there existed no incentive for any national member state to incur the financial and political cost of farm structure reform.

The EU Milk Market

All that was to change with the introduction of milk quotas in 1984. It is both true that, virtually since its inception, the CAP has been subject to proposals for reform and that the CAP has appeared to be resistant to substantial reform, a case in point being the tackling of the problem of surpluses. The milk market reforms proved no exception and are of particular interest in the context of this paper which features a case study of Normandy, well known for its lush green grass, dairy cattle and Camembert cheese. CAP dairy sector reform was, quite simply, too little, too late. It had a negligible impact upon output, yet at exactly the wrong time provided a sharp impetus for structural reform, an issue which had by now disappeared from the agenda of EU policymakers. This was because in a time of recession, there was little point in moving uneconomic farmers into urban unemployment (Kay, 1998). Furthermore, outside the farming community there was mounting dissatisfaction with the wastefulness---both in monetary cost and environmental damage terms---of the CAP. To sum up, just when it was appropriate, from the societal and environmental perspective, to slow down the rate of structural reform, a coincident device was introduced which was calculated to accelerate it.

Thus in France in 1984, 400,000 dairy farms produced an average of 60,000 litres or roughly 24,000 million litres of milk in total. By 1996, 160,000 farms were producing an average of 140,000 litres, making a total of 22,400 litres, i.e., 60 per cent fewer farms were producing 7 per cent less milk---a magnificent achievement from the point of view of efficiency gains, whether from the sectoral or the national perspective, but hardly from the socio-environmental or wider European perspective. It is not surprising that national policy in France, just as in Ireland, was subsequently directed towards arresting the pace of restructuring and preserving the fabric of the rural economy (House of Commons, 1996); it is also ironic that Clout in 1984 was citing France as an example of how national structural policies had failed to produce a revolutionary change (i.e., increase) in farm size. Yet regardless of which direction France is, at any given time, attempting to move the direction of the size of her farms, the tension between national and EU policy remains a constant. By effectively playing the one off against the other, the financial burden of an increase in agricultural production in a member state is externalised through the EU budget. As Kay (1998: 36) explains, so long as a member state is a net beneficiary of the EU budget, there exists an incentive to use national structural policies to boost national production: "the costs are spread through all member states, but the benefits are concentrated in that particular member state".

Diversification

It has been argued elsewhere that in the UK at least, the McSharry reforms allowed part-time farming to become respectable (McCleery, 1992). Further, it has been suggested that CAP reform was mainly responsible for the redefinition of so-called "part-time" farming as "pluriactivity" (Fuller, 1990). In France it was specifically milk quotas which legitimated diversification. And if it was its environmentally-friendly image which commended pluriactivity in the UK, it was presumably its traditional associations and future potential---what the Arkleton Trust summed up as a long-established, widespread and varied way of life and as such an enhancing feature of the rural economy---which appealed to the French. Either way, occupational pluralism is well-known as a survival device in the crofting areas of the Highlands of Scotland and the Irish Gaeltacht. Seldom a transient feature, it demonstrates both stability and durability, at the same time accommodating an essential dynamism in the possibilities for combinations of both activities and actors (Walker and McCleery, 1987; McCleery, 1992).

At any rate, 1984 did not see the end of the world for the French dairy sector, nor indeed its ex-practitioners hanging around Paris street corners. Rather it saw necessary modernisation for some, but, importantly, inevitable marginalisation for others---a situation strikingly similar to that pertaining to Irish farmers in their responses to the CAP and its reform, as described by Walsh (1991), although in the Irish case, the marginalisation was neither elective nor benign, arguably as a result of less favourable geographical and economic circumstances. In France, it is suggested, genuinely strategic marginalisation has occurred---achieved through dedicated pursuit by the

French government of EU policies at one level and national ones at another. For enterprising small farmers, this presented a tactical opportunity for the possibility---or certainty---of gentle economic adjustment rather than sudden financial dislocation, in the form of "creative restructuring"[1] of their farm-household activities. Moreover, because of the emphasis on rural economy and society, as distinct from environment, with a head start of almost a decade, France has managed to steal a march on the rest of the EU fifteen. Only much more recently, with the publication of the Buckwell Report (European Commission, 1997), now translated into Agenda 2000, has the wider focus shifted towards a Common Agricultural and Rural Policy for Europe (CARPE).

There has been a supreme logic at work on the part of the French, whose reputation for making EU policies work well for them is not altogether undeserved. For although the twin policies---of agricultural modernisation and farm rationalisation on the one hand and agricultural marginalisation and farm diversification on the other---were both applied at the national level, the one was largely promoted and financed by Europe and the other by France herself. With the dairy regime allowing half of France's dairy farms to disappear without appreciable diminution in output, what else was there for the French Agriculture Ministry to do, but to reorient itself to the important business of preserving the fabric of rural life? And with the latest emphasis on a CARPE as distinct from the outdated and discredited CAP, it looks as if France can increasingly look to Europe to foot the farm diversification bill as well. This is calculated not to go down well across the English Channel where the assorted media need little encouragement to give French small farmers a bad press, painting them as disruptive, dyed-in-the-wool, lazy and inefficient. Yet the study below of farm diversification in Normandy paints a different picture---one of considerable enterprise and energy as well as a desire to accommodate rather than antagonise.

Study Area Profile

The area with which this study is concerned is the Bessin-Bayeux arrondissement [district] of the Department of Calvados, itself part of the larger Region of Basse-Normandie (Lower Normandy). Typical of a western European rural area, Basse-Normandie is subject to the twin demographic phenomena of desertification and densification, the former characterising inland sections of deeper countryside, the latter manifesting itself in and around service centres---loosely defined as those communities which can command a range of small retail outlets and support a weekly market, thereby defining themselves as key settlements. Densification equally applies to a well-defined coastal strip bordering the English Channel and important for its fishing, its ferry links with southern England and its well-developed tourist industry centring on family seaside activities and the historic landing beaches of the Second World War. The City of Caen functions as both Regional and Departmental capital and constitutes a post-1945 creation, having been razed to the ground in 1944. The principal town of the Bessin district is Bayeux, famous for its tapestry depicting the Norman Conquest. Bayeux is located on the extreme eastern edge of the district, some twenty miles to the west of Caen.

Of the three constituent *départements* [counties] of Basse-Normandie, Calvados exhibits the most favourable economic and population profile, both incorporating the important coastal zone and the regional capital of Caen, and located nearest to Paris. Growth is focused on the northern half of the department, containing three of the four principal towns, as well as the busy coastal zone. Growth in the towns and their environs is balanced by rural depopulation, although there is evidence of this slowing. Nevertheless, a joint INSEE/CNRS (French National Statistics and Economics Agency and National Centre for Scientific Research) publication of the mid-1990s was still waxing lyrical about the contrast between rural decline and urban dynamism: over the whole region two-thirds of communes had a lower population in 1990 than in 1954 (CNRS/INSEE, 1994). However, this polarised picture oversimplifies the situation which is characterised by varied processes of demographic change rather than homogeneity. At the last census the population of the Bessin was 62,300 of which 15,000, almost one-quarter, lived in Bayeux, whose periphery continues to expand rapidly. The north-east third of the Bessin, which contains Bayeux, expanded at a rate of 25 per cent in the fifteen years to 1990, while the rest of the district was stagnant or declining, by up to 15 per cent in the same period. A particular problem has been the loss of well-qualified young people aged 18-30 (INSEE, 1998, 1999).

Despite the best efforts of CAP reform, the agro-alimentary industry remains the jewel in the economic crown of the Bessin, with tourism playing an important supporting role. One in two people work in the service sector, and a further one in eight in the retail sector. Otherwise, employment is dairy-dependent---one in five jobs is in either agriculture or the agro-alimentary industry. Hotel and restaurant work makes up over 20 per cent of employment in private sector commercial services. Agriculture, despite losing nearly one quarter of its workers since 1990, nevertheless accounts for 13 per cent of economically-active inhabitants, including nearly half of self-employed people in the district. Local unemployment is below both the departmental and regional figures. Rural by virtue of its economic orientation and landscape, the Bessin is nevertheless heavily subject to urban influences. Eight out of ten of the largest employers in the Bessin are located in Bayeux or its periphery. Within Calvados generally, and the Bessin specifically, the zone of influence of the city of Caen extends widely. Notably the Caen-Bayeux dual carriageway (scheduled for upgrade to motorway as part of the A13 extension plans), together with the equivalent section of the Paris-Cherbourg railway, constitutes an important development axis, incorporating both the regional airport of Caen-Carpiquet and a flourishing industrial development zone at the eastern edge of Bayeux. This axis also provides for a significant interchange of daily commuters---some 1,800 from Caen to Bayeux and twice that number in the opposite direction (INSEE, 1998, 1999).

Research Methodology

Farmers in the European union operate in a decision-making space which is sandwiched between the constraints imposed by supra-national agriculture policy on the one hand and the opportunities afforded by local situations on the other. Both may be mediated to some extent through the vehicle of national government interpretation of the former and central and local government legislation or regulatory practice in respect of the latter. So, for example, policy in both France and Ireland is directed towards arresting the pace of restructuring, but in France this is achieved through regionalisation of quota and in Ireland by restrictions on the movement of quota from less-favoured areas (House of Commons, 1996). The shape of the framework for payment of grants for rural development purposes and the regulations concerning compatibility and zoning of particular economic activities similarly either constrain or promote certain behaviours on the part of farm households. From an examination of relevant published farm statistics, it is possible to identify aggregate trends in an area. However, to gain an insight into underlying processes, and into the motivational drivers initiating these processes and attitudinal perspectives reinforcing them, it is necessary to delve deeper. To this end semi-structured interviews were carried out with ten farm households in the Bessin. Respondents were asked about the size, type and history of their operation, as well as the reasons for the implementation of any changes, level of satisfaction with the outcome of any such evolution and general views of, and attitudes towards, current developments in agriculture and agriculture policy.

The conduct of this type of research necessarily raises the question of positionality and self-reflexivity as it affects the researcher-respondent relationship and, by implication, the results of the investigation. The researcher in this case was well known locally, having spent some ten years of summer holidays in self-catering accommodation in the study area on three different farms. Her spouse and children constitute familiar faces in local shops, and at the bank, post office, weekly market and annual fair and fireworks display. The pharmacy, doctor's surgery and local hospital have all dealt with one or other of the children over the decade. The four children, all French speakers to a greater or lesser degree, are at minimum recognised by, and at maximum accepted as belonging to, a large loose subset of local children who attend or have sometimes attended a children's holiday activity scheme based on a *ferme equestre* (farm-based riding stables). The owners of this establishment, long-standing and highly-respected members of the local community, who have become family friends over the years, were instrumental in securing appropriate introductions to other farm households where the researcher was usually known by repute. It is therefore argued that in conducting the interviews, the researcher was credible in the role of insider-outsider: insider, in that she knew and was known in the local area; outsider, in that she spoke accented French, came from abroad and lived in a city. This combination proved invaluable in allowing respondents both to feel comfortable confiding in a person familiar to them and to speak with unchallenged authority on French agriculture and rural practices.

Results

A majority of the farms where interviews were held had started off as dairy enterprises, with the balance comprising mixed operations, incorporating some arable and/or beef cattle, poultry and pigs. Similarly, a majority were owner-occupied, but as a result of complicated landholding patterns, owed in part to complexities of inheritance arrangements, farmland was not necessarily consolidated around the farmhouse but might be dispersed across several parcels several kilometres apart. There was one interesting example of a farm held as a secure tenancy, the arrangement having persisted between the same two families for over 200 years. While it would be unrealistic to expect any of the farms not to have changed at all during ten or twenty years, nevertheless it was possible to distinguish qualitative from quantitative change and situations of major investment and development from those where activities were more or less ticking along.

That having been said, it should be noted that the categories of change are by no means discrete; rather they shade into each other along a continuum from total disengagement with farming at one extreme through partial disengagement---with either agri-tourism an adjunct to serious farming or farming an adjunct to serious rural tourism---to agricultural specialisation and development at the other, where commonly one partner works off-farm and provides a possibility for cross-subsidised farm development or, less commonly, both partners are engaged exclusively in the work of the farm, this being the most agriculturally intensive of the various forms of household-farm relationship. Nor is position on the continuum of particular combinations of activity necessarily fixed: on the one hand it is difficult to state whether, within a household, off-farm subsidy of agricultural activities represents more or less engagement with or disengagement from farming than farm-based non-agricultural diversification; on the other hand, such situations are not static but continuously evolving. The results of the interviews should therefore be interpreted in the context of the provisos set out above.

Of the ten farm households interviewed, one each might be described as respectively, wholly disengaged from agriculture and exclusively engaged with agriculture, i.e., representative of the opposite extremes of the gradient of involvement in farming activity. The former household, in recent retirement, continued to live in the farmhouse, having sold both land and dairy quota to a neighbour, none of the children having evinced any interest in carrying on the modest farm enterprise. All had departed to work in Caen while continuing to live locally in rural properties. The farmer continued to rent out a *gîte rural* [holiday cottage] in an adjacent commune, attached to the *corps de ferme* [farmhouse and dependencies] belonging to his elderly mother-in-law, where until very recently he had maintained a small dairy herd. Great regret was expressed to the researcher about the movement of young people out of farming and into the cities, the concomitant increase in farm size, and the accompanying reduction in the agricultural population as well as in trees and hedgerows, all of which was seen as threatening rural life.

At the opposite extreme was the case of a large mixed farm producing grain for the local agricultural cooperative, cider for local supermarkets and sale direct to the public, and milk for the dairy cooperative. Both the farmer and his wife were fully involved in the work of the farm, along with hired help at harvest time. Despite the reduction in farm-gate prices and the difficulties in obtaining additional milk quota (land had to be purchased with quota attached), nevertheless it was envisaged that a daughter, who was currently undertaking a post-school agriculture diploma, would join the family business. It was emphasised that the farm enterprise would need to expand to take her on in a full-time permanent capacity, rather than that she would be succeeding her parents, who were still 20 years away from retirement. Any such future expansion was placed squarely within the realm of agricultural development or diversification and not tourist-related, the latter being argued to be unfeasible since farming took up all available time and energy.

In between these two poles were arranged the other eight farm households. Two of these demonstrated near-total disengagement with conventional farming, having shifted over completely to farm-based diversified rural activities; in one case an expanding farm-based equestrian enterprise, and in the other case a multiple holiday-cottage-letting activity combined with a bed-and-breakfast operation. Both were households with older children at the crucial time of committing to change, but of these subsequently grown-up children, only in the first household was a daughter now involved in the business. In the context of advanced plans for major investment in the physical fabric of the stables and associated riding arena, the daughter was now marrying the son of long-standing family friends. He worked in the media industry in Paris, but she was being made a partner in her parents' business, where she would remain on site. Her future husband was already commuting weekly, and would continue to do so, the prospect of a comparable regional opening being slim at this stage in his career. In connection with the development plan, frustration was expressed at the classification of the commune as urban, which effectively debarred the venture from rural development assistance and meant reliance on a bank loan. The second rural business had also expanded over ten years to incorporate an adjacent farmhouse and dependencies, converting these traditional farm buildings sympathetically into summer holiday rental units. A higher and lower rate respectively of government assistance had been applicable to the first two conversions, while two of the four resultant properties were sufficiently well appointed to be suitable for winter lets for visiting foreign academics to the university at Caen. As diversified income had expanded, so farm income had been allowed to shrink and the milk quota sold off to a neighbour.

Both these households had endured the opprobrium of neighbouring farmers during the early and uncertain days of their farm transformations and had experienced social isolation as well as financial insecurity. While both condemned the effects on farmers of CAP reform, nevertheless both (with the hindsight of now successful business operators as distinct from either struggling farmers or failed entrepreneurs) also perceived the imposition of the milk quotas as the trigger which was to set them on the road to a new, more interesting and less harsh working life. Both households practised evident gender specificity in terms of tasks undertaken in respect of the business, although the one involved daughter divided her time fairly evenly between "male" and "female" activities. The men in both households were involved in work which was at the same time more solitary, more outdoor and more physical (e.g., haymaking, exterior maintenance, etc.) while the women undertook domestic-related activities such as cooking, shopping, general household organisation and accounts management. Critically, it was the women who were operating at the interface with the public, and both women specifically mentioned the benefits of the interest and stimulation provided by meeting a variety of people from different places and walks of life. Furthermore, each of the revamped rural enterprises had reached the point where some of the unskilled domestic chores could now be delegated to hired help, thus freeing up the women themselves to interact more with their clienteles.

Of the remaining six farms, three combined fairly traditional mixed farming activities with provision of tourist accommodation. The level of importance of the agri-tourism displayed its own gradient, confirming previous findings relating to diversification and stage in the life cycle (Shucksmith and Winter, 1990). On one farm where there were still school-age children competing for the attention of their parents, the farmer's wife looked after two tourist gîtes only; on a second, where one grown-up son had just left home and set up as a farmer in his own right with his agriculturally-trained wife---while also continuing to put in work on his father's farm---the farmer's wife offered a full-blown bed, breakfast and evening meal service; and on a third farm where all the children had left home and eschewed any involvement in agriculture, a mixed organic farming operation was integrated with the operation of a guest house---*chambres d'hôtes*---where the owners prided themselves on being able to serve evening meals which were 90 per cent own-farm produce. A small fully-serviced and attractively=situated orchard camping site was run in parallel, of itself barely breaking even, but maintained for the sole purpose of facilitating the direct sale of home-produced cider, pommeau and calvados [apple-based liqueur and spirit respectively] to the resident tourists. Contracts for the supply of quality farm produce to various local restaurants had also been secured, eliminating the need for middlemen. The farmer was at pains to explain the farms's historic associations dating back to Roman times and to emphasise the importance to environmental and personal health of organic produce. His twin interest in *patrimoine* [heritage] and *produits du terroir* [regional food specialities] is a perfect example of how *"la notion de patrimoine s'est élargie pour intégrer le paysage"* [the idea of patrimony has expanded to incorporate the countryside] (CNRS/INSEE, 1994) and both reflects and reinforces the key status of the rural idyll in France.

The final model of how farming could adapt and survive was provided by the examples of three "dual career" farms (Blekesaune et al., 1993, quoted in Hoggart et al., 1995: 220) where a remodelled engagement with agriculture by one partner was allied with constructive non-engagement by the other. On each of these farms positive change had been facilitated by cross-subsidy from the off-farm professional activities of the farmer's wife. Thus a librarian was supporting a changeover to organic farming; a hairdresser the development of a state-of the-art high-tech veal enterprise; and a nurse a reorientation towards arable farming. All three households had managed to combine significant business specialisation with a steady improvement in their standards of living, at a stage in the domestic life-cycle of increased financial pressure associated with growing children. None of the three households was interested in pursuing any on-farm tourist activities, either because it was both impossible and unnecessary where a wife had off-farm employment, or because it would also have been wholly incompatible with an intensive stock operation, which for all its cleanliness and modernity, scarcely smelt of roses. In this context it is worthwhile noting that the proprietors of the farm which had converted to a holiday cottage letting business had actually considered the possibility of high-tech veal production, but had not been able to pursue this avenue because of the geographical situation of their farm at the edge of a small settlement.

Discussion

In all three of the cases of agricultural diversification, including the organic farm where adoption had been "*par philosophie ... respect de la nature*" [out of principle ... concern for nature] there was a clear and sharply-focused sense of the farm as a business, with no sign of any romantic nostalgia for the softly-focused (false) perception of rurality of days gone by. The latter was a posture more typical of the agri-tourism enterprises, where it was necessary for survival, despite what has elsewhere been referred to as the inevitable tension between the (necessary) mess of farming and what the tourist expects (Hutson and Keddie, 1997). In the case of those farms which had diversified into fully-fledged rural businesses, if the commodification of rurality needed to be more aggressive then the complicity in the rural idyll was at least able to be more thoroughgoing, precisely because there were no longer many---or perhaps any at all---processes of agricultural production with which to clash. For these households, not surprisingly, CAP reform was viewed less as a constraint than as a catalyst presenting a positive opportunity for creative restructuring of the farm business. "*Je pense que nous c'est un peu un choix ... ouais, parce que la fatigue, la dureté du travail de l'élevage ... hein?*" [I think that for us it was partly choice---yeah, because it was so tiring, so hard, working with stock . . . d'you see?] Disillusionment was less with "*la politique de Bruxelles*" [Brussels bureaucracy] itself than with the changing nature of farming, the lifestyle and pace of which no longer appealed.

Those who continued to farm---whether supported by off-farm employment or by on-farm tourism---could not afford to admit that they were disillusioned, yet confided their regrets both that contemporary farming had lost touch with nature and that it had changed beyond recognition and was now awash with paperwork. It was also generally agreed that running the farm was harder work than 10 or even 20 years ago, although this is unremarkable just because all these were now pluriactive households combining two or more jobs. However, the librarian who was cross-subsidising a change to organic farming was inclined to be more circumspect, suggesting that it was not so much that things were now more difficult, but that they were different. Apart from acknowledging that farming today was much more dominated by forms and bureaucracy, "*ça n'arrête pas, ça n'arrête pas"* [it never stops, just never stops]---she would concede only that *"ça a beaucoup changé"* [things have changed a lot], adding that it was difficult to be objective, while straight comparison of now and then was impossible, not least because she and her husband had changed as well. *"On est dedans, on oublie . . . nous étions plus jeunes, nous vieillissons"* [You're in the midst of it, you forget . . . we were younger, now we're getting older].

Given that off-farm or non-agricultural income on such farms was compensating for falling farm-gate prices, it was not unexpected to find the farmer on the large mixed/dairy enterprise, which had eschewed all non-agricultural diversification (with the exception of direct sale of cider products to passing tourists), complaining that he had to run to stand still, because of falling prices. *"Il faut faire plus pour avoir le même revenu"* [You need to do more to make the same income]. Of agri-tourism, he conceded that while it was fine, it meant work---*"c'est bien, mais ça représente du travail"*. In view of this, and despite the belief that farming now was much more difficult then previously, his alternative for viability, as indicated above, was a large and (agriculturally) diversified unit which he and his wife would continue to work at developing and expanding with a view to incorporating their daughter in the business presently. However, with a herd of seventy cows already, this enterprise was both comfortably above the threshold which had necessitated hard decisions on the part of neighbouring small farmers and could absorb the impact of falling prices, at least in the short term.

The importance of the socio-personal dimension, observed by Cawley et al. (1997) to apply as much to the adoption and direction of farm diversification as to purely agriculture-related decision-making in Ireland, was evident also in the French case. The various choices of diversified farm---support activities being carried out---both agricultural and non-agricultural, on-farm and off-farm---as well as the particular ways in which these were being combined, reflected more than just the life-cycle stage of each of the farm households, noted by Shucksmith and Winter (1990). The nature and extent of the creative restructuring demonstrated a layered contextuality, with external constraints and opportunities common to all, internal size and structural aspects specific to the farm, and finally individual personal and domestic circumstances peculiar to the household. In respect of the latter, the critical importance of unique family biographies---combining prior life experience, education and training with life-cycle stage---in influencing the nature and timing of diversified activities adopted is underlined. Therefore, on a Bessin farm of given size and type, the state and stage of evolution of the farm business may be viewed as a product of the interplay of the history and circumstances of the lives of the proprietors or tenants with the date and type of changes in agriculture policy.

A particular course having been set, the propensity of the various farm households to promote a commodified and less than authentic rurality was, as noted earlier, closely related to the degree of importance of tourist consumption to the household's finances. It is worth reiterating that for those farms turned diversified rural businesses, this was unproblematic; but where the ongoing activities of the farm clearly threatened to expose the rural idyll as a falsity, dissatisfaction of the respondents with their lot appeared greatest, the strain of living a lie adding to the pressures of trying to do two jobs simultaneously. Another paradox of farm-based tourism, peculiar to this area, also emerged. The specific reliance of his business on its proximity to the Second World War landings beaches was matter-of-factly acknowledged by the most progressive of the agri-tourism farmers, but the other farmer's wife running a farm-based guest house clearly felt slightly uncomfortable about making money from mainly English visitors to the war cemeteries. She rationalised what she perceived as a slightly embarrassing form of heritage tourism as the silver lining to a terrible cloud for the people of that part of France, as much as for the families of the British soldiers who died there.

An evident danger with agri-tourism was that households could drift into farm-based tourism with no positive decision actually having been taken, and without any clear sense of future direction. With increasing disenchantment with the farming side of the business and without any strongly motivating factors underlying the tourist activities, the dissipation of energy in trying to keep up both activities could produce a sense that neither the tourism not the agriculture side of the business was being done especially well. In the case of the farm which also rented out two holiday cottages, for example, investment in farm modernisation was deemed pointless unless one of the children was definitely going to take up farming, yet to offer bed-and-breakfast as well as renting out gîtes was just too much work. Furthermore a vague desire to go *bio* [organic] (or more specifically para-organic because a fully organic farm was deemed too much work), allied to a feeling that modern conventional farming was out of tune with nature, was felt to be frustrated by the proximity of the activities of what were described as enormous neighbouring agribusinesses. *"C'est le stress"* [it's stressful] summed up this situation only too well.

Greater satisfaction with working life and a more positive outlook was evident in those households which had diversified wholly into rural businesses or had specialised and developed using off-farm income. Where a calculated risk had been taken and a farm transformed lock, stock and barrel into a diversified rural business, there was considerable sense of achievement that both partners had emerged at the other end emotionally unscathed with a successful business under their belts to boot. Comments such as *"C'est une bonne ambiance de travail"* [It's a nice way to work] captured a current contentment which did not dismiss acknowledged hard times which had had to be faced during the period of transition. (The sense of autonomy and ability to direct their own lives which was conveyed in the cases of the farms turned rural businesses contrasted markedly with the feelings of avenues being foreclosed which were expressed by the farmer's wife who rented the two gîtes.) In the case of the cross-subsidising specialisers, there was a comparable pride in having managed the changes while enjoying protection from any undue financial and psychological stress. The wife's independent off-farm professional existence was highly prized---"*moi je ne suis pas du tout fermière---je suis l'épouse du fermier---c'est très différent*" [I'm not married to the farm---I am married to the farmer---that's quite different!] and the income thus earned was regarded as the passport to the autonomy that eluded the agri-tourism diversifiers. The latter, as indicated, were at risk of feeling trapped in a traditional gendered experience of diversification, with freedom of manoeuvre limited and the farm and tourist enterprise coexisting, but not necessarily happily. Yet, such farm households could equally revel in being able to carry on with what was a genuine vocation and could also take a real pride in the fact, as they saw it, that to them was entrusted the important task of assuring the education in local history and rural environment of a culturally impoverished urban public.

Conclusion

Structural marginality produced by European political bureaucracy, as distinct from physical marginality experienced at the north Atlantic geographical periphery, while exhibiting comparable features and eliciting similar responses, is characterised by a much higher degree of externally-derived autonomy residing with the marginalised farm households. Proximity to the metropolitan boundary and concomitant access to markets as well as to cheap raw materials offers choices and allows farm households to plan for strategic marginalisation in the form of creative restructuring, tailored both to suit the household profile and to meet personal aspirations. At individual farm household level, the internal degree of choice is also very important; being obliged by circumstance to run a farm business as well as a tourist enterprise is not necessarily conducive to psychological well-being. Development as well as diversification is facilitated by the possibility of access to urban service sector employment, to a clientele from urban centres either adjacent or suitably plugged into the motorway network, and to external economies produced by a well-developed tourist infrastructure as well as internal economies derived from the availability of competitively-priced foodstuffs and household goods.

Where off-farm public or commercial sector salaried employment is in short supply is also where tourists fail to penetrate, so that the potential of rural tourism to restore economic prosperity in the deep heart of the depopulated French countryside has been argued to have been overestimated (Tiard and Mallon, 1995). *L'Exode Rural* [Rural Exodus][2] never did apply to coastal Normandy, nor even in its most extreme form to the neighbouring Brittany, which constitutes an unequivocal example of a north Atlantic marginal region. Basse-Normandie is therefore something of a chameleon; it is both close enough to the Atlantic coast to enjoy some of the regional development advantages of EC less-favoured area status, yet near enough to Paris to be able to benefit from significant trickle-down effects. This is critical to the cross-subsidising specialisers and to the rural business developers, while for practitioners of agri-tourim in the Bessin, to be located inside the distance decay threshold for tourist driveablility to an unspoiled combination of safe beaches and remarkable heritage coastline is fundamental to the viability of their businesses. Even the retired farmer rented out a holiday cottage and the large agriculturally-diversified farm relied upon direct or indirect tourist demand for its cider products.

To sum up, the development of a farm business, farm-based enterprise or a combination of the two represents a negotiated and evolving path carved out between the constraints imposed by structural-level policy change on the one hand and individual-level opportunities within a given farm household on the other. This process takes place within a particular window of spatial opportunity in which, in the case of the present study area, a visible, albeit changed, rurality overlies a much more complex rural-urban marginal-metropolitan substrate of relationships. Yet if place matters from a geocode perspective, it matters just as much as a social construction of reality. In the particular situation analysed here, complicity in the rural idyll leaves both sides of a financially and psychologically important bargain content: the rural suppliers of goods and services depend upon it to attract and retain their largely metropolitan market; and the urban consumers of rural goods and services rely upon it to reassure themselves that traditional values persist. Thus the image of France as a rural romantic idyll has survived CAP reform to fight another day. *La vache folle* [mad cow disease] may yet deal it a mortal blow.

Notes

[1] I am grateful to an anonymous colleague at the Fourteenth International Seminar on Marginal Regions for proposing the use of this term.

[2] *L'Exode Rural* is the title of a classic *Que sais-je* series book by Pitié, which

documents and interprets rural depopulation in France.

References

Cawley, M., D. Gillmor and P. McDonagh. 1997. Farm Diversification and Sustainability: The Perceptions of Farmers and Institutions in the West of Ireland. In R. Byron, J. Walsh and P. Breathnach (eds.), *Sustainable Development on the North Atlantic Margin*. Aldershot: Ashgate.

CNRS/INSEE. 1994. *Atlas Social de Basse-Normandie.* Caen: Presses Universitaires de Caen.

European Commission. 1997. *Towards a Common Agricultural and Rural Policy for Europe.* (The Buckwell Report). <http://europa.eu.int/comm/dg06/publi/buck_en/>.

Fearne, A. 1997. The History and Development of the CAP 1945-1990. In C. Ritson and D. R. Harvey (eds.), *The CAP*. 2nd edition. Wallingford and New York: CABI Publishing.

Fuller, Anthony M. 1990. From Part-time Farming to Pluriactivity: A Decade of Change in Rural Europe. *Journal of Rural Studies* 6 (4): 361-73.

Gilg, A. W. 1991. Planning for Agriculture: The Growing Case for a Conservation Component. *Geoforum* 22 (1): 75-79.

Hoggart, K., H. Buller and R. Black. 1995. *Rural Europe: Identity and Change.* London: Arnold.

House of Commons. 1996. *The UK Dairy Industry and the CAP Dairy Regime.* Agriculture Committee Session 1995-6, First Report. London: HMSO.

Hutson, J. and D. Keddie. 1997. Tourism and Alternative Employment among Farm Families in Less-favoured Agricultural Regions of Wales. In R. Byron, J. Walsh and P. Breathnach (eds.). *Sustainable Development on the North Atlantic Margin.* Aldershot: Ashgate.

INSEE. 1998. *Cent pour cent Basse-Normandie.* No. 43 (juillet).

INSEE. 1999. Regard sur le Bassin de Bayeux. *Onze territoires pour une région.* Caen: INSEE.

Kay, A. 1998. *The Reform of the CAP.* Wallingford and New York: CABI Publishing.

Lowe, P. and M. Whitby. 1997. The CAP and the European Environment. In C. Ritson and D. R. Harvey (eds.), *The CAP.* 2nd edition. Wallingford and New York:

CABI Publishing.

McCleery, A. 1992. Countryside Conservation through Farm Diversification. In A. McCleery and D. Turnock (eds), *Geography and Conservation.* Edinburgh: The Colinton Press.

O'Riordan, T. 1987. Agriculture and Environmental Protection. *Geography Review* 1 (1): 35-40.

Pearce, J. 1983. The Common Agricultural Policy: The Accumulation of Special Interests. In H. Wallace, et al. (eds.), *Policy-Making in the European Community.* London: Wiley.

Pitié, J. 1979. *L'Exode Rural.* Paris: Presses Universitaires de France.

Ritson, C. 1997. Introduction. In C. Ritson and D. R. Harvey (eds.), *The CAP.* 2nd edition. Wallingford and New York: CABI Publishing.

Robinson, G. M. 1990. *Conflict and Change in the Countryside.* London and New York: Belhaven Press.

Robinson, G. M. 1991. EC Agriculture Policy and the Environment: Land Use Implications in the UK. *Land Use Policy* 8 (2):95-107.

Shucksmith, M. and M. Winter. 1990. The Politics of Pluriactivity in Britain. *Journal of Rural Studies* 6 (4): 429-35.

Tiard, M. and P. Mallon. 1995. De la difficulté d'analyser le tourisme rural. *Cahiers Espaces* 42 (Tourisme Rural): 23-26.

Walker, C. A. and A. McCleery. 1987. Economic and Social Change in the Highlands. *Scottish Economic Bulletin* 35 (June): 8-20.

Walsh, J. A. 1993. Modernisation and Marginalisation under the Common Agriculture Policy: Irish Agriculture in Transition. In T. Flognfeldt et al. (eds.), *Conditions for Development in Marginal Regions: Proceedings of the XI International Seminar on Marginal Regions.* Lillehammer: Oppland College.

Winchester, H. P .M. 1993. *Contemporary France.* Harlow: Longman.

PART III
RESOURCES AND CONSTRAINTS
IN COMMUNITY DEVELOPMENT

7 The Problem of the Outsourcing of Service Provision and its Impact on Marginal Regions

PETER SJØHOLT

Introduction

The focus of this paper is on the issue of organisation and purchase of services by public authorities (mainly municipalities) and large corporations (mainly located in small one-company towns in peripheral areas). The main theme is restructuring of service provision, notably the increasing outsourcing of different types of services from institutions and corporations to private providers and the concomitant regional and local impact upon employment. It is hypothesised and partly verified that effects in the local communities may be both positive and negative, depending on the types of service and location of the buyers. The discussion is based on rather comprehensive literature from several countries, mainly in the industrialised part of the world. It is theoretical as outsourcing is viewed both in its preconditions and effects as outcome of economic, social, cultural and political factors and other driving forces in society at large. It is empirical in the sense that the paper describes the state of the art at the close of the twentieth century mainly in northwestern Europe and seeks a verification of claims put forward in specified hypotheses. Some of the verification is synthesised from the research literature on a rather broad basis. Some selected empirical cases from Norway are included, however, in order to analyse more closely beneficial or adverse regional economic and employment effects.

The Theme

Organisation of production has, over the last 15 years or so, increasingly attracted the attention both of scholars, corporate people, politicians and the public at large. One of the reasons for this concern is the important impact different organisational forms may have in a wider context than just upon production systems alone. Among the aspects of the organisational structure which has been subject to increased interest is the issue of the corporation (or institution) as a self-contained entity, producing or providing the majority of input factors itself or as a part of a system of vertical disintegration, buying in and integrating input factors from different sources. It is the dynamics of this process, the shift from the former to the latter mode of production which is the essence of the concept of outsourcing. A rather comprehensive scholarly debate has been conducted on the problematic---largely instigated in the early 1980s by Piore and Sabel (1984) and continued in a discussion on post-Fordist production systems and flexible organisation of production by Scott and Storper (1986), Storper and Christopherson (1987), Scott (1988 and 1988b), Gertler (1992) and many others.

The details of this debate need not bother us in our present context. It is sufficient to state that a new attention has been focused on the various effects of the restructuring processes in the organisation of production. In the regional field, which is an important part of our concern, centralising and decentralising impacts have been particularly been brought to the fore. The organisational discussion has rekindled the importance of agglomeration economics, taken up a hundred years ago by Marshall (1891), followed up by Weber (1909) and becoming a hot issue in the late 1980s and the 1990s, Scott (1985, 1986), Scott and Storper (1996), Amin and Robins (1990), Krugman (1991), Amin an Thrift (1992) and Asheim (1996).

The organisation of production and its concomitant many-dimensional effects are issues common both to the private and public spheres of the economy. We have, in our reasoning, tended to dichotomise very much the two parts of the economy. Certainly, great differences are apparent in the two sectors in goals and motives, the former being wholly or largely concerned with return to capital and profit in order to survive, whereas the latter mainly acts as a welfare agent and will for redistribution and equity reasons in certain cases have to disregard motives of cost reduction and profit. These viewpoints are highly relevant for the discussion in the present context. However, by emphasising the dichotomy too much we may run the risk of failing to see the similarities which undoubtedly exist. To a much larger extent than we generally think public bodies are engaged in production processes which call for productivity and efficiency, particularly in the field of service production.

Services are also the main concern of this paper---in particular their role in the wider actual and potential process of production in the private as well as the public field. Services have generally grown in magnitude and importance in both spheres. In the corporations of the private sector both the upstream and downstream part of the production chain has contributed to this development, although with great variation between types of production and hence enterprises. Most pronounced has been the increase in the service economy in corporations undergoing fundamental restructuring processes, brought about by a combination of fierce competition and substantial technological changes. In the public sphere the services in question are interesting in a double sense. They are partly inputs into production processes, very much akin to the ones demanded by private enterprises. More conspicuous though in this sector are the services rendered to the general public or to selected persons and groups as a part of the public welfare and redistributional systems. Some of the public services are therefore collective, others more individually directed.

Theoretical issues are naturally both important and interesting when discussing reorganisation of service provision. Even more relevant for our purpose are the impacts of the act of outsourcing. What are the consequences for employment in economic and social terms, among these job security and and overall labour conditions? What are the regional repercussions and, ultimately, what are the impacts on marginal regions? Questions should also explicitly be raised whether impacts are consistently negative or whether there under given conditions may be positive entrepreneurial effects seen in a regional perspective.

Apparently, a propensity to indifference exists for producing and providing service inputs in-house or through external sources. Trends are somewhat confusing (Illeris, 1996). Most scholars having studied the phenomenon agree today that there is an increasing tendency to outsource part of the production, at the same time as retention or, in some cases, growth of internal production is clearly evident. This both-and structure of transactions has its clear logic. Growth in external purchases and external production and distribution of services always presupposes that the internal organisation of a firm or an institution is capable of initiating, organising and handling the transaction and put it to practical use. In most cases this is tantamount to having an internal production potential. These facts call for great caution in explaining transactions and transactional histories.

Common both to corporate and public activities are rational economic-strategic considerations. In the private corporations it is increasingly becoming common to retain the core activities in-house and shedding more peripheral tasks by farming them out to more specialised economic units. The firm can thereby specialise in competence both internally and in external transactions and simultaneously wield maximum strategic control. In public institutions the picture is somewhat unclear but transactions are undergoing change also in this sphere. This restructuring, which may apply both to goods and services, is part of corporate strategies, the genesis of which very often can be traced back to particular theoretical systems.

Theoretical and Conceptual Background

Internalisation and externalisation of production, whether of goods or services, has been an issue under debate from early in this century. Most of the early theoretical contributions, which have also persisted over time are pure cost considerations. Coase (1937) was the first to try to explain organisational options and their outcomes in economic terms as a cost-driven process. The starting point of his theoretical reasoning is the relative costs of organising production internally versus using the market by buying in input factors for realising specific production purposes. The main contention is that firms and their internal organisation tend to expand until the cost of organising an extra transaction within the corporation exceeds the cost of using transactions on the market for the same purposes. From being a vertically integrated production unit (organisation) firms thus tend to take part in a process of vertical disintegration. This theoretical framework, which describes different models of organising production, includes costs which were absent in the tenets of the neoclassical equilibrium theorists, like search, information, bargaining and decision costs.

Stigler (1951) tried to keep the discussion within the neoclassical equilibrium tradition by explaining the different transactional forms from the point of view of the theory of the firm. Without directly taking recourse to transactional forms, he emphasised that production systems tend to be moulded as a response to economy of scale. The vertical disintegration strategy is thus a means of maximising economy of scale for firms not being able to realise it internally. Stigler was later criticised for his overall mechanistic explanations among others by Levy (1984). In the models of Williamson (1979, 1985) the institutional economic explanation initiated by Coase is developed and expanded. By introducing markets and hierarchies as core concepts of organisation of production and isolating the determining variables, he built a system to show under what circumstances different choices are made. Crucial to Williamson's transactional system are factors like asset specificity in the production process, market uncertainty, frequency of operation (or use) and bounded rationality. As the above factors increase in importance, cost of market exchange will rise to a point where internal production will be favoured as an organisational principle.

Notwithstanding the illuminating concepts developed by Williamson, the theoretical system is difficult to operationalise empirically. Buckley (1988) thus never found estimates of transactional costs. The system is also inherently static, and, as contended by O'Farrell et al. (1993), underestimates the external assets available to the firm. Use of these resources which may explain dynamics in production processes may take several organisational forms. Thus vertical disintegration, not primarily as a transactional cost-reducing measure, but as a learning process may be one solution. Good examples are sourcing out of IT services and high quality consulting in order to infuse internal production processes with new knowledge and competence. This is also dynamic in the sense that the co-production realised is a pressure on the external service provider not only to produce cheaply, as a result of more optimal economies of scale, but to offer better quality and be a constant innovator in order to be attractive to the client. This is, according to Barcet and Bonamy (1994), an everlasting dynamic dialectic, the absence of which, as shown by Larsen (1992) may result in decreasing vertical disintegration.

The growth of vertically disintegrated production systems is also dynamic in another sense, as an expression in a wish for greater flexibility, not only numerical flexibility as a means of substituting variable for fixed costs, but according to Sayer (1989) by producing flexible labour markets, flexible working practices, flexibility in restructuring and flexible organisational forms. These may fulfil various purposes besides pure cost reductions, among other things contributing to the spreading of risks. Another manifestation of organisational dynamics is increased networking and alliance building between firms, a sort of intermediate form of transactions in the Williamson scheme. This mode of organising paves the way for a better understanding of innovative dynamics as it functions as an agent for mutual sharing of new technological and processual knowledge. The essence of this system of explanation is emphasis on mutual trust in contrast to Williamson's opportunism. In this way networking can make use of synergetic potential for mutual implementing action (Cunningham and Calligan, 1991). No coherent theory is built around this transactional dynamic, but many elements have been developed by among others Thorelli (1986), Jarillo (1988), Håkansson and Johannson (1987) and summed up in Håkansson and Snehota (1995).

Finally, the strong dichotomy between in-house production and external provision of services needs some modification as far as practice in the production process is concerned. As already touched upon, linkages to external service providers, either through different forms of alliances or market deliverers, may take the form of mutual innovative exchange. This is particularly the case in services on higher cognitive levels. Advanced service provision today may often, as contended by de Bandt (1994, 1995), be a complex, integrated and interactive problem solving process between client and provider. Overriding goals in this process will be not only to hire competence but generate competence.

Organisational forms and their dynamics in service provision have increasingly come to be seen in an institutional-political context. Karlsen (1999) argues strongly in favour of contextual studies for disclosing linkages between industrial strategies, institutions and structures in local settings in order to enhance our understanding of organisational processes and behaviour.

When actors in firms and institutions step out of the internal organisation and leave provision of services to subcontractors and other external providers, much responsibility, among others for the work force, will become less restrained and even disclaimed. Outsourcing may in this sense be an instrument of reducing social costs.

Many or most of the above motives of choosing organisational forms are applicable both to private firms and public institutions. Among the latter cost reduction is generally the overriding motive of outsourcing. We should not overlook the motive of an innovative learning process also in this sphere of activities, however. Neither can it always be denied that elements of risk avoidance and of softening of labour relations may be part of the strategy also in the public sector. The latter consideration naturally varies with political colour of the organisation in question.

The relationships so far illuminated have mainly concerned service behaviour in a decentralised context, at the firm or local institutional level. The issue of outsourcing versus in-house production, particularly in the public sphere, is also linked to a higher level, increasingly moulded by national policies, which have set rules and regulations for transactions on the market and extended possibilities of or set limits to the degrees of freedom within which to operate for enterprises and institutions. The opening up of possibilities may be political-ideological in origin, as a means of enhancing market relations generally at the expense of the public economy and the internalised relations and transactions characterising it. Originating in the US and the UK under neo-liberal regimes in the 1980s, systematic promotion of market mechanisms, and thereby externalised relations initiated by federal or state authorities was introduced, only to be halted locally to some extent by opposing political regimes. Marshall (1990) and Marshall and Wood (1995) emphasize in this context the role of the new public agencies and other devolved forms of management implemented mainly for cost effective reasons even in spheres which have been retained by public authorities. From the mid-1980s particularly this has become part of globalised strategies. The OECD has spearheaded a new management programme involving a separation between public policy-making and policy implementation by leaving it to parastatal or private operative units to implement the decisions. Finally, during the last few years a compulsory tendering system has been lifted to a supranational level as part of the economic policy of regional blocks. An EU wide tendering system, also including the EEA area, has been instituted for public purchases as a means in promoting further market integration. Conversely, laws and regulations on the labour market favouring rights of employees may work in the direction of setting limits to the operations of individual firms and public bodies and will tend to conserve an organisational structure with maximum internalised relations. It is against this background paramount to see the organisation of service transactions not only as a result of market forces but also, as pointed to above, in a contextual perspective.

Methodology and Propositions

From this rather brief overview of concepts and theories of organisation of production and particularly of the part played by services, it is natural to proceed to describe how restructuring of this organisation manifests itself in the real world. We will seek to achieve this by analysing problems and conflicts in and impacts on production systems. Particular interest is focused on impacts on employment in a regional context.

Many approaches are available for the purpose. One possible way would be to formulate clear hypotheses on the issue and apply these to a more closely-defined study area. This approach was for several reasons dropped. In order to give an overview and some tentative answers, the issue was explored by means of an extensive literature review, which included journal articles in the economic, social and regional disciplines and a few books as well as reports from specific research projects. Most of the background material is British and Nordic, with the main focus on findings from Norwegian research in the field. This should give a tentative state-of-the-art review of the present situation and the conditions leading up to it. In order to get answers to specific questions about recent developments in organisation in large corporations in remote regional locations and in smaller local administrations, in depth interviews have been conducted with managers and administrative leaders in the respective bodies. The interviews cover nine enterprises and five municipalities. Thus they cannot be considered representative, although being typical and will only give indications, not final answers. The results collected should therefore be interpreted with the utmost care.

On the basis of the background data collected, by a systematic study of literature as well as through personal enquiries, we aim to comment upon the following propositions:

- That the restructuring of firms by outsourcing of several types of services has tended to create a leaner structure in enterprises in the processing industry;

- That the impact on overall employment in the local area varies according to structure, size and location of the local economy and social environment, making one-sided, peripheral industrial communities particularly vulnerable to losses in overall employment by the outsourcing process;

- That losses in local employment are more pronounced when outsourcing higher level advanced services than in the case of externalisation of lower skill operations, common both to the private and public sphere;

- That larger market oriented enterprises and local governments in more populous municipalities have generally higher rates of externalisation than smaller ones, the local area being simultaneously able to absorb redundancies; and

- That smaller public administrations are more culturally inhibited in outsourcing services, the employment balance in these municipalities often being positive.

The State of the Art: In-house Production and Outsourcing on the Threshold of the 21st Century

What then are the manifestations of outsourcing in the real world in western countries? In trying to answer this, we meet with great difficulties in generalising. Systems of organisation in corporations and public administrations have developed over time, partly in response to the requirements of a general market economy, partly as a historically-determined development path, which, moreover, is contextually embedded. Some of the structures reflect a long history. In the private sector, and primarily in manufacturing industry, the roots are to be found in complexes of enterprises developed around a core activity---such as iron processing, sawmilling, later pulp and paper processing and textile production. These enterprises organised and provided most of the inputs needed, commodities as well as services. This pattern was to be found in most British manufacturing towns, the East Coast mill towns of the US, and in the Scandinavian world in the legendary Swedish «brukssamhällen», often modelled on paternalistic principles. In Norway the so-called company towns, nuclei of processing industries, largely built on cheap energy supply, were organised and functioned pretty much in the same fashion. Extensive service hierarchies thus originated, catering to the needs not only of the enterprises, but also of the local population from the cradle to the grave.

Modern industrial corporations, although more differentiated in their set-up depending on more intricate value-added chains and gradually more inclined to sub-contracting, are by and large also organised as hierarchies, tending to maximise internalisation of their economic activities. The integration of corporate and public political strategies, as illuminated in the Fordist and regulation discourses (e.g., Piore and Sabel, op. cit.; Lipietz, 1986) tends to reinforce these tendencies by harmonising state and union interests in redistribution policies. In the public services sphere, where the model of corporate organisation has been followed, the organisation of provision has developed in a similar way. It was only in the aftermath of World War Two that government on different levels, but mainly the central institutions of the state, assumed a wider responsibility for different welfare services in most western countries. A mixture of Keynesian economic principles (1936) and left-liberal planning ideas (Mannheim, 1945; Beveridge, 1944) lay behind the vetting of responsibility for welfare in public bodies, built on principles of social equity.

It was the crisis of the Keynesian demand economy model, surfacing in the early 1970s, which brought turbulence into the system and paved the way for reorganisation. Both the emergence of new types of economic activities, among these industries springing up in the wake of the IT "revolution", more flexible production for segmented markets and new, looser pattern of organisation in old industries set the pace for new organisational drives in production systems. Manifestations like increased divisionalisation, more flexible production and increasing sub-contracting in a lot of enterprises developed alongside a neo-liberal resurgence in the field of politics in many western countries, permeating even traditionally political radical movements and weakening the earlier stabilising institutional frameworks like the trade unions.

There has on the whole been a transition from mass organisation to looser contractual relationships in many parts of the economy. The modelling of new relationships came to affect both the industrial structure and the public service systems. The latter had, in most industrialised countries, grown tremendously during the Post World War Two period, often to make up huge entities, being frequently difficult to handle. Factors reinforcing the transition to a looser organisation of production systems are also linked to a general societal restructuring. The private firms have been exposed to a climate of merciless, even ruthless competition, a fact which has strengthened the need for restructuring of their activities. Thus a need has arisen for buying in specially adjusted components that can be produced more cheaply in specialised enterprises (Nesheim, 1996). The public institutions have on their side increasingly come to face a scarcity of funding.

It is not convincingly conclusive, however, whether an overall externalisation is gaining ground or if a strong internalisation is still rather prevalent. Although there is evidence of industrial corporations even externalising most of the former core activities in commodity production and retaining mainly the more "invisible" strategic functions (Quinn, Doreley and Paquette, 1990), this is clearly an exception. Certainly, a recent Norwegian case in the same direction has been described by Nesheim (op. cit.). Conversely there is clear evidence of reinternalisation as a reaction to the recession of the 1990s (Barcet and Bonamy, 1994; Sjøholt, 1994). O'Farrell et. al. (1993) observed a similar trend in a survey undertaken in Britain. Still it is beyond doubt that externalisation simultaneously belongs to the order of the day. Specific functions, both high and low in competence requirement, thus advertising, Gruhler (1990), repair and cleaning (Rekkavik and Spillum, 1990) are increasingly being farmed out. Perry found a slight tendency of externalisation in his inquiries in New Zealand (1990, 1992) and Beyers and Lindahl (1997) came to the same conclusion using empirical evidence from the US.

In other cases both internalisation and externalisation are growing simultaneously. This led Illeris (1996) to conclude that empirical evidence indicates no strong tendency towards either externalisation or internalisation in producer services in the corporate sector. Put together, there is an increased use of services more or less equally provided from external and internal sources with a slight preponderance of outsourcing.

In the public sector the picture is also somewhat unclear. There can be no doubt that the earlier very homogeneous hierarchical structure is giving way somewhat to more loosely organised service provision, either relying on separate public agencies or on privatised providers. This transition is partly cost-driven and partly ideological in origin. On the European scene the UK has been the instigator and has today the longest tradition in a systematic outsourcing. The new drive was initiated by the Conservative government in the early 1980s and was heavily ideologically-laden. It was successively extended by means of new laws up to the early 1990s. The development has thus been planned and implemented from above. As a compulsory tendering system the outsourcing process, where also specially organised public bodies were allowed to participate, predated the EU directive of the 1990s, which was introduced as a measure of further market integration. In Britain, as described by a number of scholars, including Milne (1993), Patterson and Pinch (1995), Allen and Henry (1997) and Reimer (1998), many services earlier provided directly by the public administration have been farmed out, and largely, although not uniformly, have been taken over by private enterprises. As also demonstrated from Australia (Hall, 1995), studies of this process have mainly concentrated on rather peripheral services, cleaning, refuse collection, catering and guarding. These services are also the ones most frequently being reorganised. A rather substantial part of these has, during the last decade, been farmed out in the UK, geographically very much coinciding with municipalities of a conservative political profile, thus on the whole creating a south/north divide in coverage. In Norway pretty much of the same pattern can be found. According to a recent report (Bogen and Nyen, 1998) refuse collection is now in private hands in more than 60 per cent of the municipalities and in more than 40 per cent of the municipalities, private firms operate in the technical sector. It should then be added that this is not exclusively a recent phenomenon. Although 34 per cent of the municipalities have had privatised services since 1991, private operations were common also before 1990 in many communes, mainly in large centrally-located ones.

The above service functions make up a rather small part of the operations within the public service sector, however. Its main part, where is to be found the substantial number of employees, investments and running costs, consist of educational work, health and social care plus public works. The core functions of these sub-sectors, and particularly of the last-mentioned, have also been subject to outsourcing, but to a smaller extent than the above mentioned "hotel services". Certainly, private hospitals and clinics make up part of the health system in many western countries and most conspicuously in the United States. The non-public institutions consist of both purely market-based enterprises and enterprises owned and run by non-profit organisations. Many of these have a long tradition, but the tendencies towards privatisation have increased in the recent past. In Germany, for instance, the health system is tending towards a basic stock of public general hospitals, supplemented with a host of privately-operated specialist clinics (Kühn, 1984). Also in the field of social services, particularly in care for elderly people, many countries have witnessed outsourcing of the services to private operators, who partly own the premises, partly lease them from the public authorities. This is also the case in the Nordic countries, most conspicuously in Sweden, where from the early 1990s several large cities and municipalities in suburban areas have transferred social services earlier hierarchically organised and performed within the public administration to smaller unit operators, either public or private (Bengtsson and Rønnov, 1996). According to estimates from 1993, 4 per cent of the total costs in care for elderly and handicapped persons in Sweden was performed by private enterprises, varying by municipalities from nil to over 40 per cent (Engström, 1997). In Norway the dimensions of privatisation are generally smaller. Less than 2 per cent of the municipalities had private operators in social care in 1997. Only half of these were recent additions (after 1991; Bogen & Nyen, 1998). This shows a rather slow pace of outsourcing, even though many municipalities today are considering a possible increase in privatisation. It is important to keep in mind that these arrangements, although differing in organisation to a certain degree, are generally subject to the public authorities' ordering, financing, monitoring and scrutinising of the operations, thus mainly outsourcing the service production proper and so retaining both social commitment and capacities for control.

Important as they are, also as innovative alternatives and as systems of a more optional nature for the general public, outsourced public welfare services, and, we might add, also some general education, are still exceptions rather than the rule in most western countries. The changes have met with varying resistance, not only from professional and other vested interests, but

125

also from parts of the general public, who see the principles of equity---socially as well as regionally---threatened or even violated.

However, as long as outsourcing meets a demand, mainly because of queues in the public system, and cost efficiency and some positive innovation in organisation and in practices can be attributed to it, the new arrangements will probably run their course. This prospect makes it paramount for the public authorities, particularly in areas of fundamental social interest, to control and monitor the new service organisation. In the next chapter we shall, through a brief discussion, throw some more light on the impacts of the changing service structure in the corporate and public sphere and also see this in a regional context.

The New Service Provision: Employment and Socio-economically Linked Impacts with Particular Reference to Repercussions in Marginal Areas

As could also be gathered from the above survey, much of the knowledge we possess of the externalisation process versus the retention of internal production tasks both in the private and the public enterprises and other bodies is rather detached, being the results of studies from different parts of the world with different methodological approaches. Hence, when we are going to knit together the threads, we are left with an inconsistency problem. Difficulties are great in evaluation of impacts emanating from the process of organisation of production, and particularly difficult are the problems of measurement. This will necessarily complicate the account that follows. Instead of giving a consistent comparison based on unambiguous data sources the discussion will have to centre around less-comparable findings, mainly isolated and contextual cases, which do not easily lend themselves to analysis and general conclusion.

The impacts discussed are largely on costs and employment, both in general terms and to the extent that data exists also regionally, particularly seen in relation to marginal areas. Employment is interesting per se in quantitative terms, but is also interesting in a qualitative sense, in relation to impacts upon conditions of the work force and to the impact on the industrial environment and local community welfare. The two dimensions, employment and cost, are closely linked to each other. Cost reductions, which is one of the reasons for outsourcing, a fact following from the theoretical models which were discussed previously, are often considered to be synonymous with reduction in employment and loss of jobs. Even though there are clear relationships, more variables are linked to cost efficiency, such as better organisation and concomitant increase in productivity, more rational purchases and other savings. Norwegian investigations thus reveal cuts in costs by more rational organisation in the order of 20 to 30 per cent in insurance expenditures and operations of IT services (Kjerstad and Kristiansen, 1996). Positive impacts on efficiency and cost reductions in internally-organised services may also follow by threats of farming out the services in question. Almquist (1996) thus records from Stockholm that prospects of competitive tendering reduced the costs in public social care for the elderly by 9 or 10 per cent. In this case there was clear evidence of a reduction in the use of manpower.

Employment changes are the most conspicuous impacts of introducing new organisational concepts into the production system. In the private sector previous in-house work force may be substituted by new personnel coming in, some of them, particularly in services on a high competence level co-working with the internal staff; others, specialised in more menial or programmed tasks, performing them either outside or inside the client firm. Few consistent studies exist which can give a clear picture of the employment balance. It is seldom a question of direct substitution. Productivity gains will on the one hand possibly reduce the need for personnel. On the other hand the new externally-organised supply may create its own new demand. Two cases from large Norwegian companies in the processing industry may illustrate this and be taken as proofs of beneficial effects. In the aluminium industry, the internal organisation at one of the one-company sites wanted to get rid of the internal production of specialised tools, among these vehicles used in the production process. A company of its own was some years ago established as a spin-off from the smelter. Besides delivering to the enterprises of the concern, this company became involved in shipments to the world market. Employment has steadily increased. The company has later been resold and is today expanding its production particularly for foreign markets to the benefit of the remote local community. Another metal smelter company in a more differentiated company town found its maintenance department too heavy a burden and wanted to get rid of it. It was sold to a private company with operations in the local area which greatly extended its expertise and capacity and is now selling services also to other companies at other industrial sites.

Experiences from Norway show great variation in employment impacts as a consequence of reorganisation of service provision in larger multi-site localised corporations. By inspecting data from one company and other specialised industrial sites we find that internal employment in the enterprises in most cases has gone radically down, some of it from rationalisation of core production activities; increasingly, however, as a consequence of outsourcing of activities more peripheral to the production process, mainly services. Among these, maintenance, cleaning, refuse collection and transport services have to a large extent been transferred to private enterprises in the local area. Experience indicates that the possibility of the local community absorbing within its industrial structure former internalised functions is largely contextually contingent. Localities having fostered entrepreneurs and sites with a more broad industrial structure more readily take up the challenge of the new demand than really one-sided sites. To some extent this is also the case with non-manual services, among these IT and even some, rather simple R & D activities. Among the latter there are problems in creating viable spin-offs locally, however. Thus a new unit for environmental technology and concomitant services at one of the Norwegian sites failed before becoming firmly established. In cases when tendering is a normal procedure in the outsourcing process experiences from Denmark show that smaller firms in the local area are easily squeezed out. Large corporations and institutions, more often than not, prefer larger service firms, generally more centrally located, and which have more resources to introduce themselves on the market (PLS Consult, 1997).

According to our own inquiries many of the more sophisticated services being shed by the enterprises appear in more differentiated places. Some of it, mainly legal services, R & D, marketing and strategic consultancy, is taken over by the corporation head office and as a rule strongly centralised. But there are examples of a more local transfer. Accountancy for all the smelters of the largest multi-aluminium corporation in Norway has thus been concentrated at one of the rather peripheral production sites.

The situation in the job market should not be dramatised too one-sidedly, however. An investigation carried out in 12 Norwegian industrial and large service enterprises (Nesheim, op. cit.) revealed that companies generally aimed at some local stabilisation. They were cautious with direct dismissals, trying to solve restructuring problems by replacement, early retirement and transfer of former work force to new externalised companies. In contrast to the situation described in British investigations of public outsourcing (Allen and Henry, 1996; Reimer, 1998), great care is shown in retaining good conditions of work. In Norway, as in most of Scandinavia and in Australia, legal restrictions also limit the scope for employers to act arbitrarily. These conditions are generally more relaxed in countries like the UK and the US.

One way of outsourcing, originally strongly restricted by law but gradually relaxed and thus having grown in importance, is more use of substitutes, organised through a bureau letting out manpower. Although originally only typical clerical work was let out by these agencies, Nesheim and Hersvik (1998) found a clear tendency in Norway towards more sophisticated competence being provided, sometimes even substituting for consultancy services. This work force was to begin with justified only as real substitutes in cases of illness and other absenteeism of the regular work force. It could, however, easily be used as a means of making the labour force more flexible, by promoting a disintegrated production system which earlier in this paper was referred to as numerical flexibility. This type of substitute organisation is still mainly an urban phenomenon both as far as supply and demand are concerned. Only one bureau has branch offices outside the three largest towns. However, there are also examples of marginal areas having benefited from this type of organisation of the work force. A Danish firm letting out physicians on a short- and medium-term basis has thus solved scarcity problems in the health sector in Northern Norway.

Still, the picture is somewhat unclear. It is difficult to make up a gross balance between loss of jobs as a result of the outsourcing process on the one side and generated local employment emanating from the same process on the other. Although varying, indications point in the direction of an overall loss of jobs in the local area. This is also indicated by the demographic development. Figures from seven municipalities in Norway, particularly dependent on one or a few processing industries, show a loss of population ever since the restructuring process started. This loss has been consistent also through the 1990s, in the worst case with a population decrease of 7 per cent during the seven-year period.

Few studies have explored the more general trends in outsourcing and impact on local communities. Rusten (1997) surveyed 450 Norwegian manufacturing firms in three lines of business, mainly small and medium-sized firms, ranging from 25 to 250 in employment. Her conclusions are moderately encouraging as far as local and regional impacts of outsourcing are concerned. The main part of services being externalised from the smaller companies of the sample was preferably bought from local supply as far as possibilities existed, partly explained by lower transaction costs (among these a simplified search process), more personal informal knowledge and a business culture favouring local businesses. Larger enterprises of the sample, having more capacity for market search, tended to make more use of extraregional sources, as was also the case with subsidiaries, whose dependence on the parent companies is more pronounced. A possible change to a more centralised outsourcing pattern was evident also among smaller firms by an emerging use of brokers. For the time being this use has mainly been adopted for rather peripheral services.

A Swedish study of outsourcing of R & D in the electronics industry also shows substantial decentralisation (Suarez-Villa and Karlsson, 1996). High technology is increasingly being produced in the hinterland of the large cities. Stockholm is still the main location of vertically disintegrated production by research-intensive electronic firms in the capital. Elsewhere spin-off benefits are found in many rather dispersed, non-central localities. Contextual factors related to labour skills and organisational capabilities as well as possibilities of co-operative transactions have favoured this development.

In the public sector, several studies from England show outsourcing to have somewhat differentiated impacts on employment. According to Patterson and Pinch (op. cit.), public service work has been intensified and job losses have not been quite compensated through the transition to a new organisational structure. More managerial jobs, which have become rather centralised, and fewer jobs on the floor are also a characteristic outcome of the process. The system of large suppliers, in some cases bordering on an oligarchic structure, thus creates a concentration in management and a fragmentation in implementation. Only in rare cases has this system paved the way for small and medium-sized local providers, which were the prospects foreshadowed in the rhetoric of the agents of change in the 1980s. Allen and Henry (op. cit.) found, on the other hand, astonishingly great continuity in employment as a consequence of the process of farming out services despite a change of hands. Reimer (1999) also found apparent stability in employment in most cases, partly because of the benefits for employers of re-employing local people. Like Allen and Henry, she found changes to be more pronounced in employment conditions than in sheer number of jobs. Through the processes of negotiating and renegotiating, employment conditions tend to become tougher and more risky. Partly it has led to a cut in hours of work, in many cases to a point below thresholds of optimal social security benefits to be gained by the work force and particularly by women. Often it has necessitated workers to engage in more than one job in order to make ends meet. In contrast to the rhetoric of the proponents of the system, the work situation is far from flexible for those concerned. That services are provided by external employers mean, in contrast to the situation when provided in-house, more fragmented social relations and less scope for collective action on the part of the workers. Patterson and Pinch conclude that the new contract system also have negative repercussions on local government and local communities by undermining efficacy, capacity and local governance. It reduces the power of the local state to act in the support of the local economy, thus restricting local multiplier effects and other positive externalities. Compulsory competitive tendering has been a strong force in "hollowing out" the local state.

In the Scandinavian countries, and particularly in Norway, the changes have been far less dramatic. Berg (1999) points to the increasing devolution and contracting in public services which are organised by the state, however without ample evidence for concluding whether this has had negative impacts on employment, particularly in peripheral regions. At the regional and municipal level of public service provision, competitive tendering has a far shorter tradition than in Britain and the US. Hence fewer public institutions have up to now practised outsourcing as part of their economic and managerial strategies. Those having reorganised their provision have also witnessed moderate changes in employment. Thus Kjerstad and Kristiansen (op. cit.)

found in a sample of 25 per cent of the Norwegian municipalities that only 26 per cent of them had experienced any changes in the manning of the public service sector as a consequence of more use of external contracts. Most of the units reporting change had witnessed a reduction in jobs, the losses generally increasing by municipality size. The larger municipalities could, on the other hand, compensate more easily for the losses with new jobs in the local area. Most manual services in public works, cleaning and refuse collection which have been contracted out in smaller communities, have also gone to small and medium-sized enterprises in the local area, possibly with exception of the last service, which in some cases has been organised on an inter-municipal basis. That higher order services have been transferred to the market may have meant loss to the local community in smaller municipalities. Until now, this has not been the case with health services, though more flexible organisation has had the additional benefit of shortening queues. But the above transferred jobs are generally very few. Greater changes may follow in the wake of outsourcing of social services. This reorganisation is still in its infancy in Norway, and it is therefore premature to jump to bold conclusions. Swedish experiences point in the direction of reduction of employment both in administration and in service production. Cheaper production has generally been claimed, but economic gains from this type of outsourcing is difficult to assess. Quality of the services is one complicating aspect to take into consideration, as is increase in the need for public management, administration and control.

Up till now there has been in many smaller Norwegian municipalities an increase in internal jobs, which have, by and large, compensated for losses due to outsourced places of work. This is particularly true of social services, ranging from kindergarten attendants and teachers to nurses in elderly care. According to our own enquiries, the politicians and administrators in these communities are reluctant to fire personnel on economic grounds, explaining that this is also a reflection of the particular employment culture. An interesting organisational arrangement is reported from a peripheral municipality in South Norway, where the communal administration has sponsored a "substitute bank" for auxiliary nurses, in this way both giving the workers better security of job tenure and the municipality greater flexibility in making use of the work force.

From 1993 for some transactions and from 1994 for others the EU directive and concomitant regulations compel government and parastatal agencies at all levels to announce purchases above certain threshold values for competitive tendering. Suppliers are eligible in the whole EU-EEA area. It is still too early to draw any firm conclusions as to the impact of these transactional changes. According to Andersen and Lunde (1997) the bulk of the local and regional governments (60 per cent and 77 per cent respectively) use tendering more frequently than before, whereas the frequency of change is lower in the statal sector due to an earlier, more widespread practice of tendering contracts. Most interesting in our context is that the suppliers are still overwhelmingly national and those winning the municipal and county contracts are mainly small and medium-sized enterprises. On the other hand purchases tend to become more centralised than before, particularly the larger purchases. These have also increased in frequency, partly as a consequence of more widespread inter-municipal collaboration in purchases. It is difficult to quantify the new trends and evaluate job gains and losses. The trends point in the direction of benefits to higher levels in the regional hierarchy to the detriment of smaller local and regional places. This is partly the background of organising a project, sponsored among others by the Ministry of the Interior, The State Regional Industrial Bank and the Association of Norwegian Municipalities with the purpose of enhancing the competence of local deliverers to take part more successfully in the tendering process (Melheim, 1998). The project (LUKprosjektet) is still in action and it is therefore premature to evaluate it. Given the potential value of public purchases in the market, cautiously estimated in the range of NOK 30-50 billion, it is good reason to monitor its further development in a regional context.

A Brief Discussion of Outsourcing in Relation to the Propositions

Due to the fragmented results we have been able to present on the process of outsourcing, it is difficult to give precise answers to the propositions put forward in the chapter on methodology. As we have seen, there are tendencies and counter-tendencies both in externalising and internalising of activities. The general decrease in employment found among the larger firms in the processing industry shows a slimming process both in core operations and in more peripheral service functions of which manual services make up the bulk. These activities are increasingly being farmed out both for cost reasons and general strategic reasons, the latter in order to concentrate more on core activities. In this process the real one-sided company towns are most vulnerable to job losses, not only directly but also indirectly, as the bulk of the outsourced jobs leak out, mainly to more central and diversified places. Outsourcing in more differentiated processing industry communities, on the other hand, has generally meant more work to new local companies specialising in the services in question. These findings seem to verify propositions 1 and 2, as these contained claims of a leaner structure in the enterprises in the processing industry and hypothesized the most problematic employment impacts in one-sided peripheral industrial communities, although experiences, particularly from the Nordic countries show a somewhat better-managed reorganisation of both core and more peripheral service functions than in for example Britain and the US. Proposition 3, stating that outsourcing of higher order advanced services leads to more losses in local employment than farming out of less advanced tasks, is not directly refuted by the findings from Scandinavia but it seems to have a rather marginal effect in smaller communities and will readily be met by local supplies in medium-sized and larger towns. This stands in contrast to findings from England, where effects on local industry is judged to be rather negligible. Proposition 4 is on the whole verified by the empirical data, its sub-section being in reality a repetition of claims put forward in proposition 3. The tendencies to inhibition of outsourcing by smaller public administrations (proposition 5) were substantiated by the few municipal interviews conducted in Norway, but are because of the small size of the sample difficult to generalise any further. It has, on the whole, been very difficult to quantify the findings, a fact that should call for great caution in the final conclusion.

Concluding Remarks and Suggestions for Further Studies

This preliminary overview has shown that the issue of outsourcing versus in-house production of services both in the corporate and public sectors is many-sided in its manifestations. The preference by management for organisational form also does not lend itself to easy conclusions. The organisation of production is certainly strongly economic in motivation, but not fully explained in terms of the classical price and cost variables. Social considerations play a role, although varying between countries and different political regimes. We have even seen the contours of cultural determinants, particularly in the production of public services. These forces often pull in the direction of internal control. Simultaneously, services originating both from market and networking sources seem to grow in magnitude, often for reasons of coping better with the dynamics of modern production and as a link in the learning process. This weight on external solutions has generally had a centralising effect, viewed in a regional dimension.

There are still many black boxes to open, and this calls for an intensified research effort. More comparative studies on impacts on employment and conditions of work as a consequence of different organisational rearrangements are particularly ripe for implementation. Comparisons of similarities and differences between corporate and public systems should be given high priority and presuppose a combination of qualitative and quantitative studies. The former should preferably be closely linked to theory, which still needs development. This is particularly necessary in order to get a more profound understanding of the dynamics of the system.

References

Allen, J. and N. Henry. 1997. Ulrich Beck's Risk Society at Work: Labour and Employment in the Contract Service Industries. *Trans. Inst. Br. Geogr.* (NS) 22, 180-196.

Almqvist, R. 1996. Effekter av konkurrenshotet- en studie av egen regis resultatenheter inom äldreomsorgen i Stockholms stad. Institutet för kommunal ekonomi, 1996:58. Stockholms Universitet.

Amin, A. and K. Robins. 1990. The Re-emergence of Regional Economies? The Mythical Geography of Flexible Specialisation. *Environment and Planning* D, 8, 7-34.

Amin, A. and N. Thrift. 1992. Neo-Marshallian Nodes in Global Networks. *International Journal of Urban and Regional Research* 16, 571-587.

Andersen, M. and H. Lunde. 1997. Offentlige anskaffelser på anbud- virkninger og erfaringer med E¥S-regelverket for offentlige anskaffelser. Tromsø: NORUT.

Asheim, B. 1996. "Learning Regions" in a Globalised World Economy: towards a New Competitive Advantage of Industrial Districts? Paper given to the first European Urban and Regional Studies Conference, Exeter, April 1996.

Barcet, A. and J. Bonamy. 1994. Internalisation versus Externalisation: Valeur et Dynamique de l'Offre. Paper given to the fourth annual RESER conference, Barcelona.

Bengtsson, S. and B. Rønnow. 1996. Marked som styringsredskap- nogle erfaringer fra hollandsk og svensk ældreservice. Kφbenhavn: Socialforskningsinstitutet.

Berg, P. O. 2000. New Public Management and Peripheral Regions. In R. Byron and J. Hutson (eds.), *Community Development on the North Atlantic Margin.* Aldershot: Ashgate.

Beveridge, W. H. 1944. *Full Employment in a Free Society: A Report.* London: G. Allen.

Beyers, W. B. and D. P. Lindahl. 1997. Paper Pushers and Data Apes: The Growth and Location of Business Services in the American Economy. *L'Espace Geographique.*

Bogen, H. and T. Nyen. 1998. Privatisering og konkurranseutsetting i norske kommuner Oslo: Fafo Report 254.

Buckley, P. J. 1988. The Limits of Explanation: Testing the Internalisation Theory of the Multinational Enterprise. *Journal of International Business Studies* 19 (2), 181-

183.

Coase, R. 1937. The Nature of the Firm. *Economica* 4, 386-405.

Cunningham, M. T. and K. Calligan. 1991. Competiveness through Networks of Relationships in Information Technology Product Markets. In S. J. Paliwoda (ed.), *New Perspectives on International Marketing*. London: Routledge.

de Bandt, J. 1994. De l'Economie des Biens a l'Economie des Services: La Production de dans et Par les Services. In J. de Bandt and J. Gadrey (eds.), *Relations de Service, Richesses Marches de Services*. Paris: CNRS.

de Bandt, J. 1995. Services aux Enterprises. Paris: Economica.

Engström, B. 1997. Nya styr-och driftsformer i äldreomsorgen. Välferd eller ofärd? In. k. Jennbert and R. Lagerkrantz (EDS.), *Äldrepolitik i förändring?* Stockholm: Socialdepartementet.

Gertler, M. S. 1992. Flexibility Revisited: Districts, Nation-states and the Forces of Production. *Transactions of the Inst. of British Geogr.* (NS), 17, 259-278.

Guhler, W. 1990. *Dienstleistungsbestimmter Strukturwandel in deutscher Industrieunternehmen*. Köln: Deutscher Instituts-Verlag.

Håkansson, H. and J. Johannson. 1987. Formal and informal co-operation strategies in international industrial networks. Working Paper. Företagsekonomiska Institutet vid Uppsala Universitet.

Håkansson, H and I. Snehota. 1995. *Developing Relationships in Business Networks*. London: Routledge.

Hall, C. 1995. Competitive Tendering for Domestic Services---a Comparative Study of Three Hospitals in New South Wales. In S. Domberger and C. Hall (eds.), *The Contracting Case Book*. Canberra: Australian Government Publishing Services.

Illeris, S. 1996. *The Service Economy: A Geographical Approach*. Chichester and New York: Wiley.

Jarillo, J. C. 1988. On Strategic Networks. *Strategic Management Journal* 9, 31-41.

Karlsen, A. 1999. Institusjonelle perspektiver på næringsomstilling. Ph.D. Thesis. Faculty of Social Science and Technological Management. Trondheim: The University of Technology and Science.

Keynes, W. M. 1936. *General Theory of Employment, Interest and Money*. London: Macmillan.

Kjerstad, E. and F. Kristiansen. 1996. Erfaring med konkurranseutsetting av kommunal tjenesteproduksjon. SNF Report 87/96. Bergen: SNF.

Krugman, P. 1991. *Geography and Trade*. Cambridge, Mass.: MIT Press.

Kühn, H. 1984. *Das Finanzierungsystem der deutschen Krankenhäuser*. Berlin: Wissenschaftzentrum.

Larsen, J. N. 1992. Teknisk Rådgivning- eksempel på samspillet mellem industri og service? In S. Illeris and P. Sj¢holt (eds.), *Internationalisering af service og regional udvikling i Norden*. København: NordREFO.

Levy, D. T. 1984. Testing Stigler's Interpretation for the Division of Labour as Limited by the Extent of the Market. *Journal of Industrial Economics* 32, 377-389.

Lipietz, A. 1986. New Tendencies in the International Division of Labour: Regimes of Accumulation and Modes of Regulation In A. J. Scott and M. Storper (eds.), *Production, Work, Territory*. London: Unwin Hyman.

Mannheim, K. 1940. *Man and Society in an Age of Reconstruction*. London: Kegan Paul.

Marshall, A. 1891. *Principles of Economics*. 2nd ed. London: Macmillan.

Marshall, J. N. and P. Wood. 1995. *Services and Space: Key Aspects of Urban and Regional Development*. New York: Longman.

Melheim, R. 1998. LUK-prosjektet. *Forsyning KSI* 2 (6).

Milne, R. G. 1993. Contractor's Experience of Compulsory Competitive Tendering: A Case Study of Contract Cleaners in the NHS. *Public Administration* 71, 301-321.

Nesheim, T. 1997. Mot eksternalisering av arbeid? Analyser av tilknytningsformer for arbeid. SNF Report 35/97. Bergen: SNF.

Nesheim, T. and I. M. Hersvik. 1998. Vikarbyråer og innleie av arbeidskraft. SNF Report 47/98. Bergen: SNF.

O'Farrell, L., A .R. Moffat and D. N. Hitchens. 1993. Manufacturing Demand for Business Services in a Core and Peripheral Region: Does Flexible Production Imply Vertical Disintegration of Business Services? *Regional Studies* 27 (5), 385-400.

Patterson, A. and P. L. Pinch. 1995. "Hollowing Out" the Local State: Compulsory Competitive Tendering and the Restructuring of British Public Sector Services. *Environment and Planning* A, 1437-1461.

Perry, M. 1990. Business Service Specialization and Regional and Economic Change. *Regional Studies* 24, 195-209.

Perry, M. 1992. Flexible Production, Externalization and the Interpretation of Business Service Growth. *The Service Industries Journal* 12, 1-16.

Piore, M. J. and C. F. Sabel. 1984. *The Second Industrial Divide*. New York: Basic

Books.

PLS Consult. 1997. Erfaringer med udlicitering i kommuner og amter. K¢benhavn: Hovedrapport til Indenrigsministeriet.

Quinn, J. B., T. L. Doreley and P. Paquette. 1990. Beyond Products: Service-based Strategy. *Harvard Business Review*, 58-67.

Reimer, S. 1999. Contract Service Firms in Local Authorities: Evolving Geographies of Activity. *Regional Studies* 33 (2), 121-130.

Rekkavik, J. and P. Spillum. 1990. Tjenesteyting for næringslivet på ensidige industristeder. Bergen: Norges Handelshøyskole.

Rusten, G. 1997. Outsourcing strategies and geography: business service use by manufacturing firms. SNF Working Paper 49/97. Bergen: SNF.

Sayer, A. 1989. The New Economic Geography and Problems of Narrative. *Environment and Planning* D, 253-276.

Scott, A. J. 1985. Location Processes, Urbanisation, and Territorial Development: An Exploratory Essay. *Environment and Planning* A, 17, 479-501.

Scott, A. J. 1986. Industrial Organization and Location: Division of Labor, the Firm and Spatial Process. *Economic Geography* 62, 215-231.

Scott, A. J. 1988a. *Metropolis: From the Division of Labour to Urban Form*. Berkeley: University of California Press.

Scott, A. J. 1988b. New Industrial Spaces: Flexible Production, Organisation and Regional Development in North America and Europe. London: Pion.

Scott, A. J. and M. Storper (eds.). 1986. Production, Work, Territory. The Geographical Anatomy of Contemporary Capitalism. Boston: Allen and Unwin.

Sjøholt, P. 1994. The Role of Producer Services in Industrial and Regional Development: The Nordic Case. *European Urban and Regional Studies* 1, 115-129.

Stigler, G. J. 1951. The Division of Labour is Limited by the Extent of the Market. *Journal of Pol. Econ.* 59, 185-193.

Suarez-Villa, L. and C. Karlsson. 1996. The Development of Sweden's R & D-intensive Electronics Industries: Exports, Outsourcing and Territorial Distribution. *Environment and Planning* A, 783-817.

Thorelli, H. B. 1986. Networks: Between Markets and Hierarchies. *Strategic Management Journal* 7, 37-51.

Weber, A. 1909. *Über den Standort der Industrien*. Tübingen.

Williamson O. E. 1979. *Market and Hierarchies: Analysis and Antitrust Implications.* New York: Free Press.

Williamson, O. E. 1985. *The Economic Institutions of Capitalism.* New York: Basic Books.

8 Crafts Producers on the Celtic Fringe: Marginal Lifestyles in Marginal Regions?

ANNE-MARIE SHERWOOD, NICHOLAS PARROTT
AND TIM JENKINS

Introduction

The role of the crafts sector in the economies of marginal regions has historically received little attention. Those involved in crafts activities have tended to be regarded as voluntarily outside the economic mainstream and hence of little academic or policy concern. Yet evidence gathered by the authors suggests that the production of local crafts can make a significant developmental contribution to marginal regions: not only in direct economic terms, but also less directly through their positive association with the cultural heritage of these areas. This chapter argues that, with increasing policy emphasis on rural diversification (see, for example, NAW, 2000; MAFF, 2000) and on new ways of conceptualising the rural economy in post-agricultural terms, crafts production may have a significant role to play in future rural development strategies. Moreover, the growth of green and cultural tourism in some remote areas, together with a market demand for local products that embody values of small-scale production, tradition and skills, all suggest potential opportunities for crafts producers.

In developing these arguments, we summarise the results of recent studies of quality handcrafts on the western peripheries of Ireland and Wales.[1] The research formed part of a collaborative European project[2] and was undertaken in the counties of Sligo, Leitrim and Roscommon in northwest Ireland, and the former counties of Dyfed and Gwynedd in west Wales.[3] Here, we examine the motivations and business strategies of crafts producers based in the study areas; their contributions to the local economy; the insights that craftspeople bring to rural development issues in the postmodern context; and the role of economic development agencies in supporting and developing local production. We explore contrasts and similarities between the two study areas, and we seek to place handcrafts activities within the "New Rural Economy" of marginal regions.

Background

Although computer-based technologies and information systems are potentially able to reduce the impact of economic remoteness created by geographic peripherality, employment and income-generating opportunities remain relatively constrained in the marginal coastal and inland regions of both Ireland and Wales. In the context of falling agricultural incomes and continuing Common Agricultural Policy reform,[4] development strategies involving both new activities and the revival of older ones are being sought in both localities. Emphasis on the local and regional has been a key feature of integrated approaches to the development of farming and tourism in marginal areas (Parrott, Sherwood and Midmore, 1999) and, typically, such emphasis focuses on local materials, regional imagery, and traditional skills and practices in production, promotion and marketing. Furthermore, in addition to such indigenous developments, both study regions have attracted in-migrants from other areas in search of a more sustainable way of life. Many of these so-called lifestyle migrants[5] are attracted by relative remoteness, high environmental quality, and the perceived persistence of authentic cultures and traditions in communities apparently living on the fringes of a modern society.

Against this background, it is hardly surprising that crafts production is an attractive option for many such people. It is creative, often locally-inspired and rooted, and can provide a way of life that appears sustainable and meaningful. From a practical viewpoint, established and growing tourist markets in situ create a demand for local handcrafts, and producers potentially have access to the institutional support and economic incentives available from regional agencies, LEADER initiatives,[6] local enterprise boards and other partnerships involved in the economic development of marginal areas.

At the outset, however, we must consider what we mean by crafts. Output from the sector is extremely diverse and there are fundamental difficulties in trying to establish a workable definition. Most people tend to identify crafts instinctively as hand-produced goods requiring practical skills---such as, for example, pottery and ceramics, some types of hand-made furniture and woven textiles---but would have some difficulty in defining where crafts end, and art or design begins. Is the producer of an imaginatively-glazed ceramic bowl a fine artist or a skilled crafts maker? Would a factory-produced, but hand-painted, vase be considered a crafts product? At what level of mechanisation does enterprise activity cease to qualify as crafts production?

These uncertainties illustrate the inexact and, to an extent, subjective, nature of crafts. Nevertheless, core ingredients do exist, and these are reflected in artisanal products, which are largely hand-made, and often culturally-specific or associated with local traditions or practices. In an important sense, therefore, crafts are the "antidote" to mass-produced, undifferentiated goods. Their value lies as much in the way they are made and in the values, real or constructed, that they embody as in their usefulness or superficial attractiveness. The existence of these more intangible characteristics, together with the inherent difficulties of precisely defining crafts, raises a number of interesting questions and has important implications for the ways in which the crafts sector might be most effectively promoted and developed in the future. On a practical level, for example, crafts producers face competition from indigenous crafts produced in low-income countries, and from mass-produced artefacts; consumers may not always distinguish between tourist "junk" and "real" crafts; and institutions must consider the particular importance of small-scale enterprise in the crafts sector.

The Welsh and Irish Crafts Sectors

Before discussing these issues in more detail, this section summarises the most significant features of crafts production in the two study areas. The evidence is based on a survey conducted in 1998 of forty enterprises (twenty in west Wales and twenty in the northwest of Ireland), chosen on a non-random basis with the help of crafts organisations working in each region. The main criteria for selection were that the enterprises be "quality" producers,[7] implying a bias towards the more established and possibly older makers. A further objective was to obtain a sample that would be suitably representative in terms of the range of crafts produced in each region and the diversity of business sizes and types. In most cases, interviews took place with the "owner-makers" themselves, and followed the semi-structured, open-ended style of questioning associated with qualitative research techniques. This approach is both sufficiently focused to identify basic conditions and (often recurring) themes, and flexible to allow for individual responses to key issues and concerns. Consequently, likely avenues for further investigation can be quickly highlighted and developed.[8] Whilst it is important to bear in mind the non-random nature of the final sample, those participating in the survey (see Table 1 for an overview of sample characteristics) provided useful insights into the character of the crafts sector as a whole, and enabled a number of conclusions to be drawn.

The first row of Table 8.1 illustrates the variety of output from the crafts sector in both study areas, and two fundamental characteristics are instantly apparent. Firstly, the use of natural ingredients predominates: wood, wool, slate, clay and other traditional materials are central to crafts activities and some of these are locally-sourced. Secondly, for quality crafts, further creative input is essential and reflects the maker's originality and individual style in, for example, graphics and three-dimensional design, painting and drawing, and sculpture or carving. It is in this sense that we encounter the blurring of what might strictly be labelled "artistic ability", with the "technical skills" content of crafts. This overlap is exemplified by the output from our sample of makers, which includes traditional handcrafted all-wood cabinets, original paintings and ceramics, and unique *objets d'art* in stone and slate. A number of makers were clearly extremely gifted and producing exceptional and highly imaginative work. Some were also multi-talented and could undertake more than one creative skill. There are considerable problems associated with defining quality production under such circumstances, and these are discussed further in the next section.

Table 8.1   Characteristics of crafts enterprises in the Welsh and Irish samples

Enterprises in:	Wales	Ireland
• Type of crafts: % of sample	Pottery and ceramics (25%); wood products, including furniture and. traditional lovespoons (20%); wool crafts and weaving (15%); jewellery (15%); slate products; candles; hand-painted glass; paintings, prints and calligraphy.	Paintings (20%); wood and stone sculptures (15%); pressed flower products (10%); pottery; jewellery; glass items; hand-painted and printed textiles; furniture; stationery; candles; pewter and enamel products.
• Location of workspace	Home premises: 65% of sample; 35% in workshops or elsewhere.	Home premises: 70% of sample; 30% in workshops or elsewhere.
• Enterprise ownership	Sole traders: 80% of enterprises (25% female-owned; 15% male-owned; 40% partnerships); companies: 20% of enterprises.	Sole traders: 100% (55% female-owned; remainder male, or family partnerships).
• Employment profile	Average number of workers: 3.7 per enterprise; a. sole traders: 2.7/enterprise; b. companies: 7.8/enterprise.	Average number of workers: 2 per enterprise; 75% engaged 1-2 people.
• Business turnover	Approx. annual average: £75,000; a. sole traders: approx. £38,000; b. companies: > £200,000.	Annual average: £10,000-£20,000; 50% under £10,000.
• Origin of owners	65% from outside the area; 30% left region to return.	70% from outside the area; 20% left region to return.
• Higher education	70% with third level qualifications (i.e. diploma or higher level).	60% with third level qualifications.

Unsurprisingly, crafts activities are largely home-based in both west Wales and northwest Ireland, and most of the enterprises surveyed were small-scale. More than two-thirds of makers worked from home, where workspace might range from a makeshift corner of the family house,[9] to workshop, studio or gallery premises in adjacent barns and outbuildings. Over recent years, emerging house price differentials have made relocation profitable, and many craftspeople are drawn to relatively remote localities where depopulation and other factors have led to a relative decline in property prices. Under such circumstances, workspace in situ is not only available but also comparatively affordable. Home-based production also creates the opportunity to sell directly from the premises, thus reducing the time spent chasing sales as well as the income lost on commission. However, isolation can also create difficulties in relation to access, advertising and marketing, and some makers identified these as problems.

With a small number of exceptions enterprises were characterised by the close involvement of one or two owner-makers, operating on a self-employed, sole trader basis. For most crafts businesses, this is the simplest choice, as there are no legal start-up costs and minimal paperwork (Crafts Council, 1985: 14). In many cases, skills partnerships were strengthened by close personal relationships, and there were few employees apart from family members. In terms of all those working in crafts (that is, the self-employed, family and non-family employees, and directors), Welsh activities employed the highest numbers at more than 3.5 per enterprise on average, compared to just 2.0 per enterprise in Ireland. However, it is worth noting that the few larger companies in the Welsh sample accounted for more than 40 per cent of the total employed, including two-thirds of all non-family workers, thus raising the overall average. Many of these non-family employees were engaged in crafts retail sales, rather than directly as makers. At the other end of the spectrum, one-quarter of enterprises in Wales were very small indeed and employed just a single owner-maker.

The extent of female participation in the sector is also notable. In the Irish sample, around 55 per cent of crafts enterprises were run by women, with the corresponding figure for the Welsh sample being around 40 per cent: however, a further 40 per cent in Wales relied on the equal participation of women as partner-makers in the business. Figures published elsewhere also suggest that women predominate in the crafts sector, at a ratio of approximately 60 women to 40 men (Knott, 1994: 11). It is therefore important to consider the implications of women's participation in crafts activities when developing suitable means of business support and other policy measures.

The relatively small-scale nature of crafts operations was also reflected in business turnover, with many makers across both study areas (but particularly in Ireland) struggling financially to make a living. The mean level of turnover in the Irish case was between IR£10,000-20,000 per year, but for half the sample the turnover was under IR£10,000. Although average levels in Wales were somewhat higher, due in part to the influence of the "outlier" companies mentioned above, 40 per cent of Welsh makers also reported a comparatively low annual turnover of around GB£20,000 or less. Nevertheless, it was clear that those with well-established reputations had been able to develop their activities into profitable enterprises. In some cases, individual incomes had been higher in the past and makers were now comfortably-off and content to maintain rather than increase business activity. Notably, four out of the top five enterprises in terms of annual turnover in the Welsh sample had their own retail outlets. However, a number of enterprises involved in exports, as well as with domestic markets, had almost ceased trading in recent years as a result of general business conditions: the effects of a strong pound at the time the research was undertaken was seen as posing a particular problem.

Given the overwhelmingly rural context of the study regions, it is interesting to note that craftspeople and farmers have a surprising amount in common. Clearly, crafts producers have fewer dealings with institutions: there is little mandatory regulation of their products; few institutionally-led marketing initiatives and no subsidy system, all of which characterise agriculture. However, in both crafts and agricultural production, output is seasonal (led by the peak demands of Christmas and summer sales in the crafts sector) and daily activities tend to be home-based. Family members are expected to assist when there is extra work to be done and it can be difficult to assess the true value of labour inputs. There is also a high degree of pluriactivity in both sectors, with producers and family members engaging in other employment activities to supplement household income. Most important, however, is the significance of lifestyles for both sectors, with a pronounced willingness to work comparatively long hours for relatively little financial reward in order to sustain the family and protect a valued way of life.

For many craftspeople, however, lifestyles tend to be the result of choice rather than tradition. Unlike farming families, who may often be associated with a particular rural locality for generations, around two-thirds of crafts producers in the Welsh and Irish study areas were in-migrants. Livelihoods had been defined at a relatively early stage in some cases, as makers had long planned to live and work in a peaceful and creative environment. For others, well-paid and potentially-lucrative urban-based careers had been abandoned in search of less stressful lifestyles, more congenial family life and a safer place to bring up children. Most of the sample showed high levels of educational achievement yet were ready to accept a relatively low level of income or of material living standards in order to enjoy a better quality of life. These attitudes reflect the fundamental cultural changes associated with counter-urbanisation and, in particular, the pursuit of the "archetypal anti-urban lifestyle, involving work creativity, use of natural materials, and self-management" (Jones et al., 1986: 25). It is in this sense that crafts production represents a culturally appealing, yet economically viable, alternative means of settling in the countryside under circumstances where high capital costs and lack of knowledge often create barriers to entry in farming. The high level of incomer involvement in handcrafts suggests that, with few exceptions, the sector represents not so much a continuation of rural traditions, but rather a reinvention of them by a new generation of country dwellers.

Crafts, Quality and the Use of Locality

In a sector characterised by heterogeneity and individual flair, it is particularly important to avoid stereotyping. However it is possible to identify two broad sub-groups of crafts makers in both the Irish and Welsh samples. The first, which we term artisanal producers, work largely for personal satisfaction and, superficially, tend to be "value-led" rather than business-oriented. However, although they are highly independent and often profess to be anti-business by temperament, it would be wrong to conclude that these artisans reject commercial considerations entirely, since some were found to have considerable business acumen and commercial awareness. Producers in the second category are more openly commercial and market-orientated, and their objectives are to serve the market whilst, at the same time, usually maintaining a strong personal commitment to quality crafts.

The concept of "quality" is central to crafts production and emerged as a key area for discussion during interviews with makers. Quality is largely subjective and with few exceptions, unlike the hallmarking of precious metals and other marks of authenticity, such as "pure new wool", objective criteria for quality evaluation of crafts do not exist. Institutional support for marketing and promoting quality products (through quality-marking, for example) can therefore be a contentious issue in the crafts sector. Although design, tactile qualities and visual appearance are the dominant quality characteristics, other factors such as methods of production, traditional and regional associations, and even the ambience of retail outlets all play a part in creating quality. Some crafts veer towards the functional, others are decorative, and product lines may also offer a mixture of the two. Hand-made souvenir-type items, such as key rings bearing ceramic fish, embody an appreciably different concept from the crafts of skilled potters, artists or jewellery-designers, yet there were quality examples of both in the sample. Further, even the most artistic makers often find it necessary to produce souvenir lines, and the two sets of markets appear to overlap in many cases. A recurring issue, therefore, is the difficulty of applying quality criteria in the face of such diversity: in terms of what the criteria might be; who might apply and regulate quality; and what the value of this might be to producers.

The issue of quality is inextricably bound up with the use of locality in crafts production. The logic of modernism and globalisation has caused many regions to perceive themselves as marginalised, while the postmodern response to regional decline suggests a re-recognition of the potentials of locality (van der Ploeg, 1992; Jenkins, 2000). Locality can manifest itself in three ways. First, it can be used symbolically or emblematically as, for example, in the use of the dragon motif (in Wales) or shamrocks (in Ireland) to promote crafts products. Such use is often considered by crafts makers to be in poor taste and associated with cheap, sometimes imported, mass-produced trinkets. Second, localities provide raw materials: for example, local stone and wood are widely used for carving, and Welsh slate and gold are showcase examples of how materials with a strong local identity may be used. However, many raw materials are sourced elsewhere, sometimes unexpectedly. In Wales, for example, much of the wool used in weaving and spinning is not locally-sourced, despite the abundance of sheep.[10] Third, and perhaps most importantly in the crafts context, makers are creatively inspired by their natural and cultural environments. Such inspiration typically derives from scenic qualities, such as colours, textures and the effects of the weather, or from Celtic history, folk tales and mythology. Again, however, such uses of locality may be cynically over-exploited: in Wales, for example, there is a widespread feeling that use of the poetry of Dylan Thomas simply reflects crude popular taste since Thomas is probably the only Welsh poet many people have heard of. In such instances, the "creative inspiration" function of locality switches to the "emblematic".[11] Nevertheless, despite the caveats, the subtle use of regional imagery, creative inspiration, and local materials can significantly enhance the value of crafts by giving them a distinctive character and sense of place.

Motivation and Enterprise

Many crafts businesses develop initially from hobby interests or practical skills, and begin as owner-maker operations or as family partnerships, developing only later full-time commercial operations. Expansion tends to be slow and employment creation is limited until a market niche or a consistent pattern of demand is established. However, a large number of crafts producers in the Welsh sample showed little interest in expanding their businesses and, in order to maintain price competitiveness, several aimed deliberately to remain below the threshold for Value Added Tax (VAT), at which a 17.5 per cent sales tax becomes mandatory.[12] In contrast, and perhaps because many were operating on a smaller scale, most of those interviewed in Ireland planned to expand their markets, introduce new product lines and increase turnover. Producers also have the option of aiming for higher revenue per unit sold, rather than increasing volume of production, but this strategy often requires an established name or reputation.

Although lack of expansionist ambition may be due in part to the anti-business temperament of some makers, it owes much to practical constraints. The costs and risks of expanding from the relative safety of a one- or two-person enterprise in order to develop markets are constraining, particularly when patterns of consumption are mainly seasonal and purchases tend towards the occasional and impulsive. Expansion may involve fresh capital outlay in extending premises and workspace; additional administrative requirements and paperwork; more time spent on marketing and advertising rather than on making (the activity most producers do best); increased training costs; and a loss of quality control through reduced involvement in production. Employment creation was thought by some producers to be a particular waste of time and money: a number of those interviewed had taken on trainees in the past only to see them set up their own competing businesses locally.[13]

Lack of expansionist ambition also has a marketing logic. The unique nature of a handcrafted item may be the main reason for its appeal, and many crafts would cease to have such appeal if manufactured at high volume. Consequently, artisanal makers may be both unable and unwilling to transform their creative efforts into a production line. For these, gaining exposure is more important than expansion, and their aim becomes one of finding a suitable platform for high value, one-off pieces of work. Hence, artisanal producers tend to target galleries for exhibition space, and individual customers for commissioned work.

Marketing and selling strategies therefore reflect product diversity in the crafts sector, and there are various options available. With regard to retail sales, producers in both samples expressed dissatisfaction with the limited number of quality crafts shops in their respective localities, and they noted the very real difficulties of competing with established suppliers. In consequence, there is an incentive, where resources permit, for makers to develop retail operations, either individually or collectively through crafts unions or co-operatives. Producers may also prefer direct control over retailing because of the high mark-ups or commissions demanded by intermediaries. Other means of selling direct, such as through regional crafts markets, affords contact with the public and the chance of useful feedback.

However, reliance on direct sales is thought by some producers to restrict their capacity to expand their sales base beyond their immediate locality thereby constraining overall business growth and limiting employment opportunities. Selling into "trade", via gift and souvenir or crafts fairs, at high volume, has therefore become an option for those wishing to expand, particularly into exports. In both the Welsh and Irish samples, there was a perception that the quality of skilfully handcrafted products is not fully appreciated in domestic markets, and that mainland European and other overseas visitors make better customers. In Ireland, for example, producers may contact trade buyers through the annual Showcase Ireland, a national crafts trade fair, organised by the Crafts Council of Ireland and Enterprise Ireland. A crafts village for quality products (appraised by a jury of professional peers) attracts buyers from around the world, and inclusion in this showpiece is an important marketing aim for some makers. However, although there are similar opportunities in Wales and in the other parts of the UK, trade events like these do not appeal to all producers.

The Institutional Framework

Many of the crafts producers' attitudes to scale of production, commercial motivation and marketing are reflected in their dealings with economic development institutions. General antipathy towards the institutional establishment and the quality of business support was a common feature of our sample, particularly in Wales. Local enterprise and development agencies are generally held to be out of touch with the requirements of micro-businesses and to have little appreciation of, or interest in, the problems they face. Agencies were specifically criticised for an apparent preoccupation with headlining, through their support for large prestige projects and inward investment at the expense of small indigenous businesses. In both study areas, there is also dissatisfaction with the type of assistance on offer, much of which is felt to be inappropriate to the needs of crafts activities and to the motivations and aspirations of craftspeople. In short, many makers feel that that the crafts sector is given neither the credibility nor the resources that it deserves by institutions concerned with local and regional economic development.

Two specific examples are instructive. First, the type of workspace made available to small businesses on industrial estates or enterprise parks is often incompatible with the nature of enterprise activities, the lifestyles and the commercial aspirations of crafts producers. Our findings indicate that many prefer to work from home; some have household and family responsibilities; and, for others, a small workshop attached to an accessible retail outlet would be a preferable option. The second example concerns financial assistance. The limited availability of small grants or loans for new equipment or other purposes is a cause of much frustration, particularly when the amounts required are often as little as £500 and rarely more than £2,000. Makers report a tendency for banks to be generally hesitant when approached for relatively small sums, and development agencies are often tied by job creation or business expansion criteria when disbursing funds. Such criteria invariably attract criticism from smaller producers who, with financial assistance, may feel able to work up to expansion slowly, but are not prepared to risk a swift increase in business size. In short, there is a feeling that institutions do not understand the unique nature of crafts activities, and that expansion to higher volume production is often encouraged without regard to quality.

Despite this cynicism, more than half of the sample in both regions had received some financial assistance from local agencies. In Wales, this was principally associated with building renovation, promotional materials or attendance at trade fairs; in Ireland, finance had largely been secured for capital funding and marketing. Generally speaking, however, it was only producers who had achieved success in the conventional business sense (that is, through expansion) who were well-disposed to the efforts of development organisations. Even LEADER II groups with their participatory "bottom-up" approach had, in the main, failed to make a positive impression. There were some exceptions: in County Leitrim, for example, the County Enterprise Board has created a development and marketing programme for arts and crafts which has been positively received by local craftspeople. To benefit from this initiative, producers must be quality assessed by a jury of peers and Crafts Council of Ireland representatives. Given that craftspeople feel that institutional perceptions of quality are either misguided or underdeveloped, the use of other producers (rather than bureaucrats) as a peer review group may account for the acceptance of the scheme.

From the institutional side, our work suggests that institutions in both study areas often feel that crafts makers lack ambition or vision and rarely have the capacity or inclination to develop their businesses or marketing plans to the degree required for eligibility for assistance. They also feel that many producers are insufficiently market-driven in their approach to enterprise. These differing perspectives clearly pose a major barrier to improving the prospects for the Welsh and Irish crafts sectors.

Crafts and the Local Economy

The crafts sector has a variety of positive effects on the local rural economy. In some cases, the contribution of enterprises to local employment is clearly significant, given a relatively low level of local economic activity. The attraction of visitors into specific localities is a further obvious impact, with varying degrees of spin-off effect depending on the size and scale of particular crafts operations. The use of local suppliers for non-specialist materials and services is also often significant, and many makers try to source local inputs and support local enterprise as a matter of principle. Over the years, abandoned farmhouses and other traditional properties have been sensitively renovated by crafts producers and these buildings are now part of the local housing stock. Many makers also operate positive recycling policies and have an acute awareness of environmental, social, community and cultural issues.

Quantifying such impacts is not always simple. However, the formation in 1993 of Crafts Forum Wales (CFW), an umbrella group for crafts producers in Wales, provides some opportunity to estimate the contribution of the crafts sector to the Welsh economy. Surveys of CFW membership (which does not cover all producers in Wales) suggest that the sector generates around £24mn in revenue annually, and provides in excess of 1,000 full-time jobs and half as many part-time ones. Given that much of the value created by crafts production is added locally, the multiplier effect of the sector is likely to be high. In Ireland, new jobs in the crafts sector exceeded 636 in 1996. At Showcase Ireland 1996, a full-time job was created for every £50,000 taken by the crafts sector and for every £120,000 in the knitwear and fashion sector, so that an estimated 73 new crafts jobs and 40 new knitwear and fashion jobs were created in that year.[14]

Apart from the direct economic contributions of crafts production to local economies in terms of employment opportunities and added value, the sector generates a number of less direct benefits for marginal areas. Linkages with tourism are often strong and positive: whilst crafts enterprises may not, in themselves, be the prime motivation for tourists to visit a region, they can provide attractions for visitors already in a locality. In Wales, there are several examples of crafts enterprises establishing themselves as tourist attractions in their own right, and of created networks of tourist "crafts trails". These potentially have spin-off impacts for local economies by generating new custom for existing businesses or encouraging new enterprises. Tourists are also an important source of sales for the better-established Irish crafts businesses in many locations.

Equally important, if less tangible, is the contribution of makers in terms of regional "image-making". Crafts, with their inbuilt associations of tradition, culture, heritage and authenticity, help to build a positive image of the regions within which they are produced. Such images are of value both to tourism and to the producers of other goods and services that are tied to localities. Many craftspeople therefore consider themselves to be "image-makers" in the sense that the quality of their work reflects positively upon the area and is used in marketing literature, product promotion or exhibitions. The corollary of this, however, is that other economic actors are "image-users", and craftspeople occasionally feel aggrieved that they receive little recognition of their flagship role from the institutions involved in regional economic development.

Conclusion: Crafts Production and the "New Rural Economy"

Crafts producers, often in-migrants, are in search of more authentic and sustainable lifestyles in which quality of life concerns tend to predominate. Many have returned to their roots after periods of work elsewhere, dissatisfied with conventional urban life. Hence, more than many working in business, they have thought about the roles of environmental quality, tradition, heritage and culture in local development, and have developed attitudes to economic activity, the market and development institutions which are often at variance with the conventional norm.

Their concern with lifestyle and quality of life suggests a willingness and ability to stay in operation doing meaningful high quality work at relatively low levels of income. Their understanding of the imperatives of making a living is often sharper than that of people in more conventional occupations, and they show high levels of resourcefulness, adaptability, independence, individualism, tenacity, willingness to be educative, and orientation towards family and community. Those with responsibility for economic development in a post-industrial society should not ignore such features and the reasons for them.

Many craftspeople are anti-business (although not necessarily un-commercial) and seek to resist the so-called tyranny of the market, which they see as obsessed with consumer sovereignty, economies of scale, and cost-minimisation. They also see it as tailored towards mass-produced consumer goods, but not appropriate to creative and quality products. Hence, they tend to be supply-driven rather than demand-led and are often cynical about consumer levels of taste and quality appreciation. Many, therefore, believe strongly in shortening the supply chain, reducing the anonymity and impersonality of the market, and reviving direct contact with customers---that is, they are strong advocates of traceability. They also believe they are "creators" rather than "exploiters" of regional image, in contrast to conventional businesses. All this may result in an unwillingness to develop in the conventional sense of expanding turnover and creating employment.

This leads in turn to antipathy towards development agencies, which they see as personifying top-down, business-oriented, environment- and community-exploiting development strategies. Such strategies are not adequately focused on the use of indigenous resources, nor on the creation of sustainable communities and satisfying post-industrial lifestyles. Craftspeople are generally in sympathy with a small-business economy in which pools of local employment are created and local resources used for the clear benefit of local communities. All in all, the crafts sector raises serious issues about the type of development appropriate to marginal regions, the role of non-economic factors in development, the place of communities, and the

151

application of conventional business and marketing criteria to development. These issues need to be confronted by policy makers and developmental institutions concerned with the future development of marginal regions in a globalised economy.

Notes

[1] The authors would like to thank Sheila Gaffey and Mary Cawley at the Department of Geography at the National University of Ireland, Galway; and Desmond Gillmor at the Department of Geography, Trinity College, Dublin, for their input into an earlier version of this paper.

[2] FAIR3 CT96 1827: Regional Images and the Promotion of Quality Products and Services in the Lagging Regions of the European Union (RIPPLE), a collaborative research programme funded under the EU's FAIR programme and involving the Departments of Geography at the Universities of Coventry, Lancaster, Leicester, Caen, Valencia, Galway and Trinity College Dublin; the Scottish Agricultural College (Aberdeen), the Institute of Rural Studies (University of Wales, Aberystwyth), Cemagref (Clermont-Ferrand), Teagasc (Dublin), Department of Economics (University of Patras), and the Institute for Rural Research and Training (University of Helsinki).

[3] For further details, see Ilbery et al., 1999; Gaffey (ed.) et al., 1999; Jenkins et al., 1998; Cawley et al., 1998.

[4] In this context, trends and prospects for Welsh agriculture are examined in Hughes et al., 1996.

[5] For an examination of the composition of migration in the case of rural Wales, see Day, 1990.

[6] The EU's LEADER (Liaisons Entre Actions de Développement de l'Économie Rurale) Programme aims to promote integrated rural development through people-centred local initiatives.

[7] The difficulties of defining "quality" are discussed later.

[8] Qualitative research methodology is examined in detail in Patton, 1990, and Midmore, 1998.

[9] In her consideration of home-based production and the "struggle to create space", Fisher (1997: 241) speaks of "the remnants and artefacts of production . . . lapping menacingly at the doors".

[10] Failure to source locally can often be the result of the rigid nature of marketing

arrangements, as in the case of wool.

[11] A similar example can be found in the English Lake District, where the use of Beatrix Potter images has become less an inspiration and more a cynical marketing ploy.

[12] At the time of the study, the VAT threshold was approximately £35,000 turnover per annum.

[13] On the whole, however, makers were keen to pass on their various skills despite these risks.

[14] We are grateful to Sheila Gaffey at the National University of Ireland, Galway for the provision of the Irish estimates; and to Craft Forum Wales for the impact figures in Wales.

References

Cawley, M., S. Gaffey, D. Gillmor, P. McDonagh and P. Commins. 1998. *Regional Images and the Promotion of Quality Products and Services in the Lagging Regions of the European Union: Producer Survey Results and Analysis, Ireland.* RIPPLE FAIR3-CT96-1827, July 1998. Galway: Department of Geography, National University of Ireland.

Cloke, P. and J. Little. 1997. *Contested Countryside Cultures: Otherness, Marginality and Rurality.* London: Routledge.

Crafts Council. 1985. *Running a Workshop.* London: Crafts Council.

Day, G. 1990. *A Million on the Move? Population Change and Rural Wales.* Occasional Paper No. 27, Department of Economic and Agricultural Economics. Aberystwyth: University College of Wales.

Fisher, C. 1997. "I bought my First Saw with my Maternity Benefit": Craft Production in West Wales and the Home of (re)production. In P. Cloke and J. Little (eds.), *Contested Countryside Cultures: Otherness, Marginality and Rurality.* London: Routledge.

Gaffey, S. (ed.), M. Cawley, D. Gillmor, B. McIntyre and P. McDonagh. 1999. *Regional Images and the Promotion of Quality Products and Services in the Lagging Regions of the European Union: Final Regional Report, Ireland.* RIPPLE FAIR3-CT96-1827, July 1999. Galway: Department of Geography, National University of Ireland.

Hughes, G. O., P. Midmore and A.-M. Sherwood. 1996. *Welsh Agriculture into the New Millennium: CAP Prospects and Farming Trends in Rural Wales.* Report to the

Development Board for Rural Wales and the Welsh Development Agency. Aberystwyth: Welsh Institute of Rural Studies, The University of Wales.

Ilbery, B., M. Kneafsey, T. Jenkins, N. Parrott, P. Leat, J. Brannigan, F. Williams, G. Clark, and I. Bowler. 1999. *Regional Images and the Promotion of Quality Products and Services in the Lagging Regions of the European Union: Final Regional Report, United Kingdom.* RIPPLE FAIR3-CT96-1827.

Jenkins, T. 2000. Putting Postmodernity into Practice: Endogenous Development and the Role of Traditional Cultures in the Rural Development of Marginal Regions. *Ecological Economics* 34: 301-314.

Jenkins, T., N. Parrott, G. O. Hughes, H. Lloyd, A.-M. Sherwood, P. Leat, J. Brannigan, F. Williams, and S. Petrie. 1998. *Regional Images and the Promotion of Quality Products and Services in the Lagging Regions of the European Union: Working Paper 8, Producer Survey in the UK covering West Wales and Grampian Study Regions.* RIPPLE FAIR3-CT96-1827), June 1998. Aberystwyth: Institute of Rural Studies, The University of Wales.

Jones H., J. Caird, W. Berry and J. Dewhurst. 1986. Peripheral counter-urbanisation: Findings from an Integration of Census and Survey Data in Northern Scotland. *Regional Studies* 20 (1): 15-26.

Knott, C. 1994. *Crafts in the 90s.* London: Crafts Council.

Midmore, P. 1998. Rural Policy Reform and Local Development Programmes: Appropriate Evaluation Procedures. *Journal of Agricultural Economics* 49 (3): 409-426.

Ministry for Agriculture Fisheries and Food (MAFF). 2000. *Rural Development Strategy for England 2000-2006.* London: MAFF.

National Assembly for Wales (NAW). 2000. *Rural Development Strategy for Wales 2000-2006.* Cardiff: NAW.

Parrott, N., A.-M. Sherwood, and P. Midmore. 1999. Strengthening Links between Agriculture and Tourism on the Rural Periphery: A Case Study of Southwest Wales. In R. Byron and J. Hutson (eds.), *Local Enterprise on the North Atlantic Margin.* Aldershot: Ashgate Publishing.

Patton, M. Q. 1990. *Qualitative Evaluation and Research Methods.* 2nd edition. Newbury Park (California): Sage.

van der Ploeg, J. D. 1992. The Reconstitution of Locality. In T. Marsden, P. Lowe and S. Whatmore (eds.), *Labour and Locality.* London: David Fulton.

9 The Economic Impact of Welsh National Nature Reserves

MICHAEL CHRISTIE

Introduction

National Nature Reserves (NNR) are designated in order to maintain and preserve areas of wildlife and geological importance. The beautiful landscapes and well-preserved natural habitats within NNRs attract a large number of visitors to the reserves. Since many of these NNRs are situated within the more remote and often economic deprived areas of rural Wales, the influx of visitors constitute an important source of income and employment to the economy of these areas. The research reported here aims to quantify, using multiplier analysis, the extent of the income and employment generation associated with three NNRs in Wales.

National Nature Reserves in Wales

National Nature Reserves are designated under the National Parks and Access to the Countryside Act 1949 (amended under the Wildlife and Countryside Act 1981) for the purpose

> of (a) providing, under suitable conditions and control, special opportunities for the study of, and research into, matters relating to the fauna and flora of Great Britain and the physical conditions in which they live, and for the study of geological and physiographical features of special interest in the area, or (b) of preserving flora, fauna or geological or physiographical features of special interests in the area, or for both those purposes.
>
> *National Parks and Access to the Countryside Act 1949*

NNRs therefore represent the "best examples of a particular habitat" (English Nature, 1995: 4). In addition to their conservation role, NNRs are generally open to the public and thus are very important natural resources for outdoor recreation and environmental education. In Wales, there are 62 designated NNRs, covering an area of 18,589 Ha (CCW, 1997). Most NNRs are managed by the Countryside Council for Wales (CCW), although a number may be managed by other "approved" bodies such as the Wildlife Trust, the National Trust and the Royal Society for the Protection of Birds. Three NNRs were chosen as case studies for the investigation the economic impact of NNRs in Wales. The reserves were chosen to represent typical NNRs in Wales. A brief description of each of these reserves is provided below.

- *Ynyslas National Nature Reserve,* situated ten miles north of Aberystwyth, comprises sand dunes, beach, saltmarsh and sandflats. Ynyslas is an extremely popular site, with an estimated 200,000 visits per year. Visitors are attracted by the beach, visitor centre, accessibility and fine views of the Dyfi estuary. In addition, the site is used as an educational resource by schools and colleges studying a wide range of subject material. During summer months, four seasonal rangers assist the site warden in the management of the reserve.

- *Cors Caron NNR* is a large inland raised bog located in the Teifi Valley close to the town of Tregaron. Access to most of the site is restricted to permit holders only, however, public access to the site is provided along a disused railway line that lies alongside the bog. It is along this route that the site interpretation and a bird hide are located.

- *Coedydd Aber NNR* lies between the Carneddau massif and the narrow coastal plain of the north Wales coast. The reserve comprises a sheltered valley with a patchwork of fields, together with deciduous and coniferous woodlands. The valley has a history of occupation, evidence of which can be seen in the relic hut circles, ancient field patterns and ruined farm settlements. The reserve is highly used for both informal recreation and bird watching. In particular, visitors often walk through the reserve to the spectacular Aber Falls waterfall. The reserve also has a visitor centre.

Multiplier Analysis

In economic analysis, multiplier methodology is employed in order to measure the overall effects of an introduction or "injection" of expenditure into an economic system (Sherwood, 1994). Multiplier methodology has been extensively used to estimate the economic impact of a wide range of conservation projects (see Rayment, 1997 for examples). In multiplier analysis, three levels of economic impact are distinguished. The initial round of spending created by the original injection into an economy is known as the direct expenditure. As the recipient businesses of the direct expenditure then re-spend this money in successive indirect rounds, the number of transactions rise and the overall output expands. With this expansion in output, comes an increase in the wealth of employees and a consequent rise in their consumption expenditure (induced effects). The overall impact on the level of economic activity is expressed in terms of the changes (a multiple of the original injection) in output, income or employment which rise in the recipient economy (Fletcher and Archer, 1988). The relationship between the value of the original expenditure and the amount generated in total is expressed numerically by the multiplier.

The concept of the multiplier was developed principally by Kahn and Keynes who identified two flows of economic activity that affected economic growth: injections into the economic systems and leakages (Ashcroft et al., 1988). The essence of the Keynesian multiplier is that an injection into the economy will lead to an increase in income over and above the initial injection. The magnitude of this increase, expressed as the multiplier coefficient (k), is dependent on the rate of leakage, where leakages are derived from the marginal propensity to consume (c) and the marginal propensity to import (m) and the marginal tax rate (t) (Ryan, 1991). Thus a basic Keynesian multiplier coefficient may be calculated as follows:

$$k = \frac{1}{1-(c-m)(1-t)}$$

Multipliers can be expressed in several ways. Type 1 multipliers only account for the direct and indirect effects, whereas Type 2 multipliers also incorporate induced effects. A further divergence relates to the divisor used. In the conventional "orthodox" multiplier the divisor relates to the direct effects, whereas a "proportional" multiplier uses tourist expenditure as the divisor (Slee et al., 1997). This variety of multiplier types have caused confusion in the past (Fletcher and Archer, 1998) and therefore care will be required when adopting multiplier coefficients in this contract. Four principal types of multiplier are recognised (Slee et al., 1998):

- Sales/transaction multiplier---s measures the relationship between expenditure and economic activity in the economy, i.e., business turnover.
- Output multiplier---this is similar to the above, but also takes into account any changes in stock.
- Income multiplier--this measures the relationship between expenditure and the resulting level of income in the economy.
- Employment multiplier---this relates employment to expenditure.

In economic impact studies, it is often only the income and employment impacts that are established since they provide the most useful indicators for policy analysis (Rayment, 1995).

Methodology

The aim of the multiplier study reported here was to estimate the additional income and employment impacts to the local economy that can be attributed to the three National Nature Reserves. This assessment required three separate surveys to be undertaken. The first survey determined the extent and nature of visitor expenditures that were attributed to visits to the reserves. The second survey determined the level of expenditure and employment associated with CCW's management of the three reserves. These two surveys therefore aimed to determine the size of the initial injection of money into the local economy. Finally, a survey of local businesses aimed to determine the extent to which visitor expenditure leaked from the local economy and hence provide an estimate of the size of the local area income and employment multiplier coefficients for use in the analysis. In addition, a review of relevant multiplier studies was undertaken to identify the size of multiplier coefficient appropriate to the assessment of the impact of Welsh NNRs. Details of each of the three surveys are now reported. This is followed by the actual multiplier analysis.

The Visitor Expenditure Survey

The visitor expenditure survey aimed to estimate the extent of visitor spending associated with visits to each of the three nature reserves. The estimated average expenditure was then multiplied by the number of visitors to each reserve to establish the total annual visitor spend associated with trips to the three NNRs. In the visitor expenditure survey two main aspects to visitor spending were identified and quantified. First, expenditures relating directly to the visit to the reserve were established for the actual day of interview. These "day trip" expenditures were aggregated by multiplying the averaged day trip expenditures with the annual number of visitors to provide an estimation of the total annual expenditures incurred by both home-based visitors and holiday-based visitors[1] on day trip visits to the NNRs. The second aspect of visitor expenditure related to the volume of spending arising from holiday-based visitors on their journeys to the holiday address and their return home from their holiday address. Again these were aggregated to provide an estimate of the annual expenditure associated with travel to and from the reserves. The estimation of all of the above spending patterns enabled a comprehensive picture of visitor spending relating to visits to the NNRs to be established.

In the survey, the visitor expenditures were allocated into four expenditure categories: food, travel, accommodation and other expenditures. Each of these categories were divided into several other sub-categories (shown below in italics) to provide more detail.

- Food expenses. Expenditure on food included spending on *dining out* (restaurants, pubs and cafes), groceries (picnic items, refreshments and ice cream) and *drinks* in public houses. All of these expenses were estimated for the day of the visit to the reserve and also for the expenditures incurred by holiday-based visitors travelling to and from their holiday address.

- Travel expenses. Travel expenses included actual spending on *fuel*, and also *fares* on taxis, trains and public transport. These expenses were recorded for the day of visit and also for travel to and return home from their holiday address.

- Accommodation expenses. Accommodation spending was categorised according to *catered* accommodation such as hotels, bed and breakfast, and also to *self-catered* accommodation such as holiday chalets, caravans and camping. Accommodation expenditure was recorded for the previous night's accommodation.

- Other expenses. Miscellaneous spending was divided into expenditure *within the NNR* and expenditure *outside the NNR*. Possible expenditures undertaken within the NNR included visitor expenditure on car parking, visitor centre and voluntary contributions where appropriate. The expenditure outside the NNR included all other possible items of spending not previously taken into account. Most common items included expenditure on goods such as maps, newspapers, gifts, crafts, postcards, camera film and outdoor equipment, or expenditure on services such as visits to the cinema and swimming pool.

In addition to identifying the type of expenditures undertaken, the survey also established where the expenditures were made. Sherwood (1994) highlights the size of the area defined as the local economy as an important factor influencing the results of the multiplier analysis. Clearly, a small area will have fewer economic interlinkages and hence a larger proportion of expenditures will be leaked to outside the defined area. To examine the impact of these leakages, four sizes of area were adopted in the analysis: the area within the boundaries of each NNR, the area within a ten-mile radius of each NNR, the area within the boundaries of Wales and all other areas outside Wales. The visitor expenditure survey, therefore, also established the zone in which the visitor expenditures were made.

The visitor survey was pilot tested during two weekend days in May 1997. Following appropriate revisions, a final bilingual (English and Welsh) version of the visitor survey was conducted between mid-June and mid-September 1997. The days in which on-site interviews took place were selected using random numbers following a formula that included two weekday shifts, two weekend shifts and one bank-holiday (if appropriate) per month. A shift was defined as a fixed six hour period covering 8.00 a.m. to 2.00 p.m. or 2.00 p.m. to 8.00 p.m. In total this constituted 13 six-hour shifts at each of the three reserves over the three-month study period. During the actual interviews, respondents were selected using a random sampling methodology that involved the surveyor waiting for a defined two-minute time period before selecting the next person passing a fixed point for interview. Where a group of people were involved, the birthday method (i.e., where the person with the next birthday is selected) was used to identify the respondent for interview. It should be noted that the individual interviewed was asked to report the total expenditures incurred by the group in which he or she was travelling with. In all cases, the respondents were questioned after they had completed their visit to the reserve. It was logical, therefore, to sample close to the major exit points of the reserves, i.e., usually within or adjacent to a car park area and/or entrance points.

The Survey Responses

A total of 419 interviews (224 at Ynyslas, 68 at Cors Caron and 127 at Coedydd Aber) were undertaken in the visitor expenditure survey. The distributions of responses between the three reserves are reported in Table 9.1, as is the proportion of home-based and holiday-based respondents.

Table 9.1   Number of responses to the survey of visitors to the three NNRs

(Number of respondents)	Ynyslas		Cors Caron		Coedydd Aber		Total Number	
	No.	%	No.	%	No.	%	No.	%
Home-based	105	46.9	28	41.2	61	48.0	194	46.3
Holiday-based	119	53.1	40	58.8	66	52.0	225	53.7
Total	224		68		127		419	

The data presented in Table 9.1 illustrate that almost half of the visitors to the reserves were day-trippers from home. This demonstrates the important contribution of nature reserves as a valuable recreation resource for the local population.

It was established that each year a total of 200,000, 20,000 and 20,350 visits were made to the Ynyslas, Cors Caron and Coedydd Aber reserves respectively (Pers. Comm., CCW reserve wardens). Based on the data collected in the visitor expenditure survey (Table 9.1) an estimation of the annual number of home-based and holiday-based visitors was made (Table 9.2).

Table 9.2   Annual number of local and tourist visitors estimated for the three nature reserves

Annual number of visits	Ynyslas	Cors Caron	Coedydd Aber	Total Number
Local visitors	93800	8240	9768	**111808**
Tourist visitors	106200	11760	10582	**128542**
Annual number of visitors	200000	20000	20350	**240350**

The mean expenditure incurred by a home-based visitor during the day trip to the reserves was estimated to be £14.65, £11.08 and £10.25 respectively for Ynyslas, Cors Caron and Coedydd Aber. This level of expenditure was slightly higher than the £8.60 average expenditure of visitors to the Welsh countryside (UK Day visits survey, 1996). The majority of home-based visitor expenditure related to purchases of food on the day of visit, although actual travel expenses incurred were also shown to be important for trips to Ynyslas. Full details of the breakdown of expenditure can be found in Christie et al. (1998).

An estimate of the total expenditures made by home-based visitors (Table 9.3) was calculated by multiplying their day trip expenditures by the estimated annual number of visitors to the reserves (Table 9.2). The total expenditure relating to visits to Ynyslas (£1.7 million) was over four times that of the other two reserves (£39,500 at Cors Caron and £35,000 at Coedydd Aber). This reflects that the greater number of visitors to Ynyslas and also the higher levels of expenditure per Ynyslas visitor. Of the original injection of £1.8 million expenditure undertaken by home-based visitors, £1.3 million was injected into the local economy (defined as being within ten miles of the reserve) of the three reserves. Again differences were found between reserves in that around 75 per cent of the expenditure at Ynyslas was concentrated within the local economy, whereas only around 40 per cent of the expenditures at Cors Caron and Coedydd Aber. This reflects the tendency of Ynyslas visitors to concentrate their expenditures in the towns of Borth and Aberystwyth, both situated near Ynyslas. It should, however, be noted that the proportion of expenditures actually made within Wales was consistent between reserves. This result demonstrates the importance that the choice of the size of the "local economy" in multiplier analysis can have on the level of leakage from that defined economy.

Table 9.3   Distribution   of   total   home-based   visitor   expenditure according to location

Total home-based day trip expenditure	Within NNR (£)	Within 10 miles (£)	Within Wales (£)	Outside Wales (£)	Total (£)
Ynyslas	80,146	1,235,286	236,952	189,910	1,742,294
	(4.6%)	(70.9%)	(13.6%)	(10.9%)	(100%)
Cors Caron	0	16,178	19,619	3,718	39,515
	(0%)	(40.9%)	(49.6%)	(9.4%)	(100%)
Coedydd Aber	0	13,490	19,326	2,062	34,878
	(0%)	(38.7%)	(55.4%)	(6.0%)	(100%)
Total for NNRs within each zone	80,146	1,264,954	275,897	195,690	1,816,687
% within each zone	4.4	69.6	15.2	10.8	100

The expenditures undertaken by holiday-based visitors were analysed according to day trip expenditures and expenditures incurred travelling to the area from their home address, and expenditures incurred during their return journey home.

The mean expenditures of holiday-based visitors during day trips to the reserves were estimated to be £56.01, £31.08 and £29.60 per person for Ynyslas, Cors Caron and Coedydd Aber respectively. Holiday-based visitors therefore tended to spend three times that of home-based visitors. The reason for this inflated expenditure mainly related to the additional cost of accommodation and also to some extent the higher expenditure on food. These mean daily expenditures were again multiplied by the number of holiday-based visitors to give total expenditure estimation of £6.63 million (Table 9.4). Of this original expenditure, £5.66 million (85 per cent) was injected into the local economy of the reserves. A comparison between reserves again demonstrated significant differences between sites with over 90 per cent of these expenditures associated with Ynyslas being undertaken within ten miles of the reserve, while only 35 per cent and 20 per cent were within ten miles of Cors Caron and Coedydd Aber (Table 9.4). These differences again largely reflect the proximity of towns to the reserves.

A total of £825,000 was spent by holiday-based visitors travelling to the reserves, of which £45,000 (5 per cent) was spent within ten miles of the reserves. This finding demonstrates that visitors clearly "stock up" in

Table 9.4   Distribution of annual holiday-based visitor day trip expenditure according to location

Total holiday-based day trip expenditure	Within NNR (£)	Within 10 miles (£)	Within Wales (£)	Outside Wales (£)	Total (£)
Ynyslas	375,131 (6 3%)	5,097,026 (85.6%)	345,359 (5.8%)	136,953 (2.3%)	**5,954,469**
Cors Caron	0 -	127,193 (34.8%)	227,705 (62 3%)	10,599 (2.9%)	**365,497**
Coedydd Aber	625 (0 2%)	64,057 (18.4%)	243,104 (80 1%)	4,687 (1.5%)	**312,473**
Total for NNRs within each zone	375,756	5,288,276	816,169	152,239	6,632,440
% within each zone	5.6	79.7	12.3	2.3	100.0

provisions before leaving home.   It was also estimated that holiday-based visitors would spent £421,000 on their return journeys, of which £140,500 (33 per cent) would be spent within the local economy of the reserves. Most of these expenditures related to travel expenses incurred.

The total injection of all visitor expenditures into the local economies of the reserves was estimated to be £7.19 million per annum. The majority of this (£6.95m) related to the Ynyslas reserve. Cors Caron and Coedydd Aber attracted £168,900 and £96,700 respectively. It is this injection of money into the local economy that is used in the multiplier analysis.

The CCW Expenditure Survey

CCW's expenditure on visitor management at the three reserves was established through interviews with the relevant staff.   In the 1996-97 financial year CCW's total expenditure on visitor management at the three reserves was estimated to be £27,100 (Table 9.5). Of this, only 21 per cent (£5,700) was retained within the local economies (within ten miles) of the reserves.   The majority of this expenditure related to staff wages.   It is interesting to note that although capital expenditure accounted for the majority of CCW's expenditure associated with visitor management, none of this capital expenditure was undertaken within the local economies of the reserves. This perhaps reflects the nature of the countryside contractors and construction firms.

Table 9.5   CCW expenditure on interpretation at the three nature reserves during the 1996-97 financial year

Expenditure Type	Annual Expenditure	% of Annual expenditure	Allocation of Expenditure by Area (£)		
	(£)	(%)	10 miles	Wales	UK
Staff salaries / wages	47299	17.5	42199	5100	0
Contractors	21620	7.9	10300	11320	0
Maintenance expenditures	40094	14.8	14381	23210	2503
Capital expenditures	157852	58.2	0	153204	4648
Other expenditures	4136	1.5	1538	1026	1572
Total within each zone	271001	100	68418	193860	8723
% of total within each zone	100.0		25.2	71.6	3.2

Estimation of the Multiplier Coefficient

The direct expenditures made by visitors and CCW into the local economy of the three reserves were multiplied by local income and employment multiplier coefficients to provide an estimate of the indirect and induced income and jobs generated within the local economy. The size of the multiplier coefficients used in the research were determined through a combination of two sources. First, a number of multiplier studies that used Welsh case studies or examined nature conservation issues were reviewed to establish appropriate coefficients for this study. Rayment concluded in a review of nature conservation economic impact studies that the income and employment multipliers obtained from such studies "provide a relatively consistent indication of the local economic impact of visitor expenditures" (1995:3). Nature conservation multiplier coefficients examined in Rayment's review ranged from 0.25 - 0.45, while employment multipliers indicated that one full time equivalent (FTE) job was created from every £15,000 to £20,000 visitor expenditure.

With regard to Welsh-based studies, Sherwood (1994) used an income multiplier of 0.385 in her evaluation of the impact of the Royal Welsh Show. Perhaps the study most relevant to the current research is Griffiths's (1996) study that examined the impact of the Kite Country Project to the economy of rural mid Wales. In this study, Griffiths adopts a local income multiplier of 0.3. With regard to employment impacts, Griffiths assumes that one FTE job is created per £18,000 visitor expenditure and that an extra 0.25 jobs are created locally per person directly employed in running the Kite Country project. The project also involved the construction of a visitor centre, where it was found that £1 million construction expenditure over three years generated 1.6 FTE jobs among local construction firms per year, with a further 0.4 extra jobs created indirectly through expenditures by construction firms and workers. It is clear from the above review that there is reasonable consistency between the multiplier values associated with nature conservation and those relating to the Welsh economy. Since the size and location of the local economy and the types of visitor expenditure associated with Griffiths's Kite Country study are likely to be very similar to those found in the current research, it was decided to use Griffiths's income and employment multiplier values in the present research.

To add further support to the decision to use of Griffiths's multiplier coefficient, a survey of local businesses was undertaken in an attempt to elicit a value for the income and employment multiplier coefficient. The businesses were chosen to represent a cross-section of the businesses used by visitors to the reserves. The businesses investigated included grocery stores, public houses, petrol stations, cafes, catered accommodation establishments and self-catering accommodation establishments. Each business was asked to state the activities undertaken, the proportion of local to tourist customers in both summer and winter, the number of people employed within the business, the level of business income and profit, and the location where inputs to the business were purchased. Although it is recognised that the number of business included in the survey was quite small and therefore the estimates of the income and employment multipliers were crude, it was considered that they would provide valuable evidence supporting, or otherwise, the use of Griffiths's multiplier coefficients.

The owners or managers of the businesses interviewed indicated that approximately 20 per cent of their business custom could be attributed to tourist expenditures, of which the majority was undertaken during the summer months. The average level of business sales attributed to tourists was estimated to be £68,800 per business, although it should be noted that the range of business sales varied greatly. The average income of the businesses interviewed was estimated to be £24,100 per year). Using the above data, a local income multiplier coefficient, derived from the ratio of net income to visitor expenditure, was estimated to be 0.35. This value is clearly within the limits of the typical values for nature conservation (Rayment, 1995) and is reasonable similar to Griffiths's (1996) value of 0.3. These findings therefore support the use of Griffiths's income multiplier for this research.

The business survey also asked business managers to report the number of FTE jobs within their business. It was shown that the average business employed the equivalent of 4.46 staff. The local employment multiplier derived from this indicates that one FTE job was created from £15,426 visitor expenditure. This value is within the lower limits of that found in the other studies, but is sufficiently close to Griffiths's value (£18,000) to indicate that Griffiths's employment multiplier is suitable for use in the current research.

The findings of the business survey were therefore found to be comparable with those found in other multiplier studies of nature conservation. In particular, the derived multiplier coefficients were comparable with those used

Table 9.6   Summary of the local income and employment impact of the three NNRs

Local impact	Ynyslas	Cors Caron	Coedydd Aber	Total
Visitor numbers	**200000**	**20000**	**20350**	**240350**
	(£)	**(£)**	**(£)**	**(£)**
Local visitor expenditure	6956606	152541	86149	7195296
Local CCW expenditure	42533	15350	10535	68418
Total local expenditure	6999139	167891	96684	7263714
	(£)	**(£)**	**(£)**	**(£)**
Local visitor income impact	2086982	45762	25845	2158589
Local CCW income impact	32054	11745	6265	50064
Total local income impact	2119036	57507	32110	2208653
	FTE jobs	FTE jobs	FTE jobs	FTE jobs
Visitor employment impact	386.48	8.47	4.79	399.74
CCW employment impact	3.32	1.83	1.17	6.32
Total local employment impact	389.80	10.30	5.96	406.06

by Griffiths in his study of Kite Country in mid-Wales. It was therefore concluded that the multipliers used in Griffiths's study would be suitable for the current study.

Application of the Griffiths's multiplier coefficients to the visitor and CCW expenditures allowed estimates of the levels of income and employment generated to be made (Table 9.6). The multiplier analysis estimated that £2.21 million income was generated and that 406 FTE jobs were created within the local economies of the reserves as a result of visitor and CCW expenditures. The majority of these impacts (£2.1 million income and 390 jobs) were associated with the Ynyslas reserve. The reasons why Ynyslas had such a significantly greater economic impact than the other two reserves were that: Ynyslas had almost ten times as many visitors visiting as the other two reserves; higher average expenditure were made by Ynyslas visitors; and there was a greater retention of expenditures within the Ynyslas economy.

Discussion

The results of the above impact assessment will be discussed from two angles. First, the actual data collected will be scrutinised in order to assess the validity of the results. Second, the implications of the research findings to CCW and also to wider environmental concerns are discussed.

The credibility of the research findings is very much dependent on the accuracy of the data collected. This data principally includes the level of economic impact determined using multiplier methodology has been shown to be influenced by three main factors: the estimate of the average visitor expenditure, the accuracy of the estimate of visitor numbers, and the size of the multiplier coefficient used.

The reliability of the level of visitor expenditure establish in the research may be checked, at least to some extent, by comparing the average expenditure made by survey respondents with that of other comparable studies. The average spend associated with trips to Wales was estimated to be £8.60 in the UK Day Visits Survey and £10 for day-trippers and £18.50 for holidaymakers in Griffiths's Kite Country study. Although the average visitor expenditure established in the NNR study was found to be greater than those found in other studies, it should be noted that the UK Day Visits Survey did not include accommodation costs. Our data is comparable with these other studies when accommodation costs are excluded.

The second aspect under consideration was the estimations of annual visitor numbers to the reserves. Although our observations undertaken during the visitor survey would, in general, support CCW's estimates of visitor numbers, it was considered that CCW's estimates of visitor numbers at Cors Caron were perhaps too high. Part of the reason for this inflated estimate related to the adoption of a new system for recording visitor numbers at this reserve. It was therefore considered that the visitor number estimates for Cors Caron were somewhat inflated, and that the actual income and employment impact resulting from visits to Cors Caron were likely to be lower than that estimated in this research. As a result of this concern, it was recommended that CCW review its system used to monitor visitor numbers at their reserves so as to ensure accurate and consistent estimates. A second issue regarding the estimation of visitor numbers related to the finding that only around 40 per cent of the visitor to Ynyslas reserve were aware of the fact that the site was a NNR; the majority of visitors were solely attracted to the beach at Ynyslas. Assuming that the aim of the research is to estimate the economic impacts generated as a result of nature conservation, then it is argued that the economic impact generated by Ynyslas should accordingly be adjusted. This would give a reduce impact of Ynyslas NNR to £1.28 million and 234 FTE jobs.

The final issue regarding the reliability of the economic impact assessment relates to the size of the multiplier coefficients used. The coefficient used in the research was based on a coefficient used in a study that examined Red Kite Country in mid Wales. Thus the actual geographic location of the Kite study and the size of the economy investigated were both comparable with the study reported here. Further evidence that the multiplier coefficients were suitable came from the business study, which also made an estimate of the appropriate size of the multiplier coefficient.

Thus the findings of the multiplier study would appear to provide a reliable estimate of the economic impact of the three NNRs to the Welsh economy. The main issue of concern related to the need to obtain reliable estimates of the number of visitors to the reserves. It was therefore recommended that CCW should review its procedures for monitoring visitor numbers at its reserves so as to ensure improved accuracy.

Turning now to discuss the wider policy implications of this research, it is useful to make an assessment of the economic impact of all NNRs in Wales and to compare this to other rural-based activities. In Wales there are a total of 62 designated NNRs. Assuming that the three reserves investigated in the research broadly represent the other NNRs in Wales, then the total economic impact of the national nature reserves may be estimated. For this calculation, it was assumed that the economic impact of the other reserves could be equally divided among the three reserves investigated. Thus, it was assumed that approximately 20 reserves had an economic impact similar to that of Ynyslas, 20 were similar to Cors Caron, and 20 to Coedydd Aber. Since it is recognised that the beach at Ynyslas may bias the results, the income and employment impacts used in the calculation were restricted to the 40 per cent of visitors who were aware of the NNR status of Ynyslas. Based on these assumptions, it was estimated that a total of £27.34 million income and around 5000 FTE jobs are created in Wales as a result of NNR designation. This finding is consistent with CEAS (1993) who estimated that the net income from nature conservation in Wales was between £39 and £52 million per annum. Total expenditure on the management of Welsh NNRs was in the region of £150,000 in 1996, while total grant aid giving by CCW on nature conservation was around £2.4 million. Clearly there is a large return from expenditure on nature reserves in terms of income and employment generation.

To put these figures into context, the income and employment impacts estimated for the nature reserves were compared to the impacts associated with other rural sectors, namely agriculture and forestry (Table 9.7). With regard to income, the Dairy sector had the greatest income generation per Ha (£1,477), with NNRs being only slightly less (£1,477 per Ha). The income generated from NNR was, interestingly found to be greater than both forestry and LFA cattle and sheep. With regard to employment, Thompson and Psaltopoulos (1993) estimated the employment impact of agriculture and forestry in Wales in terms of jobs created per 1000 Ha. Job creation associated with nature reserves was found to be twice that of lowland agriculture and forestry, and about three times that of LFA agriculture. These findings highlight the economic importance of nature reserves to rural economies, suggesting that they may have a greater economic impact than the traditional rural sectors.

Table 9.7   Comparison of income and employment generation per 1000 Ha between different rural sectors

Sector	Income £/ Ha	Sector	Employment FTE Jobs / 1000 Ha
NNR[1]	1477	NNR[1]	269
Dairy[2]	1749	Agriculture / Food[4]	19.3
LFA cattle / sheep[2]	474	Agriculture / Food LFA[4]	40.1
Lowland cattle / sheep[2]	753	Forestry[4]	26.0
Forestry[3]	873		

Sources: [1] derived from author's study; [2] MAFF, 1995; [3] derived from FICGB (1994) study; [4] Thompson and Psaltpoulos, 1993.

However, it should be highlighted that most of the income and employment generated from the NNRs relate the indirect visitor expenditure. The actual direct impacts associated with NNRs are much less.

European and UK rural policy is increasingly focusing on environmental and rural development issues (e.g. Agenda 2000), rather than traditional agricultural support. This paper has demonstrated that NNRs, which have traditionally been considered only for their environmental benefits, can also effectively generate substantial income and employment benefits in remote rural areas. The size of these benefits are comparable to those found in the more traditional rural sectors. These findings therefore provide evidence that supports the new direction of rural policy in Europe.

Note

[1] Home-based visitors were defined as those respondents who stated that they were on a recreation day trip or on a routine activity. Holiday-based visitors were classified as those individuals who had travelled to the nature reserves from a holiday address, i.e., main summer holiday, short break holiday or weekend break.

References

CEAS. 1993. *The Economy of Landscape and Nature Conservation in England and Wales.* Report to CCW, CC and English Nature. CEAS Consultants (Wye) Ltd.

Christie, Keirle and Scott. 1998. *The Economic Impact of Welsh National Nature Reserves.* Bangor: CCW.

Countryside Council for Wales. 1997. *Annual Report 1996.* Bangor: CCW.

English Nature. 1995. *National Nature Reserves.* Peterborough: English Nature.

FICGB. 1994. *The Forestry Industry Yearbook 1993-94.* London: Forestry Industry Committee of Great Britain.

Fletcher, J. E. and B. H. Archer. 1988. Input-output Analysis and Tourist Impact Studies. *Annals of Tourism Research* 16, 514-529.

Griffiths, K. K. 1996. The Economic Impact of the Kite Country Project in Mid Wales. Unpublished MSc thesis, Oxford Brookes University.

Ministry of Agriculture, Fisheries and Food. 1995. *Farm Incomes in the UK, 1993-94.* London: HMSO.

Rayment, M. 1995. *Nature Conservation, Employment and Local Economies.* Sandy (Beds.): Royal Sciety for the Protection of Birds.

_____. 1997. *Working with Nature in Britain: Case Studies of Nature Conservation, Employment and Local Economies.* Sandy (Beds.): Royal Sciety for the Protection of Birds.

Ryan, C. 1991. *Recreational Tourism: A Social Science Perspective.* London: Routledge.

Sherwood, A.-M. 1994. *The Economic Impact of the Royal Welsh Showground.* Report for the Royal Welsh Agricultural Society: Aberystwyth.

Slee, B., H. Farr and P. Snowdon. 1997. The Economic Impact of Alternative Types of Rural Tourism. *Journal of Agricultural Economics* 48 (2), 179-192.

Slee, B., H. Farr and P. Snowdon. 1998. Agrotourism and Synergistic Pluriactivity. Unpublished report: University of Aberdeen.

Thompson, B. and P. Psaltopoulos. 1993. The Rural Employment League: Agriculture vs Forestry. Discussion Paper to Annual Conference of Agricultural Economics Society, Oxford, April 1993.

UK Day Visits Survey. 1996. Cardiff: Countryside Recreation Network.

10 The Politics of Local Land-Use Planning in Norway

JØRGEN AMDAM

Introduction

In Norway there has been for some time a debate going on about how well physical planning works. On the basis of studies up to the present, it is pretty unambiguous that the overall planning works well as a control instrument for land development in "virgin territory". To the extent that there are discrepancies, these are related to the fact that conflicts, in particular with conservation interests, but also with nature and outdoor interests, have been sufficiently clarified during the planning process. In these cases the planning process has not led to the key actors developing common visions about how land use actually ought to be and subsequent reviewing of the overall plans has had the role of a replay. This illustrates how important it is that the planning process involves broad participation from involved parties in the commune and from "veto-bodies" and that during the process it is possible to develop common visions and compromises on the rough long-term land use.

On the other hand, these studies reveal little about how physical planning works in existing built-up areas in Norway. There is an ongoing process of in-filling and land use change which to a large extent would appear to be characterised by chance and piecemeal development. These are areas where all changes in the actual land use as a rule involve a conflict where there are many interested parties. Planning requires large resources and considerable involvement from all the key actors, to make possible the development of visions that will control the use of land. It is obvious that we also lack good methods or practices for the way in which such planning should be carried out. In today's situation, where the "occupation of the prairie" is more or less over in most towns and population centres, we must pay more attention to the existing structures and see how they can be further developed on, among other things, welfare, aesthetic and environmental grounds.

The Volda study indicates that if the commune formulates detailed plans which it alone or in an alliance with landowners or other strong economic interests does not have the ability to implement, then such plans are hardly realistic. Even though our survey is not very broadly-based, it would appear to be true to claim that the more detailed and long-term a physical plan is, the less realistic it is. Attempts at long-term detailed control of land use would

173

seem to work best when these plans aim to keep the situation as it is.

Radical alterations that require the demolition of property etc., which are not already agreed upon and where there are no financial means to allow for this to be implemented at once, are at best interesting, but unrealistic utopias. On the other hand, there may be the need to plan in detail strategic changes that are important for the total situation, even though the changes cannot take place right away. An example is the development of the road system in the centre of Volda. Today, almost 65 years after the main road system in the centre of Volda was first mapped out, there is hope that the last stretch of road can be put into place, if the commune's economy allows. It is the fact that detailed plans have always stuck to this choice of alignment for the road that has meant that land has been reserved and has been available for development roughly as it had been planned.

My main conclusion is that, for the time being:

- planning for the expansion of built-up areas on "virgin territory" works; but also that

- planning for the development of built-up areas on previously developed land works poorly and new knowledge and methods are needed.

Background

I will therefore look more closely at the case "Volda centre" and use this example and some other work in the MILKOM-programme (Kleven, 1997) to discuss and formulate some future research tasks in connection with physical planning. In this paper I have included only the main points in the planning development of Volda centre, drawn from a recent working report (Amdam, 1998). The key issues here are whether in fact it is the case that the planning and development legislation after 1965 has had a more controlling function and has had greater effect than earlier planning, or is it the case that society has visions of its future and its land use which dominate and govern regardless of the legislation? And is it the case that planning legislation works best for expansion in the "wilderness", while we lack tools for planning and implementing changes in established areas?

The latest study in Norway done by Saglie and Lyssand Sandberg (1997) has shown that in communes like Elverum and Sandefjord, the answer is "We are sticking to the plan". On the basis of their work, there is good reason to claim that communal physical overall planning has worked well in connection with the preparation of land for development in the period 1970-1990. But at the same time, new questions are raised about how the physical planning actually works. Is the reason why planning during the 1970s worked so well in their survey that the communes made an effort and planned the development of all land that in some way could be released for such development? If the target is really big, it is very difficult to miss, especially if you are using a shotgun.

Whether or not it is the intention of physical planning to control land use in an overall context, Saglie and Lyssand Sandberg (1996a, 1996b; 1997) have not given us a detailed answer as to whether it works. What we have been told is that it works well as far as planning for the growth of built-up areas is concerned. Does this mean that physical planning prepares the ground for growth in rings round the centre, while the core is left untouched by planning efforts? The problem is of course that it is difficult to generalise from just a few examples, but examples can help to throw light on processes that are on-going and which can produce different results from place to place. It is also vital to decide what demands should be made of a physical plan in order to be able to say that it works. An extreme demand can be that it is not successful until it has been fulfilled 100 per cent. This is probably too strong a demand, since physical plans are seldom based on time and process. They reflect a picture of a desired situation in an indefinite future. The more comprehensive and detailed a physical plan is, the less chances there are that it can be put into effect, because the demands on land use and the challenges to society alter.

Unitary plans, on the other hand, are meant to control the overall development of land use in an area and this will be dynamic over time, during which plans must also be updated on the basis of needs. Therefore it can be expected that a unitary plan approved e.g. in 1970 will not be implemented 100 per cent; normally later planning will lead to amendments. What must be expected is that development that takes place during the period to which the plan applies is in accordance with the plan or at least with its main intentions. It is this that Saglie and Lyssand Sandberg have checked in the case of land for expansion and have found that plan and development correspond well. But physical plans can also present visions for land use, structures and situations that may influence the development later and serve as guidelines for later planning and development. Even where plans are not put into effect as intended, one can ask whether such visions have "caught on" but have been expressed in ways other than that which was originally planned.

The Case of the Village of Volda

Volda is a rural community, half town, half village, in Sunnmøre with about 5,000 inhabitants and in addition about 2,000 students as of today (1998). The commune has a population of about 8,000 excluding students. Volda is

Figure 10.1   Volda in 1993 (photo: Per Eide)

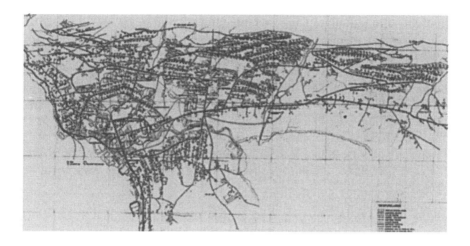

Map 10.1   Map of built-up areas and roads, Volda, 1997

dominated by public sector activity in the form of a college, hospital, upper secondary school, etc., but also by mechanical industries. Figure 10.1 shows an overview of the centre and the development pattern around 1993. Some housing estates on the hillside on the left of the picture are not included; apart from that the picture shows the area in which around 7,000 people live and work on an average day, with the exception of the summer. What strikes one when looking at the picture is the large green areas, the spread of institutions in between the housing areas and the key position occupied by the sea and the harbour.

Map 10.1 shows the features that formed the basis of the commune section plan for the centre of Volda from 1997, covering roads and buildings. The dotted lines show roads that were planned but not built in 1997. The map underlines the structure as it appears in Figure 10.1. While key land area near the centre is agricultural land, most of the expansion in recent years has taken place on the southern slopes of the valley up towards 240 metres above sea level. This is a strategy that a colleague compared with trying to fill water round the top edge of a bucket in the hope that the bottom would remain dry.

At the same time this strategy has meant that there is farmland near the centre which would allow the expansion of service area, new housing development and not least important for Volda---the development of public institutions. An example is the farmland between the two original college buildings. The land situated on a line between these two building complexes

177

is now being used to construct a new college building, among other things, to underline the fact that this is now an amalgamated college. Without the restrictive conservation policy as regards farming land in the 1970s and 1980s which prevented planned development, this would not have been possible because the area was then earmarked for industry and housing. The question I pose is: to what extent have these structures materialised as a result of planning and what can we learn from almost 80 years of planning in a small town like Volda? Volda centre was legally a fire commune with a certain enforced planning even before 1900 as a result of a fire here in 1899. At the same time Volda is an example of a built-up area in western Norway at the level beneath towns, actually a typical commune centre in a medium-sized Norwegian commune---with the typical tensions between the traditional and the new.

Planning Efforts in the Centre of Volda from 1920 to 1947

Ole Berg, who had a military background, formulated the first known plan for the centre of Volda in 1920. As with the 1970s plans for Elverum and Sandefjord, this was for its time a very expansive plan with great emphasis on the development of town quarters and blocks of buildings and the forming of a town---ideas which were bound to fail in a farming community like Volda.

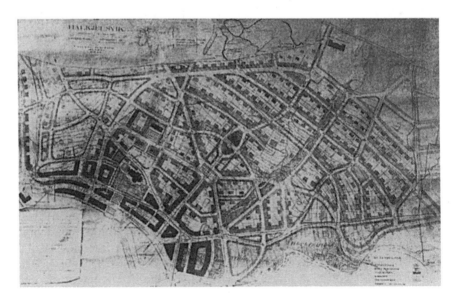

Map 10.2   Prof. Sverre Pedersen's plan for central Volda, 1933

The next major planning attempt in the centre of Volda was organised by Sverre Pedersen in 1933, a plan that was not approved until 1940 (see Map 10.2). This plan was less comprehensive than Berg's, concentrating roughly on the central core of the area round the centre of Volda (the farm known as Halkjelsvik) north of the river and northwards as far as the Teacher's Training College. Yet again the plan is based on concentric squares or blocks of buildings with great emphasis on road lines which follow the contours and therefore also form a circular structure. The visions of Volda as a town are still there, but on a somewhat smaller scale. Blocks of buildings have been drawn in the centre combined with a market-place or square which provides an opening between the church and the sea, similarly a "mini-Karl-Johans-street" (the main thoroughfare in Oslo) leading up to the courtyard at the Halkjelsvik farm, where a "palace" was drawn in.

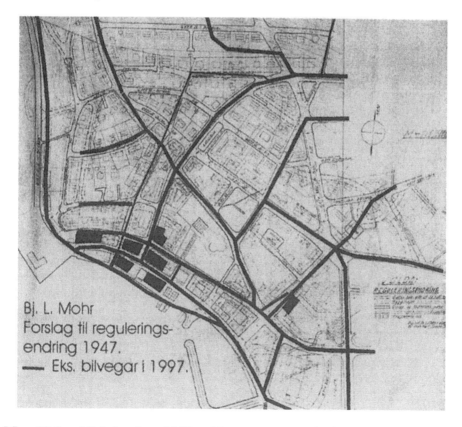

Map 10.3 **Mohr's plan, 1947, with roads and buildings built according to the plan shown in black**

Architect Bjarne Lous Mohr drew up a local plan in 1947, approved in 1949. On map 3 the existing roads from 1997 have been added and buildings that have been erected in accordance with Pedersen and Mohr's plans away from housing areas which were only marginally affected by this local plan amendment. Mohr's contribution is mainly associated with the linking of the road northwards from the church with a street with dwelling houses as far as the present lower secondary school. At the same time this map illustrates Pedersen and Mohr's great visions and that little has been implemented in the centre. When I (in Amdam, 1992) claimed: "Only a few buildings have been erected according to the physical plan from 1950 for a typical rural community like Volda, in spite of the fact that the central area and the total amount of buildings have increased at least five-fold today", this is with reference to Mohr's local plan which in fact applied until 1987.

What then have been the effects of these planning efforts in the centre of Volda from 1920 to 1947?

- Plans which depended upon making alterations to the existing building mass have generally been unsuccessful. Only 6 buildings were demolished in the period 1920-1997 in Volda on the basis of public initiative, two due to road plans put forward by the highways authority, and four on the initiative of the commune. The four "communal" buildings were already derelict and demolished on the basis of voluntary agreements with the landowners (S. Hessen, personal information).

- Planning efforts have mainly involved maintaining and in-filling of the road network that existed around 1920. The fact is that cart-tracks and rough farm-tracks that existed in 1920 have had more to say for the road system in the centre of Volda than the above-mentioned plans. It is the State Highways Authority that has created the major improvements to the road system with their construction of roads adjacent to water in two stages, the road along the river and the construction of the main road along the shore of the fjord towards ¥rsta. The major plans for the development of a street structure in the centre of Volda have not been put into effect.

- The plans have put forward ideas related to a harbour wall, promenade, market-place, localisation of public buildings, etc., which have all been put into effect in another form, but where the actual putting forward of the ideas as part of the planning process has without doubt been extremely valuable.

- To the extent that the plans from the period 1920 to 1950 have acted as guidelines for the development of the centre of Volda, this has been on land which was not already developed and on agricultural land of farms that were run less intensively. Arable land was only to a small degree

180

developed, and in those cases for public institutions like the college and other purposes in the town centre.

Local Planning from 1950 to 1970

The first clerk of works in Volda (Arne Sommernes, appointed in Volda from 1948 to 1957) initiated a close co-operation with Bjarne Lous Mohr's architect's office in Bergen, which drew up a whole series of local plans for Volda in the period 1953 to roughly 1965. Around 1965 the new clerk of works Sigbjørn Hessen put together a mosaic of these plans. This map is a conglomerate of at least 7 different local plans which together covered most of the area in the present centre of Volda. The local plan mosaic shows that the ideas about a concentric Volda-town based on the development of farming land were still very much alive in the 1950s and 1960s. But the vision had altered from a "block town" to a "villa town".

A common feature found repeatedly in connection with the implementation of the local plans in the 1960s is that there are great visions of house-building on agricultural land near the centre, but land that was in active use in farming was only developed as an exception. Part of the reason for this was that the commune was not willing to use force in order to implement the plans. Development took place on land which the owners were prepared to sell by voluntary agreement with the commune or by leasing it direct to the house-builder. In other words, it was the land-owners who controlled the actual implementation of the plans.

Not until 1970 did the commune council vote to make a compulsory purchase. The background was a conflict with the land-owners on the terms of leasing. Not until this point in time has the commune been willing to use force to put into effect its plans (S.Hessen personal information). There are probably several reasons for this political change of policy. The planning and building law of 1965 focused far more than earlier on the importance of the co-ordinated planning and implementation of changes in land use. Volda was in the middle of a period of great expansion due to the development of the school system and the hospital, with a strong increase in demand for housing. At the same time, politicians were elected to the council who were more concerned about conservation and protecting the environment than "protecting the land-owners". Overall planning came into focus instead of "postage-stamp planning".

Regional Planning from 1965 to 1973

Pursuant to the new building regulations of 1965, the neighbouring communes of Volda and Ørsta started joint regional planning. In the period 1965 to 1968

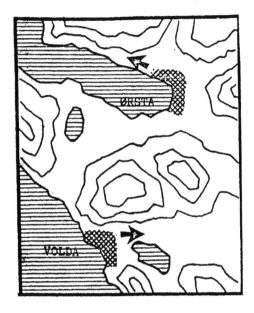

Figure 10.2   Regional plan 1973, alternative 2

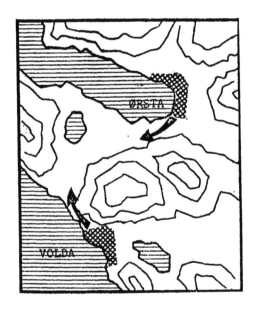

Figure 10.3   Regional plan 1973, alternative 3

the work was carried out by a joint committee appointed by both councils. In 1968 this was replaced by a regional planning council with members in accordance with the new building regulations, and chaired by the district stipendiary magistrate. The regional planning council appointed Andersson and Skjånes As as planning advisors and up until 1973 several analyses and sketches were drawn up. This work was summarised in the Ørsta/Volda regional plan 73 (Andersson and Skjånes 1973). In the draft plan, three main strategies were outlined for the development of the two centres which are situated just 10 kilometres or 6 miles from each other, see Figures 10.2 and 10.3. Three alternatives were formulated: (1) Concentric growth round the two centres; (2) "Opposite growth", i.e., Ørsta was to grow westwards along the fjord and Volda eastwards up the valley; and (3) "Growing together", i.e., Ørsta was to grow on the south side of the Ørstafjord towards Volda and Volda correspondingly towards Ørsta.

The main arguments were in favour of alternative 3 in the plan (picture 3), which was also supported by the regional planning council and the county commune (Andersson and Skjånes, 1973):

• To improve the two built-up areas' competitive ability and to support efforts to establish their status as a first-rank centre in the county, with specialisation and integration of the two centres of population.

• Deliberate localisation of jobs and housing between the two existing centres will make it easier for the central area to function as one residential and job market.

• An integration would be advantageous as far as the communal technical services were concerned. "The Ørsta-Volda regional draft plan, pressure zones and mains system" recommend that the two communes build a joint reservoir on the ridge between the two centres.

• The localisation of the airport between the two centres means that this area is made ready for development and therefore attractive for others who might wish to establish business in Volda and Ørsta.

Volda and Ørsta are two neighbouring communes, covering a wide area and with populations of 8,000 and 10,000 respectively, of whom over 10,000 today live in the central area and/or in the area between them. But the good intentions in the regional plan are far from being fulfilled. Let us therefore look more closely at what has happened to the proposals in the regional plan.

The building together of the two centres has been partly implemented, but in fact Ørsta has developed residential areas towards Volda in Hovdebygda (alternative 3, mainly because of the avalanche danger associated with alternative 2), while Volda has developed its residential areas up the valley

183

(alternative 2). The idea was to develop large areas for residential and industrial purposes in the Mork area close to the boundary with Ørsta and at one point in time, there was also a plan to localise the regional college there. Volda organised a "coup" during the last localisation process around 1970 by erecting an "industrial building" for the college east of the present boundary with Volda. This localisation with its associated halls of residence and dwellings for the staff, has laid the foundations for development in Volda at later stages. A residential estate was developed at Mork, but the major plans that involved developing good farming land were put aside. The wooded area on both sides of the boundary has been used as an industrial area, generally in accordance with the regional plan.

The integration of communal technical services has been put on one side. Both communes have built their own waterworks. In reality it only needs a 600-metre pipeline along the length of the airport to connect the two waterworks together, but proposals to do so in connection with the increased demand for water have been rejected, in particular by the Ørsta council.

The local airport was built when the regional plan was put forward; in fact it was a noise zone map linked to this that was used by Volda to reject development of the regional college in the area near the boundary with Ørsta. The vision of the fourth town in the county of Møre og Romsdal has in effect been rejected by both the local councils. Many arguments have been used to explain this, but threats that a joint investment here could lead to an amalgamation of the two communes has undoubtedly been important, and not least the elder generation of politicians in both communes have strong feelings directed against the neighbouring commune. So even though the regional planning council, the commune councils and the county commune in principle were positive towards a building-together, the actual development has been a mixture of building together and apart---the visions have only partly made an impact. Joint regional planning stopped completely after 1973.

Overall Planning after 1975

In 1975 Volda presented a new zone plan for the centre of Volda with a growth area up the valley. At first sight this plan appears to pretty expansive in the same way as corresponding plans for Elverum and Sandefjord, but as the added boundaries for the town centre show, the zone boundaries had been overrun as early as 1980. In reality the zone plan from 1975 is a summary of the local plans produced up until 1970, with certain adjustments.

The next overall plan for the central area was formulated in 1989. This plan was also in the main a registration of existing land use with areas drawn in which were already designated (residential area to the east) or in the process of being designated (residential area to the northwest). The main difference between the 1975 zone plan and this communal sub-plan is that the institutional area has been reduced, partly because halls of residence and old people's homes are now registered as residential area, partly because the central agricultural area between the regional college and the teacher training college is registered as mixed public and service area. To the south the farmland earlier designated for residential purposes has been returned to agricultural purposes. The proposed line for the new main county road through the middle of the town centre has been dropped.

A characteristic feature of this plan is that more distinct boundaries have been established between the central area and the surrounding agricultural land. In reality the plan contains very little expansion into new land development. If the plan is based on a vision, that must be in-filling and use of vacant land within the limits of the centre. This corresponds well with development trends in other population centres and towns in the 1980s, as shown by among others Lyssand Larsen and Saglie (1995). To a greater extent than from 1970 to 1980, the period from 1980 to 1990 is characterised more by in-filling than expansion onto new land, but also by less pressure for development. In Volda this becomes apparent in the way new land is no longer offered for development with the help of local plans outside the unitary plan area, as was the case for example with the northwestern residential estate just after the zone plan for Volda in 1975 had been approved.

The next stage in overall planning in Volda was in 1997, see Map 10.4. The alterations in the overall plans from 1989 to 1997 are remarkably small. With a tiny exception, the outer limits between the commune sub-plan area and the surrounding agricultural, mountain and sea areas are exactly the same.

Detailed Planning in the Centre: Consequences

Let us turn our attention to the central area for which Berg and Pedersen had such great visions. The last local plan for the centre was formulated by Architect Einar Ridderstrøm in 1985 and it was adopted by the commune council in 1987. Einar Ridderstrøm was employed at the regional university college and was for a period round 1980 leader of the communal committee that gives planning permission in Volda. In this role and as a self-employed architect he had a vital role in the development of the centre of Volda in the 1980s. Before the last plan for the centre was drawn up, he was closely involved in the last major developments, the Lothe-block on the sea road and the development of the old dairy east of the river as a supermarket for the Co-op. But these two developments probably provided enough land for business purposes for the next 15-20 years, because only one building for business purposes has been erected after Ridderstrøm's local plan was adopted, namely the Holte block in Storgata, hatched in black on Map 10.5.

185

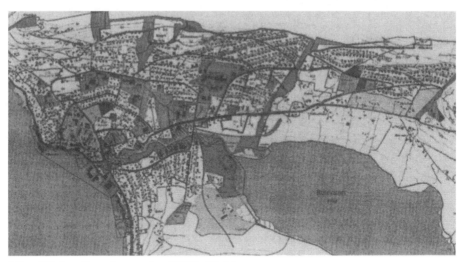

Map 10.4   Land use plan 1997, Volda

If one looks at the results of almost 70 years of planning in the central area defined as on Map 10.5, it is remarkable how little has been changed with the help of planning efforts, also in the period after this plan had been adopted.

Changes in the road system have taken place on the basis of special national highway planning such as the highway along by the sea, otherwise the road and street pattern is in fact by and large the same as before 1920. The new roundabout (Ridderstrøm) at the top of Map 10.5 with its accompanying new roads has not been built. The main reason for this is probably a lack of funds, but also a failure to give it priority in relation to other projects.

"We Stick to the Plan"?

In Sandefjord the politicians claimed that "We stick to the plan", and the researchers accepted that this was the case (Saglie and Lyssand Sandberg, 1996b). The same can be said as far as Volda is concerned for the period after 1975, but certainly not to the overall plans alone. On Map 10.6, I have drawn in the various residential estates developed in Volda and also added in which decade the estate development started. I have divided roughly into estates and it will also include previously scattered dwellings, farmhouses, etc. The land developed before 1940 has not been included; that is, I commence with Pedersen's overall plan. I will first comment on the residential areas, then the institutional areas and one industrial area.   The major features are:

Map 10.5   Detail of land use plan for central Volda, 1987

- The residential area marked 1945 was developed in the period 1945-1960 by and large in accordance with Pedersen's plan approved in 1940 and Mohr's local plan from 1947. Pedersen had placed considerably larger housing estates in this area, but probably due to conflicts with farming interests, these were not taken into use. Instead the commune "jumped over" these areas and continued housing development outside Pedersen's plan area after 1960.

- The residential areas marked 1960 were developed from about 1960 to about 1970 in connection with the expansion of the school system (upper secondary and teacher's training college), the hospital and industry and related activities. The development was carried out in accordance with housing plans and local plans without any basis in an approved overall plan.

- The residential area marked 1970 is to be found again on the overall plan of 1975. The basis is local plans drawn up early in the 1960s (they are part of the local plan mosaic), i.e., before the new planning and building law of 1965, and drawn in on the zone plan from 1975.

- The residential area marked 1980 was not part of the zone plan 1975, but development started early in the 1980s on the basis of a local plan for the area. Not until the commune sub-plan from 1989 is the area to be found sketched in at overall plan level.

- After 1989 no housing estate has been developed outside the boundaries of the commune sub-plan, in fact there was very little new housing development until after 1995.

- The building of institutions has to an even greater degree been characterised by localisation without any conformity with overall planning. It started back in the 1920s when the teacher's training college was localised to a housing area in Berg's plan from 1920, right on the outskirts of his plan area. The area was drawn in on Pedersen's plan of 1933. The hospital was built in the 1930s outside Pedersen's plan area. The old people's home was built in the 1960s in an area designated for residential purposes in Pedersen's plan. The new upper secondary school (1964) and the regional college (1970) were developed partly in accordance with limited local plans in which the majority of this land was designated for industrial use. The town hall, telecommunications centre and community hall were built in the 1950s and 60s in areas that were planned partly for housing, partly for school purposes by Pedersen.

- In 1975 considerable areas of land were designated for institutional purposes and subsequent institutional development has been in accordance with this land use (new hospital and new nursing home in the 1980s, further development and amalgamation of the colleges).

Industrial development from the 1950s and onwards took place partly on land designated for industrial purposes by Pedersen, but also outside his planning area and partly on land designated for residential purposes.

While Sandefjord and Elverum made use of the unitary planning instruments provided in the planning and building law of 1965 to designate large areas of land for expansion, this was not done in Volda. Up until 1989, the overall planning has in effect been way behind the actual expansion of land development. The development instruments after 1950 have instead been major and minor "postage stamp planning adjustments" as the need arose. Up to about 1970 "postage stamp planning adjustments" served the purpose of the visionary element in Volda commune, the sum total of these plans reflects a vision of the compact population centre with the heavy development of agricultural land near the centre for housing and industrial purposes, see map 2. One vital reason why this vision was never fulfilled was that the commune was not willing to use force in relation to the landowners.

Even though in the period up to 1989, it has not been possible to control particular housing developments with the help of existing overall plans, development has been planned and probably the authorities making the decisions have had visions and principles on which to base those decisions. What appears to be decisive is that housing development is less important than cultivated land, but also that the landowners who controlled the development by way of voluntary agreements and leasing did not want greater development for financial reasons and they kept hold of their cultivated land in the end. This meant that such land was avoided and the expansion was allowed on grazing and forest land on the slopes to the north and east of the centre. Only the development of institutions was allowed on farmed land near the centre, and then on the basis of voluntary agreements with the landowners.

These "principles" correspond well to the attitudes we found in the land administration authorities and among politicians in a survey in 1980. Footpaths and cycle tracks, functions in the town centre and public roads were all seen to be more important than land conservation. Housing estates and industry were considered to be just about as important as land conservation in the bodies whose task it was to administer the conservation laws and as a little more important by those bodies administering building laws and by the communal administration (Amdam, Amdam and Olsen, 1981). In Volda they were clearly even more restrictive, which may be related to the fact that farmers and landowners had great influence politically. If we look at he way the planning has worked, it is possible to see at least three periods with distinct theoretical links (Amdam and Veggeland, 1991, 1998).

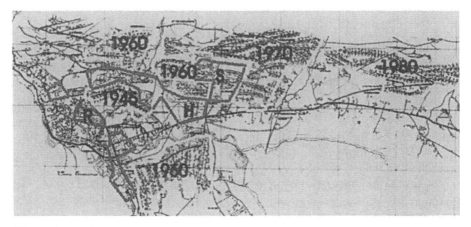

Map 10.6   Central Volda, building sites and year development begun

The Utopians. From 1920 to 1960, planning is characterised by big plans to develop Volda as a town with streets and compact housing development. The planning was instrumental and authoritarian and involved "an urban occupation of the village" from the top (a normative, rational planning: see Banfield, 1959; Friedmann, 1987). This planning was scarcely successful. Just a few town quarters, a few stretches of road and a little housing development were the result---but the visions were never accepted by the local villagers themselves. The plans in effect required a "great fire". Plans were "nice things to have", but useful only in so far as they fitted in. The commune was not willing or able to put the plans into effect itself. Probably this unrealistic planning was also the basis for negative attitudes to overall planning on the part of key politicians right up until the 1990s.

The incrementalists. From about 1960, when land expansion started in earnest and up to about 1990, the planning has been characterised by "piece by piece" development (Lindblom, 1959; Friedmann, 1987). While one in larger places like Elverum and Sandefjord made ready large areas for development through overall planning with the help of the Building Law of 1965, Volda was always behind with this overall planning. The regional planning council's intentions of building Ørsta together with Volda had been clearly rejected by Volda in reality. The local plans from the period up to about 1960 were made use of to the extent that they fitted in and were not in conflict with cultivated land in use.

Instead the centre has been expanded in just about the way one could expect, taking into account the conservationist and landowner interests combined with the great need for land on which to expand. The Law on Land Conservation has probably been just as important as a planning instrument as the Planning and Building Law, even in areas that had already been designated for other purposes. As the need has arisen, considerable areas of land for housing development have been made ready with the help of "postage stamp planning adjustments". Overall plans like the zone plan of 1975 were to a large extent a "summary" and adjustment of existing local plans, without making ready new land for expansion. It is the municipal services department together with the leading politicians and conservationists and highway authorities who have been responsible for this planning.

Early on, "standard agreements" were drawn up with landowners which meant that the latter were awarded a certain number of the house plots as compensation for land in housing development areas, even in cases when the land was taken by force of law. Key politicians, who themselves were landowners and farmers, negotiated agreements as the need arose in connection with giving up land for the development of public institutions. Not until after 1970 were politicians willing to make use of the law allowing enforced acquisition of private property as a means to an end. In reality I believe that many of the leading politicians in Volda in this period had a joint image of the development process that involved protecting cultivated land which was only to be used for "distinguished purposes". Housing development could take place on outlying rough grazing land.

"The horse-traders" or collaborative planning. With the existence of the commune sub-plan from 1989, which generally registers and fills in existing land use, the main guidelines for land use for the centre of Volda have probably been established for many years to come. Some land may be added through expansion on agricultural land and by further development northwards "up the mountain". The main challenge is to find satisfactory negotiated settlements on farmland that has been enclosed and for land which is of little use, which will require negotiations with various groups of owners. Such negotiations have, among other things, led to housing development on land planned for public institutions in order to free such land voluntarily. There seems to be little willingness to make use of the powers inherent in approved plans, apart from when it suits Volda politically. The poor communal economy has probably also played its part, among other things in the case of the lack of road development. Such negotiations are on the part of the commune generally dominated by key politicians, with the municipal services department as a "secretariat". Their opposite numbers are partly landowners, but also the highway authorities and to a lesser extent environmentalists and conservationists, since their interests have generally been taken care of in the planning adjustment process. The strategy is to aim

at broad agreement on necessary development through various forms of "give and take" and negotiations, in ways that are typical of politicians as "horse-traders" (positively meant) and well described by Offerdal (1992).

This increased emphasis on co-operation, public and private partnerships, negotiations with strong private and public interests etc (collaborative planning) are also typical of physical planning in other countries than Norway at the present time, see e.g. Patsy Healey (1997).

Physical Planning and Key Findings in Volda

A normal starting-point is that it was not until the introduction of the Planning and Building Law of 1965 that an instrument existed for physical planning and its implementation outside urban areas. The question that arises is whether Volda is atypical, or is it the case that we planners have exaggerated the significance of the Planning and Building Law of 1965? Was it in fact the case that the idea of planning had been introduced in rural areas as early as the turn of the century in Norway and that it in reality worked, even with poor support in legislation? The studies by Saglie & Lyssand Sandberg (1997) would seem to indicate that a new era arrived with the introduction of the planning instrument that the Planning and Building Law of 1965 represented, which revolutionised the physical planning in Elverum and Sandefjord. This study of the situation in Volda would seem to indicate the opposite; there was no revolution, but rather an evolution towards more and more precise drawn records of planned areas.

One hypothesis might be that it is Volda that is atypical---that this village on the fjord which had the first printing works in rural Norway, was ahead of its time. It may also be that in this village surrounded by mountains, fjords and lakes, land was such a scarcity that "everyone" realised that planning of the use of the scarce land resources was necessary. But many population centres and small towns in coastal Norway experience a similar situation as regards land resources as that in Volda, some even have less land---others somewhat more. Even if we lack good historical studies of physical planning at a detailed level, we know that professor Sverre Pedersen and his disciples from around 1920 put in an incredible effort in formulating plans for the centres of most of the population centres in Norway (Jensen 1980). Perhaps it is rather the case that there is difference between coastal and inland regions of Norway? Or is it perhaps more the difference between urban and rural communes that we see again as the differences between Volda and Sandefjord/Elverum? Was it so that urban communes like Sandefjord had taken into use most of its available land by 1965 and that the amalgamation of communes at the end of the 1960s came simultaneously with the overall planning instrument and made possible a rapid and expansive planning of---

for the urban communes---"newly acquired" land, that is, a sort of "imperialistic" planning?

Whatever the case, I believe it is necessary to study land use and visions of such use in a longer perspective than simply the period after 1965. The study in Volda seems to indicate that important guidelines and visions were established as early as just after the First World War and emphasised through planning efforts from the 1950s onwards. Let me therefore quote from the abstract of Rolf Jensen's (1980) Ph.D. thesis *The Birth of Modern Norwegian Planning*:

> Traditionally the towns had attempted to solve their growth problems by urban expansion, which was not very popular among their neighbouring communes. Conflicts between town and country were intensified. Therefore attempts were made to find other solutions or forms of solutions, yet again by looking at what other countries had achieved. For although "regional circumstances" was still an unknown term in Norwegian planning, the international garden city movement had adopted it (see page xvi). Planning became a matter of course during the 1930s. The reason was to be found in the cultural heritage was free from problems and indisputable. The practical picture of the planning was that it combated speculation, restricted the free operation of economic forces, guaranteed the population at large sanitary and technical standards and exercised control over the development of society. Planning was to act as a political instrument (page xix).

> . . . Wartime led to a break in continuity for Norwegian planning. Agreement on rapid reconstruction of society left little time for deeper reflection with an historical perspective. Not until the beginning of the 1970s did the need arise again for such activity (page xx).

Was the Planning and Building Law of 1965 so revolutionary for Norwegian planning as it is easy to get the impression of from the studies linked to the MILKOM-programme? The example from Volda illustrates two issues and circumstances:

* Planning of the expansion of population centres on "virgin land" works--- i.e., the spread of built-up area onto land that previously has been used for other purposes which are not "development", such as agricultural and untouched land of various types. The study in Volda shows that especially the local plans have controlled this land development and that after about 1960 there is general conformity between planned and actual development ---if one allows for running adjustments through amendments to the plans.

* Planning of the development of population centres on developed land

193

works poorly---i.e., plan proposals that involve the demolition or alteration of existing elements in the built-up area. The study in Volda reveals that it is almost impossible to implement such plans, if the owners do not agree with the commune on such changes. It is only the Highways Authority that has managed to implement such "enforced changes" in connection with the extension of the main national highway. The same applies to a certain extent proposals for the development of cultivated land which the owner stills wishes to use for that purpose, even though it has been planned for development. Instead the planning has gradually been adapted to fit in with this reality.

If one is to generalise from these findings in Volda, one has to check whether this is a general tendency in Norway. Are there examples that invalidate these hypotheses? If one is to answer unambiguously that the physical planning works, it must apply to both types of situations of planned land use change.

The Studies in Sandefjord and Elverum

Saglie and Lyssand Sandberg's findings (1996a, 1996b) correspond with the first hypothesis. They have shown that of the land that was developed in the period 1970-1990, 98 per cent in Elverum and 91 per cent in Sandefjord is in accordance with the overall plans from around 1970. There is a watershed before and after 1970. Prior to 1970 the figures for Elverum and Sandefjord respectively were 67 per cent (Elverum 1964-70) and 79 per cent (Sandefjord 1961-70) of land developed in accordance with plans. One limitation they make is:

> We have limited the study to apply only to extensions of the population centre, i.e., changes in land use that result in the outer boundaries of the population centre are moved. We have for example not registered land use changes within the built-up area's boundaries that existed at the beginning of the survey period . . . . (1996b: 32)

This means that they have not tried to provide an answer to the other hypothesis in their studies of Elverum and Sandefjord; therefore their comments that the physical planning works in these towns limited to planning of the expansion of the built-up areas.

Sandefjord was amalgamated with Sandar commune in 1968. No "existing overall plan" was to be found for the area before the general plan of 1970. The planning was limited to local plans, even though some of these would appear more like minor zone plans rather than local plans that apply to individual development projects. As in Volda in the same period, local plans are the

194

instrument used to control land use for the whole of the built-up area. In the period 1961 to 1972, 21 per cent of the built-up area expansion was not in accordance with existing local plans. In the period after 1972, 9 per cent of the expansion of the population centre has not been in accordance with overall plans, but the figure is only 4 per cent if the local plans are included. This reflects a strict control of the development of the built-up area through planning after 1972.

The study indicates that most of the planning efforts in Sandar commune were characterised by planning of plot development, usually on the initiative of the landowners, and that no "local plan mosaic" existed that in reality was an overall plan, as in Volda (Saglie and Lyssand Sandberg, 1996b). On the one hand Sandefjord had an urban commune that was more or less fully developed and surrounding the town was Sandar commune with ad-hoc planning of short-term development. Not until after the amalgamation of communes in 1968 was it possible to see the land use in context and to start planning that was easy to follow. This is a different situation from that in Volda, where commune amalgamation has also taken place at the same time, but where the "newly acquired" land was very peripheral compared to the population centre.

In the detailed and well-presented study of overall planning in Sandefjord after 1990, it is very clear that it is the expansion of development in previously uninhabited areas that is in focus in the overall planning. Even though in-filling gradually becomes a theme, this applies to "closed-in agricultural land". There is little trace of active planning of changes in land use in areas that have already been developed in this survey of the overall planning in Sandefjord, but this may be due to limitations made for the research work.

Planning work in Elverum shows many parallels with Volda up to 1940. The population centre was designated a "building commune" (given responsibility for local town planning) in 1898 and the first planning commenced (Saglie and Lyssand Sandberg, 1996a). A utopian local plan (which was really a layout drawing) was drawn up in 1924 with great and dramatic visions, just as in Volda---and probably with small consequences as in Volda (individual houses and short stretches of road).

Elverum was bombed in 1940 and large parts of the central area burned down. Sverre Pederesen and Karl Grevstad drew up a local plan for this area in 1941, which was adopted in 1946 with certain adjustments---and with more radical adjustments in 1948. This plan became very important for the reconstruction work---it worked well where there were no existing buildings. An important principle was that it was based on the existing infrastructure of streets and underground pipelines, which meant it was realistic but which also had consequences for the size of the buildings. But at the same time, the reconstruction work proceeded apace and it was easy to be given exemption from the plan. The "building commune" became part of the rural commune in 1955. Prior to this, the administration had been too weak to manage the planning and implementation in the population centre.

Strong expansion after the war lead to 13 local plans initiated by landowners in the period 1963 to 1969 which covered a combined area of 670 acres, of which 540 was housing development. This planning also involved expansion onto "virgin territory" and land that the owners wished to develop (as in Volda). But as opposed to Volda, this "sum of mosaics of local plans" only partly represents an overall plan for land use within reasonable limits for the built-up area.

The zone plan of 1970 represents a drawing in of the adopted local plans and in addition a further expansion onto virgin territory. "The wish was as far as possible to avoid compulsory purchase, and the plan therefore showed development on more untouched areas. Building on virgin land also meant that it was easier to control the financial aspect, because the costs of preparing the plots were added to the price of the plots" (Saglie and Lyssand Sandberg, 1996a: 79). Obvious parallels with a similar strategy in Volda are apparent here---but the zone plan was more expansive than the corresponding plan for the centre of Volda in 1975--that covered a total area of 1,235 acres.

The further overall planning in Elverum has mainly involved adjusting the zone plan from 1975, partly through further but less comprehensive expansion, partly by selecting areas on the periphery of the population centre. The zone plan from 1970 applied to 2,750 acres, the general plan from 1979 3,840 acres and the sub-plan from 1991 3,350 acres, but roughly the same housing area as in the zone plan from 1970 (1,662 acres and 1,647 acres respectively).

Physical planning in Elverum has been a real success story. Just 2 per cent of the development in the period 1970-1990 has not been in accordance with the existing overall plan. On the other hand, large areas of land, especially for industrial purposes, have been laid out which have not been developed and the development is such that there remain large areas available for in-filling (as in Volda). It is clear that a vision has existed among key actors as to how Elverum was to develop and the layout drawings have reflected these visions---and with a development company as an important instrument of implementation. Conflicts about land have been rare. But these visions concern expansion onto "virgin territory". With the exception of discussions and conflicts related to the future route of the national highway (as in Volda), there is little of this planning that is documented by Saglie and Lyssand Sandberg (1996a) that concerns restructuring and altering existing buildings. Here the vision appears to have been "to leave things as they are".

The examples from Sandefjord and Elverum do not provide any basis for rejecting the first hypothesis, that physical planning works well in the case of growth on virgin land; in fact they support similar findings in Volda. But neither do they provide a basis for rejecting the second hypothesis: that the planning of the development of population centres (changes in the form of the place) on developed land works poorly.

Green Belts and the Planning of Land Use: Hønefoss

The studies by Nyhuus (1996) and Halvorsen Thoren (1996) are interesting because they have studied changes in land use within the boundaries of population centres, but limited to green belts. They can therefore indicate whether the second hypothesis must be rejected.

Generally speaking they also find that plans and actual changes in land use correspond well in the case of expansion of the built-up areas in Sandefjord and Hønefoss. On the other hand, the picture is more complicated in the case of green field sites and planning in the centre itself, a topic that has been studied closely in Hønefoss.

In Hønefoss, Halvorsen Thoren discovered (1996: 61):

> Most interesting here is that of the 182 individual developments, only about half of them, or 92 to be exact, taken place in accordance with the general plan or after local plans, while the rest have been developed as individual partitioning off land or purely and simply in opposition to the general plan and the planning of the town centre. ... It is the public sector itself that is responsible for almost half of the developments in areas which have been designated as green field sites. By that we mean both open and free areas and land used for agricultural purposes. The purposes of the development are schools, sports facilities and various types of state institutions, for example the Norwegian Mapping Authority and Norwegian Telecom. Business and industrial use and residential development are roughly equally represented in the other half of the land developed in opposition to the general plan.

This expansion is on "virgin territory" like other development planning, but in this case planned green field sites within the boundaries of the built-up area. But another 15 per cent of the expansion onto farming land happened in Hønefoss on land outside the overall plans, much of this by way of individual plan adjustments. Measured in area, the amount of such redeployment of agricultural land is 47.5 acres, while 237.5 acres of agricultural land has been developed in accordance with the plan. As the quote above mentions, the biggest culprit is the public sector itself. New schools, kindergartens, etc., are considered more important than green belts even though they have been planned for these purposes. A certain change has taken place over time. In the period 1976 to 1983 22.5 acres designated as open and free areas or parks were developed, as opposed to only four acres in the period 1983-94. It is not clear whether this is due to better planning or less pressure for development. All told, about 225 acres (of which 160 acres in accordance with the general or local plan) were developed in the first period, as against about 115 acres in the second period (of which 80 acres in accordance with the general or local plan). Of interesting findings I would like to mention in particular that the planned open, free recreation areas appear to have better protection than the others. The area of publicly owned green field sites was doubled from 1975 to 1985.

> This has happened without the commune itself having a full overview of the structure that in this way was established. ... The planning has among other things been important, but has taken place as an incremental process. The green belt has developed step by step and more or less by chance. (Halvorsen Thoren, 1996: 118)

> Even so, the changes in content are primarily the result of "the not approved variety" based on small gradual changes without any root in the communal overall planning. Here it is the individual landowner's taste and the planners' professional ability that have decided how green it will be and how much natural beauty is created. The administrative practice among the green experts is also important here. The passing of time also leads to the town becoming greener and getting several layers, at least after periods of development. Most of what happens on the agricultural land happens completely divorced from communal planning. This arena has been left to agricultural policy and the landowners' own decisions. (ibid.)

As in Volda, these green belts function as reservoirs with which to be able to meet future needs for town centre purposes, institutions, industrial areas, etc., and such changes often take place as exemptions from plans. As Halvorsen Thoren (1996: 115) points out: "As opposed to the expansions in area, part of the developments within the town centre take place in accordance with the not-approved variety as a series of gradual and unplanned changes".

The findings support this first hypothesis, that the planning works well in the case of the development of virgin territory. But neither do they provide a basis for rejecting the second hypothesis, the findings give indirect support to a hypothesis that planning on "developed built-up area" works poorly: in-filling and changes in land use appear to a large extent to happen by chance.

Overall Plans and Actual Land Use

At the Institute of Geography at the University of Bergen, five Masters' theses have been written in which planned land use in overall plans is compared with actual land use. As in most other studies, it is the planned growth as compared with the actual growth that is studied. Sætre (1991) and Aanderaa (1995) studied rural communes close to urban areas (Randaberg compared to Stavanger and Søgne compared to Kristiansand). Typical for both these communes was that the planning work started early, a number of plans have been formulated, there has been consensus about conservation and full conformity between the planned and actual land. In these two communes it is clear that early on in the process, common visions of how the land was to be used were developed and that these have governed the overall land expansion with minor adjustments.

Sætre (1991) also looked at Stavanger, where he found great emphasis on the planning of land use, but also large conflicts between the commune's vision of future land use and the visions of higher authorities specially linked to conservation and natural and open air recreation areas. Therefore there is divergence between the commune's own plans and the actual land use development. Magerøy (1992, Kvinnherad), Jacobsen (1994, Bømlo) and Merok (1997, Stranda) have studied more rural communes with relatively few plans. The communes cover a wide area, have a disjointed structure and clearly separate villages. The zone plans for the commune and village centre therefore have a normal physical form of plan, in addition to general layout drawings with few details for the general plan/commune plan and local plans at the detailed level (these have not been studied). Kvinnherad is a large commune in area and has 13,000 inhabitants and 10 villages with no dominating centre. The first general plan that was formulated in 1967 was a typical plan "for the desk drawer" with large divergences between the plan and the actual development. The reason was according to Magerøy (1992) that this first plan did not take into account the conservation interests and that there was a considerable over-dimensioning of land for housing and industry in Husnes. The planning process was characterised by great conflicts between the interests of the various villages etc. The next general plan from 1979 paid more attention to the conservation interests and the conformity between plan and later development was far greater.

Bømlo was studied by Jacobsen (1994). In this island commune with almost 10,000 inhabitants in Sunnhordaland, it is clear that visions were developed at an early stage of how the land was to be used. Few plans have been drawn up and the planning processes produced few conflicts, among other things because conservation was respected at an early stage. His overall impression is that the planned and actual land use development corresponded well in Bømlo.

Merok (1997) came to the same conclusion in Stranda. This industrial commune in Sunnmøre was one of the first to commission an overall plan from a consultant and only Molde commune was ahead of them in approving a general plan. There is a high degree of conformity between planned land use in the four zone plans in Stranda and the actual land use. Deviations are for the most part connected to the fact that considerably more land was designated especially for residential development than has actually been made use of. While the general plan planned for a growth in population, this growth has to a large extent not taken place.

Also in these surveys there is a high degree of conformity between planned land use in overall plans and the actual land use, but as in many communes it is obvious that in the first generation of overall plans, things were exaggerated somewhat. Volda appears in fact to be an exception in so far as the zone plan for the centre of Volda in 1975 seems to be far less expansive with regard to land use than was usual in the 1960s and 1970s.

When there is a deviance between overall plans and subsequent land use, this appears to be related to unresolved conflicts, especially with conservationists. It is clear that no common vision of land use has been developed either locally or in co-operation with higher authorities. This means that the fight for land continues even after plans have been approved and adopted, that especially politically little attempt is made to follow up the plans and that later reviewing of the plans serves as a replay until joint "compromise visions" on land use have been developed. It is not the case in these studies either that detailed attention has been paid to the planning and change in use of existing buildings.

Discussion and Theoretical Implications

In this article I have shown that Norwegian overall planning has worked best as "cowboy planning", i.e., as an "occupation" of land outside the built-up areas which there may be use for some time in the future in order to expand the built-up areas, but without any concrete detailed plans for when and whether the land will be needed. Such a very expansive land use policy can stimulate the development of more land area than is necessary and desirable and can also increase works traffic and thereby result in damage to the environment.

On the other hand, these studies reveal little about how physical planning works in existing built-up areas in Norway. There is an ongoing process of in-filling and land use change which to a large extent would appear to be characterised by chance and piecemeal development. These are areas where all changes in the actual land use as a rule involve a conflict where there are many interested parties. The local community, commune or region as a political and administrative institution only controls some factors that decide the development. Individuals, corporations, organisations, government, regional authorities etc., also have power. Whatever they do the commune generally has to adjust to it. Ideally a system would be developed where all actors agreed upon what had to be done, in total and individually, in order to achieve the desired future (a kind of co-operative strategic management based on negotiations and understanding).

It is obvious that we also lack good methods or practices for the way in which such planning should be carried out. In today's situation, where the "occupation of the prairie" is more or less over in most towns and population centres, we must pay more attention to the existing structures and see how they can be further developed on, among other things, welfare, aesthetic and environmental grounds. The planning requires large resources and considerable involvement form all the key actors, to make possible the development of visions that will control the use of land (Amdam, 1992).

We must see conflict and conflict resolution as normal activity in planning instead of trying to escape from them. In all situations with many decisions makers and participants, we will have conflict about facts, interests, values and persons (Amdam and Veggeland 1998). It is not possible or necessary to solve all conflict. Some conflicts are needed for prosperity and development---to encourage initiative and a change of paradigm. Other conflicts are bottlenecks for local development. An important goal for local strategic planning is to identify such situations. It must try to develop strategies and actions for conflict resolution together with strategies and actions related to issues where there is little conflict but a real lack of knowledge and understanding of what must be done.

Communicative planning theories like social learning and social mobilisation concentrate on a learning dialogue between participants (Friedmann, 1987; Amdam, 1995). We must first concentrate on facts and interests. What do we agree and disagree on? What can be done to get new facts if facts are unclear? What compromise can be reached in interest conflicts? This means that this planning is based on communicative processes between participants (Sager, 1993, 1994).

A communicative negotiation strategy presupposes that there is conflict of interest and that the aim is to arrive at a compromise which guarantees the interests of each party to some reasonable degree. Such processes function most often as "slow-moving" learning where each participant evaluates effects from earlier steps, and takes a new step according to her/his own interests. Through such learning processes over time the participants can learn to trust each other and to understand which questions are best not asked and on what issues real co-operation is possible. The co-operation changes from negotiation to discussion and change is easier to introduce and implement. A strategic planning process can work like this if we use what time is necessary, to go through more than one stage or "circle" and concentrate on issues where a solution is possible; a true collaboration must be developed (Healey, 1997). The change from normative to "horse-dealing" planning strategy in Volda is a typical example of this change in planning attitude.

A local community or commune is---naturally---full of tension and conflict about how the situation is and how they should be (Healey, 1992, 1997). Local politics is about values, interests and solutions. Local politicians are elected to put forward specific interests. To some extent politicians must disagree to attend to their voters' interests. But the political process also produces compromises that are acceptable for at least a majority. Policymaking is a learning process just as planning is.

References

Amdam, J. 1991. Lokal planlegging i praksis. In J. Naustdalslid (ed.), *Kommunal styring*. 3rd ed. Oslo: Det norske Samlaget.

Amdam, J. 1992. Local Planning and Mobilization: Experiences from the Norwegian Fringe. In M. Tykkyläinen (ed.), *Development Issues and Strategies in the New Europe*. Aldershot;: Avebury.

Amdam, J. 1995. Mobilization, Participation and Partnership Building in Local Development Planning: Experience from Local Planning on Women's Conditions in Six Norwegian Communes. *European Planning Studies* 3 (3): 305-332.

Amdam, J. 1998. *Fungerer (heller ikkje) den fysiske planlegginga?* Arbeidsrapport nr. 58. M¢reforsking og h¢gskulen i Volda.

Amdam, J., R. Amdam and A. Olsen. 1981. *Meiningar om jordforvaltninga.* Møreforsking rapport nr. 8105. Volda.

Amdam, J. and N. Veggeland. 1991. *Teorier om samfunnsplanlegging. En teoretisk introduksjon for planlegging av samfunnsendring.* Oslo: Universitetsforlaget.

Amdam, J. and N. Veggeland. 1998. *Teorier om samfunnsplanlegging. Lokalt, regionalt, nasjonalt, internasjonalt.* Oslo: Universitetsforlaget.

Anderson and Skjånes As. 1973. *Ørsta/Volda regionplan* 73. Sandvika.

Banfield, E. C. 1959/73. Ends and Means in Planning. In A. Faludi (ed.), *A Reader in Planning Theory.* Oxford.

Friedmann, J. 1987. *Planning in the Public Domain.* Princeton: Princeton University Press.

Halvorsen Thorén, A.-K. 1996. *Grønnstrukturens vilkår i kommunal*

202

Local Land-Use Planning in Norway

arealplanlegging på Hønefoss fra 1965-1995. MILKOM notat 12/96. Oslo: NIBR.

Healey, P. 1992. Planning through Debate. *TPR* 63 (2): 112-136.

Healey, P. 1997. *Collaborative Planning. Shaping Places in Fragmented Societies.* London: Macmillan.

Jacobsen, S. E. 1994. *Etter sytten års arbeid: Generalplanen er nå ferdig. Et studie i generalplanarbeid i Bømlo kommune med vekt på arealplanlegging.* Hovedfagsoppgave i geografi. Universitetet i Bergen: Institutt for geografi.

Jensen, R. 1980. *Moderne norsk byplanlegging blir til.* Trondheim: Nordplan.

Kleven, T. 1997. *Et forsøksvis testamente.* Plan nr. 1 og 2.

Lindblom C. E. 1959/73. The Science of "Muddling Through". In A. Faludi (ed.), *A Reader in Planning Theory.* Oxford.

Lyssand Sandberg, S., and I.-L. Saglie. 1995. *Tettstedsareal i Norge. Areal pr. innbygger 1970-1990 i 22 tettsteder i Norge.* NIBR-rapport 1995: 3. Oslo: NIBR.

Magerøy, N. M. 1992. *Plan og resultat. Ein studie av generalplanarbeidet i Kvinnherad kommune med hovedvekt på arealplanlegging.* Hovedfagsoppgave i geografi. Universitetet i Bergen: Institutt for geografi.

Merak, E. 1997. *Fra planlegging på papiret til virkeligheten. Et studie av general--- og kommuneplanarbeidet i Stranda kommune med hovedvekt på arealplanlegging.* Hovedfagsoppgave i geografi. Universitetet i Bergen: Institutt for geografi.

Nyhuus, S. 1996. *Grønnstrukturens vilkår i kommunal arealplanlegging på Hønefoss 1965-1995.* MILKOM-notat 12/96. Oslo: NIBR.

Nyhuus, S. og A.-K. Halvorsen Thorén. 1996. *Grønnstrukturens vilkår i kommunal arealplanlegging 1965-1995.* MILKOM notat 15/96. Oslo: NIBR.

Offerdal, A. 1992. *Den politiske kommunen.* Oslo: Det norske samlaget.

Sager, T. 1993. *Paradigms for Planning: A Rationality-Based Classification.* Trondheim: Norwegian Institute of Technology.

Sager, T. 1994. *Communicative planning theory.* Aldershot: Avebury.

Saglie, I.-L. and S. Lyssand Sandberg. 1996a. *Elverum tettsted 1964-1990. Planer og arealutvikling.* NIBR-rapport 1996: 7. Oslo: NIBR.

Saglie, I.-L. and S. Lyssand Sandberg. 1996b. *"Vi holder oss til planen." Sandefjord tettsted 1961-1993. Planer og arealutvikling.* NIBR-rapport 1996: 14. Oslo: NIBR.

11 Differing Agendas in Community Development: The Case of Self-build

SUSAN HUTSON AND STUART JONES

This paper arises from a two-year evaluation of a self-build scheme in Wales run by a children's charity in which vulnerable young people built six two-bedroomed houses. These houses were developed and owned by a Housing Association and four of the twenty-nine young builders rented houses at a reduced rent when they were completed. There were various problems throughout the two years---notably in a time over-run. The original scheme was meant to last twelve months. In the end it took double this time. The total cost of the scheme was originally estimated to be £350,000. In the end it cost £500,000. What, apparently, went wrong? The main answer lay in the lack of fit between a one-off community scheme and the UK housing and labour markets as well as mainstream training structures. A second answer lay in the different agendas of the housing, support and training agencies who necessarily combined in community self-build. This raises broader questions about community development.

Self-provided and Self-built Housing

Surprisingly, self-provisioned housing makes up the majority (around 70 per cent) of detached, owner-occupied houses in many western European and Scandinavian countries (Duncan and Rowe, 1993). This is not so in the UK, where they make up only 18 per cent. The main reasons for this are the predominance of speculative building which combines with complex planning laws and building regulation as well as the high cost of land (Clapham et al., 1993).

Until the last decade, self-build housing in Europe has been largely the preserve of individual households with sufficient income to obtain a mortgage, together with some initial construction skills who have built, part-built or simply contracted out the building processes of their house for their own ownership. Such households have been in employment, often building in the evenings and weekends. Where the household contracts out much of the building processes, the term "self-provisioning" is used and it may involve putting up a kit house on a ready-prepared site (Barlow, 1992). Pure "self-build", where all the construction is taken on by the owner, is a minority option within self-provisioning.

The advantages of this kind of self-provision and self-build are principally in the savings which can be gained through the input of self labour. This varies from between 5 and 30 per cent depending on the labour input. Higher standards, larger unit size as well as choice and control can be gained in this type of housing. Duncan and Rowe (1993) go on to say that, contrary to many opinions, self-provision is not associated with backwardness, peripherality or lack of market development. They point out that self-provision lowers the money cost of housing and usually ensures higher quality. The self-provision sector will compete directly with the capitalist economy and present a different market environment. Housing cycles may be calmed and spatial polarisation less severe. The net result is likely to be a decline in speculative behaviour and a concentration on longer-term efficiency.

Even in countries where self-provisioned building is much more of a mainstream route into housing, single people, lone parents and unemployed people are unlikely to be involved (Duncan and Rowe, 1993). This is explained by their lack of finance, self-confidence, time and energy. A similar lack of advantage in the black economy is highlighted, in the UK, by Pahl (1984) who showed that it is working people who can gain here because they have the necessary skills, contacts and tools. Ironically, people in housing need are not generally in a position to self-build or self-provide housing because they do not have necessary financial backing or ability to undertake a long-term project.

Community Self-build for Disadvantaged Young People

The Community self-build movement in the UK began in the 1980s and was a deliberate attempt to promote self-build and bring into it people who were in housing need but lacked the necessary financial resources or the skills. Many schemes targeted disadvantaged and unemployed young people. Using the "empowerment model", community self-build has tended to involve people with chaotic lifestyles, already distanced from training and the labour market. Thus community self-build differs from housing self-provision in its history, its structure, its objectives and its target group.

The aims of community self-build were clearly to change society although this element can also be evident in self-build by individuals. However, in community self-build, with its particular client group, the underlying aim is more about changing lives rather than society (Holman and Gillon, 1994). A

206

similar mix of missionary zeal, philanthropy and practical community work has supported much of the UK voluntary sector since the 19th century.

The first scheme, Zenzele, was distinctive in being a scheme for ownership and it was also distinctive in its success (Holman, 1996). In the early 1980s, a group of twelve young unemployed people were brought together in the aftermath of race riots in Bristol to build a block of twelve flats. Several of them had had previous construction industry experience. Social Security (DHHS) agreed that they were eligible to receive benefits whilst working on the project. Mortgages for purchase were arranged with a building society and interest payments were covered by Social Security. On completion, all but one of the builders gained full-time employment in the construction industry. Most significantly, the value of the flats rose from £12,000 on completion in 1985 to £45,000 in 1988 (Serventi, 1994). The owners sold up and moved on. It was clear that success rested on external market forces.

Unfortunately, the Zenzele scheme proved hard to replicate. The two building societies which had entered self-build withdrew as a number of houses were abandoned in the housing slump. At the same time, Social Security payment of mortgage interest was not available for the first nine months. From this date, community self-build schemes built for rent only. From the mid-1980s, general economic trends worsened in the UK. Youth unemployment deepened, leaving little hope for employment for unskilled school leavers. Youth homelessness soon became a recognised social problem as Social Security restrictions hit young people, particularly those under 16. In some ways, the need for community self-build was even greater---to provide training and housing for increasingly disadvantaged and disenfranchised young people. At the same time, market forces---in their influence on mortgages, property prices and jobs---became less favourable, creating problems for community self-build (Holman, 1996).

At this time, a number of pressure groups entered the arena---Walter Seagal, Community Self-Build Agency and CHISEL. Their pressure led the Housing Corporation to make housing money (HAG) available through Housing Associations on condition that projects showed 20 per cent savings over contractor construction costs. By 1995 there were twenty-two such self-build schemes in the north of England alone (Holman, 1996). Over the same period, Charity Projects, in a programme named "Building Young Lives", put aside £333,000 to fund development workers in 10 young people's projects (Levine, 1994).

Community Self-build Looks Like an Ideal Solution

The area of south Wales where the particular community self-build scheme was situated was in the valleys. Here the closure of coal mines from 1945 to

1989 had left high rates of unemployment and the economic raison d'être of the area disappeared. Relatively poor communication with the prosperous capital city, Cardiff, and the M4 corridor from England, as well as a lack of flat land for development, worked against new industries. The valleys had an ageing population with poor rates of health and high rates of welfare dependency.

With a lack of external investment, it is not surprising that "community" is envisaged as performing such an integral role in the area's regeneration. Like other ex-mining communities, those of the valleys have been noted for their close-knit social structures and the mechanisms of reciprocity and solidarity which these support, although there has undoubtedly been a tendency towards the romanticisation of these structures (Adamson, 1997). More recently, European money has been targeted at the valleys where indicators of poverty qualify the area for Objective 1 money, available in only five other UK areas.

Against this context of economic restructuring and social exclusion, what better way to address the problem facing young people than community self-build? A report in 1995 found high rates of homelessness and rough sleeping in the valleys, particularly amongst 16- and 17-year-olds (Hutson and Jones, 1997). What better way to address the homelessness problem than to provide homeless people with the skills and opportunity to build their own homes? It is, in essence, an idea of ideological and pragmatic appeal. Importantly, it arouses considerable public resonance and support.

The Valleys' Self-build Scheme

The Valleys' self-build scheme was launched in 1994. Initiated by a children's charity, the aim of the project was to provide a "roof over their heads, a chance to learn, a sense of involvement and a genuine involvement" (Serventi, 1994). In partnership with a local housing association, six two-bedroomed houses were built on a site close to the town centre. The houses were built of Masonite---pressed wooden sheets which can be cut and manipulated by relatively unskilled labour. The majority of the young builders were under 18 years old and a number were care-leavers. A third were women.

During the building period, the young builders spent a day a week in college and qualified for a training allowance of £45 a week. In fact, the training broke down after a year because the young builders were alienated from a college environment, the training was at too high a level and, although efforts were made to modify the course, delays in this lead to apathy. Although qualifications were not passed, the young builders gained some training on the building site and this was one of the strong points of the scheme. As one young man said (Hutson and Jones, 1997): "In college we just build stuff up just to knock it down. Up here at least we see something at the end of it. I don't just want to work for fuck all".

This contrasts markedly with attitudes to the government "training opportunities" of the time (Furlong, 1992). Accounts (Craine in McDonald, 1997) show considerable dissatisfaction and cynicism amongst young people and a deep reluctance to enter into schemes perceived as "slave labour" or "working for nothing" (Jones, 1994).

The Success of Community Self-build

The evaluations of a number of self-build schemes in the UK (Turok, 1993; Levine, 1994; Lee, 1996), together with the experience of the Valley's scheme shows that the main success of community self build is in improving the self-esteem of the self-builders. This arises from the long-term commitment achieved, the specific skills acquired as well as being involved in a job which is seen to be important and worthwhile. Turok (1993: 47) says, of a scheme in Glasgow: "Most participants gained a sense of achievement and interpersonal skills from working as a group on a practical project" and, in evaluating ten schemes funded by Charity Project, Levine (1994: 7) states that self-build contributes not only secure housing but also "serves to boost their confidence". Young people on the Valleys' project did not usually talk about self-esteem but the following comparison by one young man of work on the site with his previous unemployed situation indicates a change. Before, he was "bored shitless and got into trouble, everything from fighting to pissing people off on purpose like" (Hutson and Jones, 1997: 17).

Practical Problems of Self-build Schemes

However, self-build evaluations and the Valleys' project show up a number of serious problems which can be summarised thus:

The Cost of Housing

In professional self-provided or self-built housing, there is saving from the input of self-labour of between 5 and 30 percent. In theory this saving or "sweat equity" as it is called, is available as a reward---either in terms of lower rents or as a lump sum to be given to builders, when the building is complete. However, very often, this sweat equity is eroded or disappears as unforeseen costs eat into the capital allocated. In the Valleys' scheme, the contractor's price for constructing six houses would have been £270,000. The cost of the scheme, including support, was £350,000 and so the "sweat equity" was lost. If it remains, problems can occur in its distribution. There tends to be a lack of clarity over how much it will be and tensions can arise over its division between builders who have put in different amounts of labour (Holman, 1996).

Commentators agree that, generally, self-build with unskilled labour does not produce cheap housing (Holman, 1996). In fact, a realistic budget may exceed a contractor-built site. This is because of the hidden costs---of extra site supervision and general social support. Extra costs may also be incurred through buying materials unusable by unskilled workers or by getting in contractors on certain elements of building in order to speed up the building process. Such extra costs are not covered by housing finance. The only option to cover them is to draw in charity sources. However, charity funding, which is being used more and more in welfare schemes, makes long-term planning difficult.

Delays and Work Pace

Holman and Gillon (1994) tell us that "each self-build group can give a list of delays---bureaucracy, funding, TEC rulings, legal contrasts, unforeseen problems on site". Holman (1996) gives us an account of two schemes that took six to seven years to set up and Levine (1994) reckons the average setting-up period as over four years. This reflects the complexity of planning and building regulations. Poor attendance, short working days and short attention spans can all lead to delays with the building process. Turok (1993) estimates that the productivity of young builders on his scheme was 20 percent that of trained labour. Delays in one scheme led funding to run out before the houses were finished which meant that the young people completed the houses in their own time. Delays can mean that self-build, already requiring long-term commitment, becomes an even longer-scale project. Most importantly, delays affect budgets and so final cost effectiveness.

It is perhaps remarkable that young people work at all on self-build projects where the only financial gain is a cheaper rent at the end for a minority. The incentive is very different from professional self-build where the outcome is the ownership of a house. Most young self-builders work on benefit rates or, in some cases, a £10 rate on top of benefit rates. In the Valleys' self-build scheme, money was a frequent cause for complaint amongst the young builders. This was not surprising as it was calculated that the remittance of £45 a week worked out at an hourly rate of 25p. All agreed that, as well as causing them financial worries, this rate of pay acted as a disincentive to turning up and working hard. In this way, poor pay, motivation, delays and the final costs of project interrelate. It is ironic that self-build, as other UK training schemes since the mid-1980s, is intended to instil labour market values without paying real wages for the job.

Entry in the Labour Market

Apart from the case of Zenzele, reports of self-builders gaining work after the scheme are generally disappointing. Turok (1993) shows, in an evaluation of a "rehab" scheme in Glasgow, that the end skills of the workers were too low to gain employment and very few had the motivation to go on to the further training which, in the 1990s, is required for permanent employment. Of the 27 young people who passed through the Valleys' scheme, five left to get casual work and five went on to college. However, it is difficult to calculate what impact working on the scheme has had as the local labour market was depressed and young people take a time to settle into work. An issue particular to self-build is the difficulty which women experience in gaining future employment on male dominated building sites.

Maintenance of Tenancies in Self-build

Where it is reported in evaluations, self-builders often leave the houses they build. This is surprising in view of the relative degree of commitment to the task reported above. In one scheme (personal communication), interpersonal conflict between the builders and lack of furniture were trigger factors in tenants leaving. In another scheme (Turok, 1993), where flats in an undesirable housing area had been "rehabbed", threats from local youths and two subsequent burglaries lead to the builders, who had come from other areas of the city, leaving. In the Valleys' scheme, four self-builders took up tenancies. One gave up his flat soon after, when he went to prison, and two of the young women put in for transfers within the year. It should be pointed out, however, that young people can be understandably mobile in housing at this stage of their lives.

Lack of Fit between the Agendas of Self-build and the UK Housing Market

In terms of delays (and their effect on costs), subsequent jobs and maintenance of tenancies, blame is often placed on the self-builders' behaviour. In fact, however, these problems arise through a lack of fit between self-build and mainstream structures---in terms of housing and labour markets as well as current training and benefit structures.

Community self-build is about building houses in a different way from mainstream speculative building which dominates in the UK housing market. For example, self-build needs to employ innovative building materials and construction techniques, since brickwork and plastering, the mainstay of the average UK house, require skilled labour. Small inner-city sites are the most common for self-build whereas speculative construction is more often on larger, green field sites. All these factors of difference can increase delays in initial planning and building regulations. Overall, to operate a highly technical and long-term project outside mainstream processes is difficult, costly and subject to delay. The amount of work involved is indicated by the statement by a housing association that "the file was three times thicker" for a self-build project than for a mainstream development (Holman, 1996). Such time is money.

Although there are several national self-build advisory groups, these do not make up for lack of knowledge in the local area. The name "self-build" gives the impression that all the necessary skills can be picked up on the job. This may be so for the young self-builders but self-build knowledge at the management and supervision level is also needed. Local building advisors, such as quantity surveyors, may have little sympathy with, or knowledge of, self-build. Pickering and Williams (1991) point out that local authorities can be supportive of community self-build but seldom are because of the complexities involved. Duncan and Rowe (1993) pin-point the mismatch between existing institutions and self-build when they state: "If planners won't allocate land and if financial institutions won't accept labour, then self-provision won't flourish".

The presence of empty houses within the valley is one indication that there are other reasons for homelessness over and above the lack of properties. Under housing legislation in the UK, single people are seldom eligible for social housing even though the demand from families is falling. There is an unwillingness to house single young people due to a fear of high turnover and abandonments, associated with this group. A second reason for this unwillingness to house single people is the pressure from neighbours because of perceived differences in lifestyle and the threat which young people are often seen to pose in terms of drug use and crime within a local area (Pearson, 1984; Hutson and Jones, 1997).

On the positive side, self-build schemes have the potential to help dispel the fears of the public in showing that young people are capable of work and commitment. Self-build can be used to enable young people to live locally in chosen areas. Self-build is an important way in which homeless young people can gain access to housing but changes in legislation and public attitudes would house greater numbers in a shorter time.

Youth Training and the Labour Market

The alienation of the Valleys' self-builders with traditional college-based training has already been noted. This alienation, originating from these young peoples' experiences of schooling continues into college and training schemes. As Jones (1999: 151) points out in her study of young people in the Valleys:

> Limited training opportunities coupled with a perception of training as poor quality or lacking any financial reward have led to a voluntary disengagement form the quasi-work spheres of youth training, manifesting in an initial refusal to participate in or premature leaving of training schemes.

Against this background, participation in the self-build scheme was quite good. This alienation from college was a factor in the failure of the self-builders to gain any formal qualifications. The lack of fit between the college-based courses and the requirements of the self-build site, the fact that the site supervisor did not have the accrediting qualification and so could not assess work on site, the delay over changing the structure of the training when it was clearly failing---all led to the breakdown of the training. This was a particular pity when the on-site delivery of training was clearly successful with the young people.

The failure of young people to enter employment after the completion of a self-build scheme is a direct reflection of the lack jobs in the local labour market. Casual work was available, such as making Christmas crackers, but entry into proper jobs for young people was largely through college and qualifications. As Jones (1999: 15) points out:

> Often young people from marginalised (communities) . . . are seen by some employers as a bad employment risk. Such young people are perceived as work-shy or from unstable families who are without the disciplines needed to sustain a job.

A self-build scheme gives the potential for overcoming this stigma by alternative training but it is difficult to link a one-off scheme to mainstream training and labour markets which are already excluding these young people.

Problems with Benefits

The low level of the Social Security benefits for young people which provided the "wages" on the self-build scheme have already been highlighted. Such low levels of income make it difficult for young people to maintain their accommodation while working on the scheme and then, to furnish and maintain the new self-build house. Few young single people on benefit can afford to live in self-contained accommodation but shared accommodation for young single people has limited success (Hutson, 1997).

Benefits create other problems. The sheer bureaucracy of the benefit system creates difficulties for anyone in a new or unique situation. The policing aim of Jobseekers' Allowance does not fit with the requirements of an innovative scheme. The change over of training benefits to New Deal, in the middle of the Valleys' project, created considerable problems for the young builders and their support worker. The time regulations on these benefits do not fit with the requirements of self-build, and the regulation that young people must be unemployed for six months in order to claim benefit rules out those who are in college or work from moving onto the scheme.

Dependence on benefit creates problems once the self-build scheme is finished. If young people enter the job market, they will lose their housing benefit. This can lead young people into making realistic decisions to stay out of the labour market (Turok, 1993). Moreover, if "sweat equity" is translated into lower rents, the self-builders will not see the gain while housing benefit is being paid.

Partnership Working and Different Agency Agendas

Self-build necessitates multi-agency co-operation, as do many statutory and voluntary projects. Community development is undertaken within a partnership model as funding requires it. Community self-build is characterised by a partnership between housing, support and training agencies. This has many strengths such as pooling resources and the learning which each agency gains of the other's work and client group. However, differences in agencies' agendas were noticeable in the Valleys' project. For example, the aim of housing agencies is to produce houses to time and to budget. The support agency, on the other hand, was working with an empowerment model where the interests of the clients were put first. Such different aims and work cultures can make working together slow and, at times, conflictual.

An example of such a difference could be seen in the selection and maintenance of the self-builders. If meeting deadlines and containing costs are crucial, as they are to housing agencies, then it would be an advantage to employ young people already used to work disciplines and to evict from the project those that fail to keep to keep these standards. On the other hand, empowerment objectives would favour targeting a more vulnerable workforce and would aim to support them rather than evict on the first occasion. Turok points out that there is a difference between a client group that can be helped by community self-build and those that can best do the job. As he says (1993: 500), "The desire for a visible product worked against the objectives of personal development and training". Levine sums up this issue in posing the question:

> Can housing associations, big business organisations, continue to identify with small-scale, participative, less well organised groups of young self-builders---who can deliver the goods but at a cost which does not fit in with housing associations' general approach to development?

Young self-builders themselves are likely to have agendas which are different from the agencies involved. In the Valleys' scheme young people tended to take part for "something to do" rather than for longer-term training aims. The gaining of accommodation was, in general, too distant to act as a motivating factor. Group working, which could be seen by managing agencies as a positive factor, can, for participants, be a difficulty. Lee (1996: 29) comments that the group of self-builders expressed little sense of community with each other after completion and that this was seen as a loss.

Self-build and Evaluation Techniques

The response to social problems in the 1990s is, increasingly, in terms of isolated projects or pilots rather than through broader changes in policies. Moreover, these schemes of pilots must be evaluated in order to ensure effectiveness and value for money. Evaluation is usually about measurement and "value for money". In such a quantitative environment, self-build schemes tend to show up badly.

The main gains in self-build are individual gains in self-esteem but such gains are hard to measure. How do you measure something as subjective and unquantifiable as "having something to do"? Moreover, individual gains are often masked by factors which can be measured, such as the turnover of builders, the gaining of employment and the maintenance of tenancies. In these actions, young people may have many reasons for not complying and so end rates may not be favourable. In the Valleys' project, the self-builders felt that the training was extremely effective. However, measured in terms of formal outcomes, it looked poor.

The success of projects like self-build tend to be measured by young peoples' behaviour---behaviour which is often around drug consumption, criminal behaviour as well as stability in work and housing. After all, these schemes are, fundamentally, about changing young people's lives. If the self-build scheme is over-running or the budget under threat, it is the young peoples' attendance and behaviour which is often blamed. Other factors, such as the structural barriers outlined above, are less visible and not looked for.

Calculating gain against cost, Turok (1993) comments that "The personal gains for the participants were a bonus gained at an extra cost of £66,000". He concludes that "Personal development was achieved but benefits were short-lived in the social circumstances in which they lived". Levine (1994: 94) clearly supports self-build. As he says,

> If self-build is such a good idea and contributes not only secure housing for homeless young people but also serves to boost their confidence then . . . what can be done to reduce the tangle of barriers which contribute to the delays and frustrations?

Is Community Development Empowerment or Exploitation?

While self-build can be seen as a positive way of people dealing with their housing problems and gaining housing of a better standard with an element of saving, it can also be seen as capitalist exploitation of unpaid labour (Walliman, 1993). The positive aspect of self-build is more likely where people have choice and exploitation is more likely to be present where, through lack of provision, self-build is the only way of gaining access to housing. The same dual standpoint can been seen in community development. On the one hand it can lead to the empowerment of individuals and appropriate provision. On the other hand, community development can be used as a substitute for state services, often through unpaid labour. What appears to benefit the local population in fact colludes with the interests of the stste. In addition, a "community" approach can lead to people's behaviour being blamed for ills which arise, more clearly, from structural problems.

Conclusions

Academics have long documented the failure of top-down economic developments and shown how the objectives of the politicians and the experts often do not correspond with the objectives and values of those people on the ground. In view of these problems, it would appear logical that community development is the answer to social exclusion. Self-build, similarly, would appear to present a successful way of solving the lack of jobs and housing for young people.

The evaluations of a number of self-build schemes and the experience of the Valleys' scheme in south Wales suggest that a number of problems occur in community self-build---notably that the housing is expensive and that there are problems of delays and poor attendance. Moreover, self-build schemes do not appear to prepare young people effectively for work and tenancies are not even well maintained.

These difficulties can be explained, in the first place, by the lack of fit between the processes of self-build and the tightly planned, speculative house-building market of the UK. Moreover, the current training programmes for young people fails to cope with the most disadvantaged. The local labour market, in areas where young people will be prepared to work on self-build, are depressed and the entry into reasonable jobs is geared though further education. The self-build experience, although valued positively on the ground, did not overcome these barriers to work for the young self-builder. Young people on self-build schemes can draw training benefits but their rates are so low that they end up working for 25p an hour which is hardly an incentive to attend regularly.

Further problems are created by inter-agency working, which is characteristic of self-build where housing, support and training agencies must work together. It is evident that a commitment to disadvantaged young people will work directly against the production of houses cheaply and to time. Moreover young peoples' agendas and lifestyles work against their labour market involvement. Current evaluation agendas work against recognising the benefits of self-build. Gains in self-esteem are difficult to measure and demonstrate but failure in attendance and increased costs easily show up.

More seriously, community development can rest on the exploitation of cheap labour. This is evident in self-build where work is rewarded with rates £10 a week higher than the benefit levels which can already be drawn. Community development can be used as a substitute for state services. Similarly, "special" projects can replace universal state provision. Lastly, the failure of community development can easily be blamed on the people at the grass roots. In self-build, escalating costs and delays were blamed on the low attendance or low motivation of the young builders. Structural factors are thus turned into personal failings---a strategy well used by both right- and left-wing politicians. What appears to benefit the local population can often provide more jobs and resources, not for the community, but only for those professional workers who run the schemes.

References

Adamson, D. 1997. *Social and Economic Regeneration in Wales: The Roles of Community Development in Community Enterprise.* ERYR Paper No. 1, Cardiff: Community Enterprise Wales.

Barlow, J. 1992. Self-promoted Housing and Capitalist Suppliers: The Case of France. *Housing Studies* 7 (41): 225-267.

Clapham, D., K. Kintrea and G. MacAdam. 1993. Individual Self-provisioning and the Scottish Housing System. *Housing Studies* 30 (8): 1355-1369.

Craine, S. 1997. "The Black Magic Roundabout": Cyclical Transitions, Social Exclusion and Alternative Careers. In R. Macdonald (ed.), *Youth, the Underclass and Social Exclusion*. London: Routledge.

Duncan, S. and A. Rowe. 1993. Self-provided Housing: The First World's Hidden Housing Arm. *Urban Studies* 30.

Furlong, A. 1992. *Growing up in a Classless Society: School to Work Transitions.* Edinburgh: Edinburgh University Press.

Holman, C. 1996. Community Self-build in England: Exploring the Potential and the Reality. *Environment by Design* 1 (2): 185-201.

Holman, C. and P. Gillon. 1994. *Making Self-build Happen.* London: The Children's Society.

Hutson, S. 1997. *Supported Housing: The Experience of Young Care-leavers.* London: Barnardo's.

Hutson, S. and S. Jones. 1997. *Rough Sleeping and Homelessness in Rhondda Cynon Taff.* Pontypridd: University of Glamorgan.

Jones, S. 1994. Social Polarisation in Mid-Glamorgan. Unpublished paper delivered to the Ideas of Community Conference, University of the West of England.

Jones, S. 1999. *Breakdown of the Work Ethic? An Analysis of Labour Force Attachment in a Marginalised Community.* Unpublished M.Phil. thesis, University of Glamorgan.

Lee, J. 1996. *They Didn't Tell Us About the Worms.* London: The Children's Society.

Levine, D. 1994. *I've Started so I'll Finish: A Study of Self-Build Schemes for Young People in Housing Need.* Worksop: Ryton Books.

Pahl, R. 1984. *Divisions of Labour.* Oxford: Basil Blackwell.

Pearson, G. 1984. *Hooligan: A History of Respectable Fears.* London: Macmillan.

Pickering, A. and G. Williams. 1991. Self-build Housing Groups and Affordable Housing. *Housing Review* 40 (3): 62.

Serventi, M. 1994. *Why Don't We Build It? A Feasibility Study.* London: Barnardo's.

Turok, I. 1993. Tackling Poverty through Housing Investment: An Evaluation of a Community Self-build Project in Glasgow. *Housing Studies* 8 (1): 47-59.

Walliman, N. 1993. A Study of Recent Initiatives in Group Self-build Housing in Britain. Unpublished Ph.D. thesis, Oxford Brookes University.

12 Fighting for Survival: A Comparison of Two Irish Community Development Movements

DIARMUID Ó CEARBHAILL AND TONY VARLEY

Introduction

While an unprecedented level of activity has characterised "community development" in Ireland over the past decade or so, somewhat paradoxically the general upsurge has not been felt across the board. In particular, some of the long-established tendencies have found themselves faltering and struggling to survive. This phenomenon will be explored in this chapter by considering two major cases---that of the Muintir na Tíre (Muintir) community council (CC) movement, whose origins date back to the early 1930s, and that of the Gaeltacht community development co-operatives (CDCs), which first began to appear in the mid-1960s.[1]

The nature of the difficulties these two traditions of local collective action have faced will be considered, as will the performance of the central bodies claiming to represent them, Muintir's national organisation and Comhlachas na gComharchumann (Association of Co-operatives). To explore the difficulties attaching to approaches of the two traditions, our discussion will consider their aims, forms of organisation and performance. Activists linked to both movements have recognised that they must assert themselves at the supra-local level if they are to prosper at local level. How their efforts at the regional and national levels have fared is therefore critical to an understanding of their overall position.

Our discussion will be arranged in four sections. In considering the background to the emergence of Muintir and the Gaeltacht CDCs, the subject of section one, we will sketch the general approaches the two tendencies have taken to "local development" and to the organisation of collective action. We will proceed, in section two, to examine the nature of the problems that have surfaced for Muintir and the CDCs in the last 20 years or so. Here the way in which these difficulties have presented themselves on two levels---the local and the supra-local---will be discussed. The topic for discussion in section three will be the manner in which Muintir and the CDCs, at the local and the supra-local levels, have striven to get to grips with their difficulties. A comparison of the predicaments faced by the two movements, and the responses these have evoked at the local and supra-local levels, will be made in our final section.

As forms of local collective action, how are the Muintir CCs and the Gaeltacht CDCs to be characterised? The common emphasis placed on membership participation and on accountability to a membership would appear to locate them among the types of organised local interests Esman and Uphoff (1984) have discussed at considerable length. These authors distinguish between local development associations (LDAs), co-operatives and special-interest associations. The community groups affiliated with the Muintir na Tíre movement in Ireland, first organised as parish councils and now as community councils, qualify as clear examples of area-based organisations. In fact, they provide what is arguably the best example of LDA-type collective action in rural Ireland. As is the case with the general run of LDAs, Muintir sees its CCs attempting to mobilise the local population in its entirety and to combine, in the activities they pursue, local self-help effort with lobbying in pursuit of a range of economic, social and cultural tasks. The CCs typically claim not only to speak on behalf of all local residents but also to confer benefits on all the people they presume to serve.

The big difference Esman and Uphoff (1984: 63) find between LDAs and co-operatives is in the nature of the benefits they produce. To the extent that the benefits that flow from LDA activity are spread widely across a locality, they are akin to "public goods". In contrast, the benefits produced by co-operatives tend, in the first instance at least, to accrue more narrowly to a membership. Hence they veer towards the private end of the private-public spectrum, at least as far as the distribution of benefits is concerned. The Gaeltacht CDCs, although organised formally as multi-purpose co-operatives, are in many ways a mixed case. They possess many of the features of the LDA. As well as being area-based, their memberships typically extend throughout a locality and the benefits of the activities they pursue may likewise be widely disseminated locally.

A pessimistic assessment of the prospects for LDA-type local actors (such as the Muintir CCs and the Gaeltacht CDCs) would be that they run the risk of being "taken over" by local elites. These elites, although they may proceed in the name of safeguarding and extending the community interest, might be said by our pessimist to be more interested in advancing either their own conception of the community interest or their own personal interests. Another suggestion about LDA-type collective actors is that they suffer from a fundamental weakness in that they are over-ambitious in trying to represent everyone and to do too much (Johnston and Clark, 1982: 180). By allowing themselves to be pulled in too many directions, they are likely to fall between stools. In consequence, they risk ending up being ineffective and finding their claims to be representative and effective compromised and contested. A claim made specifically for Ireland in the 1980s is that LDA-type groups (such as the Muintir CCs) were giving way to a more specialised community action organised along interest association lines (see Crickley and Devlin, 1990: 54).

The identity of interest associations, according to how Esman and Uphoff portray the last and most diverse of their three types of local organisation, is drawn from a source other than the sharing of a sense of attachment to a local community or the pooling of resources. Class, gender, ethnicity and religion provide some of the many social markers around which interest associations may form. To the extent that they are capable of accommodating social as well as economic interests and producing public as well as private benefits, interest associations fall somewhere in between LDAs and co-operatives in the sort of aims they pursue and in the sorts of benefits they are able to create.

Background and Early History

Behind the two approaches of Muintir and the Gaeltacht CDCs we can find distinctive perspectives relating to the shape local development should take. These perspectives, at one level, are grounded in deep-seated ideological preferences; at another level they express themselves in the aims of what passes for legitimate collective action and the form it takes. The Catholic social movement that drew its inspiration from the so-called social encyclicals heavily influenced Muintir's basic ideological orientation.[2] Another source of inspiration was the perceived necessity of its founder, Fr. John Hayes, to create an organisation capable of transcending the divisions which civil war (1922-3) had caused in Ireland. Assuaging the effects of class conflict, especially those surrounding the bout of intense syndicalist-style class conflict that broke out between farmers and farm labourers during the revolutionary period (1917-23), was another of Fr. Hayes's pre-occupations. Interestingly, Fr. Hayes's initial idea was to create a federation of producers' co-operatives. As things turned out, the conflicts between different types of producers and, the reluctance of labourers to participate in this co-operative federation, meant that his enthusiasm for co-operative-based organisation quickly waned.

Despairing of organising rural interests along co-operative lines, Muintir had reinvented itself as a national movement of parish councils/guilds by 1937. The expectation of Fr. Hayes and his associates was that these councils, which were to be put together along vocational lines, would pursue the common good by taking on a wide-ranging programme of collective self-help activity. At the start, Muintir was committed to remaining strictly independent of the state. In the event, the activities that the parish councils turned their attention to---such as organising war-time fuel and food provision schemes and assisting in the effort to achieve post-war rural electrification---came quickly to reflect the national priorities of the Irish state. After Fr. Hayes's death in 1957, Muintir moved closer to the state and ultimately came to embrace the UN's conception of community development. This revolved around the ideal of creating partnership-type relationships between official and voluntary bodies. The rapid pace of social change in the Ireland of the 1960s coincided with Muintir's decline. It was against this background that dissatisfaction with the vocational system of representation grew among some Muintir activists. Ultimately, the national organisation agreed in 1970 to the abolition of the parish councils and their replacement by what were regarded to be more genuinely representative popularly elected "community councils".

As formulated in the early 1970s, Muintir's view of community development was based on the principles that its local councils should be representative, be capable of assembling and giving voice to a local consensus and be effective in the pragmatic sense of being able to get things done. What the national organisation had then to say about local-level representation was focused greatly on how the CCs should be constituted so as to be properly representative. As of old, the theory of community development informing the new CCs continued to envisage the creation of a broad alliance at local level, capable of giving expression to the general will of the local community and so advancing the common good in numerous tangible ways.[3] Aside from the importance of using regular elections as a means of demonstrating representativeness, local councils were urged to strive to be effective by planning a certain type of programme of activity. They were enjoined to achieve a mix of long and short-term projects that would reflect a locality's 'social, cultural, economic, educational and recreational needs" (Muintir na Tíre, n.d.: 4-5). In thinking about the conditions for effective community development, the importance of the CC working in tandem with the state was heavily emphasised.

In contrast to Muintir, where an attempt to launch a national movement preceded the formation of the first parish councils in the 1930s, the first of the Gaeltacht CDCs was to appear in Kerry in 1966. Very significantly, the same year had seen the introduction of a state grant to encourage the formation of agricultural improvement co-operatives by providing funding to cover administration expenses and pay the salary of a full-time manager. This grant was to prove critical to the formation of subsequent Gaeltacht CDCs, a total of 16 by 1977 (see Table 12.1).

What also seems to have been relevant to the appearance of many of these co-operatives (7 were created in 1970-1) was the brief flowering of a civil

Table 12.1   Gaeltacht community development co-operatives: shareholdings and employment

Name of CDC	Year of Foundation	Accounts (1)	No. of Share-holders	Paid up Share Capital (£IR)	Share Capital per Member (£IR)	Full-time Employees (2)
Chorca	1966	1983	891	40,320	45.3	9
Dhuibhne•		1998	968	89,929	92.9	5
Iorrais	1967	1981	846	13,346	15.8	19
		1997	956	58,364	61.1	28
Cleire	1970	1983	505	10,916	21.6	8
		1997	646	26,039	40.3	5
Dhuiche	1970	1980	511	9,083	17.8	7
Sheoigheach		1997	567	121,883	215.0	5
Acla (lapsed)	1970	1981	734	8,962	12.2	4
Thorai	1970	1983	56	1,400	25.0	-
		1997	62	5,200	83.9	6
Arann/Inis Mor	1971	1980	375	15,215	40.6	8
	1991	1997	137	8,865	64.7	6
Caomhan	1971	1983	184	6,820	37.1	13
		1996	312	23,057	73.9	7
Chois	1971	1981	596	21,586	36.2	43
Fharraige/Shailear na	1984	1998	907	113,845	125.5	1
Rath Cairn	1971	1983	837	15,000	17.9	7
		1997	1091	74,360	68.2	4
Naom Fhionain	1973	1982	244	17,001	69.7	10
		1994	265	66,109	249.5	-
Leith Triuigh	1973	1983	156	857	5.5	2
		1997	267	3,962	14.8	1
Lar Thir Chonaill	1974	1979	480	6,516	13.6	2
		1997	775	47,073	60.7	-
Inis Meáin	1976	1983	123	5,426	44.1	20
		1997	191	21,975	115.1	6
Na nOilean (lapsed)	1976	1981	1,389	35,708	25.7	47
Arainn Mhor	1977	1980	172	8,050	46.8	7
		1998	186	15,350	82.5	5
TOTAL		1979-83	8,099	216,206		206
		1994-98	7,330	676,011		79
AVERAGE		1979-83	506	13,513	26.7	13
		1994-98	524	48,287	92.2	6

Sources and notes: [1] Data for recent years taken from returns to the Registrar of Friendly Societies; comparable date for earlier years from Breachnach, 1986. [2] May not include employment in subsidiaries and associated companies.   •55 were temporarily employed in FAS schemes and student summer employment in 1997.

rights movement in the Gaeltacht districts (particularly Conamara) of Ireland. Breathnach's (1986: 83) suggestion is that it was the local development groups established by civil rights activists in the late 1960s that "in some cases formed a springboard for subsequent CDC formation". Those active in the CDCs believed that the stress laid on manufacturing industry in the state's strategy for Gaeltacht development was excessive and that more attention should be paid to development based on indigenous natural resources (Breathnach, 1986: 84). "For many CDC activists", Breathnach (1986: 84) suggests, "the preference for natural resource development is ideological: i.e. that the development of indigenous resources under indigenous control offers better prospects for the preservation of the distinctive cultural characteristics of the Gaeltacht".

Another dimension of the Gaeltacht's declining position that the CDCs were to focus upon was the absence or inadequacy of a range of services considered vital to the survival of rural areas. Here the CDCs sought to do something practical about market failure and the reluctance of the state to commit resources to the direct provision of vital services. This they did by turning their attention to "installing and maintaining private water supply systems, generating electricity (especially on off-shore islands), supplying agricultural and hardware requisites, running retail shops and providing community facilities" (Breathnach, 1986: 85).

Constraints and Difficulties

Muintir's difficulties, no less than those of the CDCs, have presented themselves at the local and supra-local levels. At local level the difficulties faced by the Muintir CCs centre around issues of effectiveness and representativeness. Effectiveness and representativeness can be highly inter-related, for once they come to be perceived to be ineffective and weak, CCs are likely to lose much of the legitimacy they possess as bodies capable of representing their local communities. Just as the CDCs have had to contend with some degeneration of the principles of co-operation, the local CCs have had to deal with some departure from the model Muintir has recommended its affiliated CCs should follow.

In particular, the injunction that representativeness is to be achieved by holding regular elections has, in a significant number of cases, tended to be either ignored or very selectively respected. The tendency for the write-in ballot to return locally popular but poorly motivated CC members has become especially troublesome.[4] The experience of some west of Ireland CC activists has been that the Muintir election system, upon which the CC's claim to representativeness ultimately rests, can become a liability when it produces a poorly motivated and inactive membership.

In relation to effectiveness, the national organisation's exhortation that the CCs should take on a wide span of work has come up against the weakness of CCs in engaging in economic activity directly. Where the CCs have been most effective has been in lobbying the local authorities to provide or improve infrastructural facilities and amenities (such as piped water schemes, community centres, etc.), providing recreational facilities and organising leisure activities and events.

Effectiveness, in view of the indifference of some of the membership, the shortage of volunteers and the apathy of the wider community, depends critically as a rule on the efforts and dedication of a small few activists. In the circumstances they find themselves in, these activists see it as lamentable if unavoidable that a few individuals should have to do the lion's share of the work in order to keep the CC going. Reliance on a small group of activists is also seen as potentially risky. The stepping down of veteran activists, in a situation where the pool of activists is always small, may precipitate a transition crisis that plunges a CC into a period of inactivity or even causes it to collapse.

The difficulties of Muintir (the national organisation) have related to the numerical decline of its affiliated CCs. They have also flowed from Muintir's inability to convince the state that it be given sole national responsibility for organising CCs. In 1970, Muintir's review committee had made a point of proposing that the Irish state bestow on Muintir national responsibility for promoting and establishing CCs and for meeting their training and information needs. What was envisaged was a professionally staffed development unit that, with adequate financial support from the central and local state authorities, would serve as the means of servicing the needs of a steadily expanding number of Muintir-affiliated CCs (Muintir na Tíre, 1971: 36-37).

In terms of its actual relations with the state, the best that Muintir has been able to achieve has been to secure intermittent funding to extend the Muintir CC-centred approach on a pilot basis. The development such a pattern of go-stop funding permits, of course, has brought its own difficulties. Another problem in Muintir's relations with the state stems from its relationship with public representatives. Local politicians in particular, who regard themselves to be the only properly constituted local representatives, have on occasion felt threatened by community interests who are seen by them as competitors in claiming to represent local communities (Roche, 1982: 303-4).

Many of the difficulties that national Muintir has faced since the 1970s---declining CC numbers,[5] an ageing activist population and the national organisation's diminishing ability to service its community councils---tended to come to a head in the 1980s. This was particularly so after Muintir's annual grant-in-aid was halved in 1987 (from IR£30,000 to IR£15,000), causing the national organisation to lay off practically all its paid staff.

Two broad and partly inter-related sets of difficulties have confronted the CDCs over their individual careers. What might be described as economic difficulties have made their presence felt in the form of undercapitalisation (see Table 12.and the consequent heavy dependence on the state for investment funds. As serious as undercapitalisation was in itself, it was greatly exacerbated by the prolonged economic recession that gripped the Irish economy in the 1970s and 1980s. In fact, the two largest of the CDCs, measured in terms of the provision of employment, were to fail in the early 1980s.

The second broad set of problems which the CDCs have had to face reflect the manner in which the theory of co-operation has tended to degenerate in the way the CDCs have come to organise themselves. Lucey (1990: 1) provides a succinct overview of the theory of co-operation when he suggests that co-operative principles require that "it is the users who own the co-op, the users who control the co-op and the users who should benefit from the activities of the co-op". As far as the element of current ownership is concerned, it cannot be said to apply in any strict sense to CDCs, given their continued heavy dependence on state subventions and their uphill struggle to survive commercially. Non-local sympathisers and supporters, who are neither patrons nor users of co-operative services, have provided a substantial proportion of CDC shareholders in many cases. The admission of non-users to membership can be taken to represent a basic departure from co-operative theory. As a practice, however, it is understandable as an expedient that has been forced upon the co-operatives by the inadequacy of their local share equity bases.

What about the issue of membership control? Typically CDCs' boards of management consist of ten to twenty elected members. The turnover of board members has been historically low (Commins et al., 1981). Membership apathy, manifested in a general disinterest in co-operative affairs and members' disinclination to exercise their voting rights, has been a serious difficulty for the CDCs, and has been especially marked in the larger ones where management is more professionalised (Commins, 1973, 1978; Breathnach, 1986). Such circumstances were to encourage a tendency for the task of formulating policy to be taken over by the paid managers.

In what senses do the members benefit from the activities of the Gaeltacht CDCs? The desire to serve the community as a whole has seen the CDCs extend their activities beyond economic development and local employment creation to embrace social service and infrastructure provision. The same desire has prompted them to pursue cultural and general community development objectives. Stettner (1986) can link the Irish CDCs with the performance of as many as 48 different activities. In terms of job creation, the

Gaeltacht CDCs were directly providing 206 full-time jobs in the mid 1980s, a figure that compares to 79 in the late 1990s. Far more important than their contribution to direct job creation has been the CDCs' ability to boost the income-earning capacities of local individuals and households.

At the same time, the benefits that accrue from some co-operative-sponsored activity---handicrafts, horticulture and aquaculture are prominent examples here---cannot always be said to have been spread evenly within the localities that the CDCs serve (Breathnach, 1986). When everything is considered, however, the contribution of the CDCs has often been critical to local economic and social survival. Not surprisingly, this has been especially so on the offshore islands; a case study of one of the island CDCs, presents many islanders as accepting themselves that the island itself might no longer be inhabited were it not for the CDC and its projects (D'Arcy, 1990).

So far we have been dealing with the CDCs individually. When Breathnach wrote his paper on the Gaeltacht CDCs in the 1980s, an association of Gaeltacht CDCs was already in existence. It then operated as a network for the dissemination of information and acted as a pressure group in relation to state agencies and politicians. As an association whose coverage was less than total, Breathnach (1986: 99) presents it as having been "constrained by the lack of time available to CDC managers to devote to it, due to the myriad other pressures under which they work". Interestingly, Breathnach draws particular attention to the fact that the association of Gaeltacht CDCs could not really look for assistance to the Irish Co-operative Organisation Society (ICOS), the national representative body for the Irish co-operative movement. The reason why this was so, Breathnach (1980: 100) suggests, was because ICOS was "dominated by large agri-business co-operatives, with little time to devote to the peculiar needs of 'small fry' such as the CDCs". The inability of ICOS to deal with the CDCs through the medium of the Irish language was also something that told against it, in the eyes of CDC activists.

Negotiating Recent Challenges

Improvisation has been central to the manner CCs have adapted to the difficulties they have encountered in operating the Muintir election system. Four of the 15 Muintir-affiliated west of Ireland CCs surveyed in the mid-1980s may initially have held Muintir-type elections, but these were to be abandoned in favour of recruiting volunteer councillors at periodically convened public meetings. Another CC had never held elections, preferring from the beginning to recruit volunteers at its annual general meeting. A merit of the system of recruiting volunteers, according to interviewed western CC activists, was the more committed members it produced. CC activists, in light of the difficulties with the Muintir system of elections and other pressing problems, saw themselves as having little option but to sacrifice some degree of representativeness (in the strict Muintir sense) so as to remain effective. A possible problem with the improvised method of relying upon what are essentially volunteer councillors is that it may contribute to the view of CCs as being under the control of cliques; as such, it may diminish a CC's legitimacy in the eyes of locals and outsiders alike. Of course, as is common with many forms of indirect representation, the holding of elections may provide little protection from the operation of tendencies that give rise to control by elites anyway.

Another condition of effectiveness, some CC activists would maintain, is that CCs steer clear of controversial issues. When issues become contentious, the claims CCs make to representativeness, and the underlying view they tend to have of the local community as a single entity, can be partly or wholly challenged. To preserve the ability to speak with one voice on behalf of the local community, a strong tendency is evident in some groups to avoid dissension-provoking issues altogether. Of course, success here cannot be guaranteed and certain types of issues---environmental ones most recently--- can pose severe difficulties for groups such as CCs that seek to represent the local community as a whole (see Allen and Jones, 1991).

Despite the potential for competition between them,[6] CCs have regularly been able to establish good working relations with individual politicians, going so far in some cases as to co-opt county councillors as CC members. A risk, however, attaches to this practice. One of the western CCs surveyed in the 1980s had been effectively paralysed when two opposed county councillors turned it into a competitive arena of party political point scoring. Many CCs, accepting the essentially clientelist nature of much interest representation in Ireland, have adapted themselves to the system by using politicians to arrange introductions with distant officialdom, or to intervene on occasion so as to expedite CC business with sections of the state bureaucracy.

There is no agreement among CC activists about the likely benefits of incorporation within the formal system of local government. While some welcome the prospect as a means of realising their desire for partnership, others are wary of the notion on the grounds that it is incompatible with the principle of voluntarism and might possibly pave the way for destructive politicisation. What experience also teaches is that the state is anything but a unitary entity and that differences in scale and capacity pose formidable difficulties to anything other than symbolic "partnership". Dealings with certain branches of the state---the local authorities especially---have resulted in considerable cynicism about the state's commitment to any sort of genuine partnership (O'Donohue, 1982; Ó Cearbhaill and Varley, 1988). The deterioration or withdrawal of state services in the 1980s caused disillusion with notions of "partnership" among members of the surveyed western CCs. It even prompted some movement towards a more oppositional stance and acceptance of the use of confrontational tactics against the local government arm of the state.

No less than for the local CCs, the difficulties experienced with representativeness and effectiveness have thrown up numerous challenges for Muintir's national organisation. The single greatest challenge it has faced has been to restore the plausibility of its central claim to be capable of building a genuinely nation-wide movement of local CCs, servicing its affiliated units and representing the "local community" interest in the wider world.

The national organisation's claim to represent the local community sector, as we have seen, has not been helped by the weakness of its affiliated CCs, both numerically and in terms of their ability to make their mark as 'serious players" in the sphere of local development. The reality is that most Irish localities lack a CC of any description, never mind one affiliated to Muintir. Nor has the historical concentration of its organisational strength in Munster and south Leinster done much for Muintir's claim to be a movement whose spatial coverage is genuinely nation-wide.

A conceivably more fundamental difficulty confronting Muintir's aspiration to be a credible national-level representative body has been the tendency for many of its affiliated CCs to stray from the path laid out for them to follow. The gap between the ideal being urged on the CCs and the realities some of them have had to deal with might be taken to indicate that the national leadership is seriously out of touch with local conditions on the ground. Nonetheless, affiliated CCs continue to be urged to hold regular elections and to furnish reports of their annual meetings to national headquarters. So as to improve its attractiveness, an attempt has been made to change the national organisation's image, expand and improve the services it can provide to its CCs and involve itself in new activities. In the early 1990s it was hoped, by sub-titling itself "Irish Communities in Action" and "The Irish Community Development Movement", to revitalise its image and achieve a wider appeal for itself.

Muintir's credibility as a national representative body has been eroded by other negative developments as well. Not alone did the difficulties that overtook it in the late 1980s find expression in a severe funding crisis; they also showed themselves in the partial collapse of the national organisation's representative structures. The response of the national organisation to this state of affairs, one that is comparable to that taken by many of its affiliated CCs at the local level, has involved considerable organisational improvisation. We thus find the National Council being replaced by a new management committee, a body not provided for in Muintir's constitution. For a number of years this management committee (with representatives from eight of the Republic's 26 counties) met two or three times yearly to prepare submissions, make policy decisions and deal with pressing business.

After the management committee failed to meet in 1994, management of the national organisation was transferred to the hands of five national officers. These came to comprise a "national executive committee". Naturally enough, the members of the ad interim management committee and national executive committee consider it desirable to restore the more broadly based National Council. Hopes that things were set to improve rose with the appointment of a full-time president in the mid-1990s. The presence of a full-time president, whose five-year tenure of office ends in 2000, has helped attract some new activists. Still, without full-time community workers, capable of expanding and servicing the network of Muintir CCs adequately, the chances of restoring the national council are regarded as slim by the national leadership.

If community workers are to be recruited, how are they to be paid? In 1992, Muintir's national leadership requested funding to support the training of six to eight community development officers to work under the aegis of the new County Enterprise Boards, which had attracted an allocation of IR$25 million in the 1993 national budget. This proposal did not succeed due to the prolonged delays in setting up these Boards. Early in 1998 Muintir did succeed, however, in securing funding under the LEADER programme sufficient to allow the appointment and training of three full-time animateurs. These have now completed a two-year period organising new CCs in three pilot areas.

In view of the proliferation of partnerships of various kinds in Ireland, Muintir's standing as a national representative body has been seen by its top leadership to depend heavily on its ability to establish partnership-type relationships with different arms of the state. Undoubtedly, the "Community Alert" scheme has been where Muintir has achieved most success in building partnership-type relations with the state in the 1990s. The origins of the Community Alert scheme can be traced to the mid to late 1980s when local vigilance groups began to be formed to protect the rural elderly from attacks by violent mobile gangs. The Community Alert scheme is organised by local community interests in association with the Gardaí (police) as a form of community policing. It has come to be seen by Muintir's national leadership as its best near term chance of restoring the movement's national profile, demonstrating its practical relevance and giving local CCs a new focus and lease of life. Up to May 1998, some 1,121 Community Alert groups had been created, and many as yet unorganised localities still await inclusion in the Community Alert scheme.

As part of its acceptance of the partnership ideal in the early 1970s, Muintir ruled out the use of confrontation tactics at all levels of the movement. Local authority and other cutbacks, however, caused some individual CCs to adopt a more confrontational stance vis-á-vis the state in the 1980s. In a parallel movement that was prompted by accelerating rural decline and state retrenchment in the 1980s, some cracks began to appear in the national movement's desire to shun confrontational tactics in its dealings with the state. We thus find the national organisation voicing concern about the fabric of rural society being destroyed as state rationalisation and financial retrenchment continued to degrade infrastructure and service provision. The proposal in 1991 to close down many rural sub-post offices provoked Muintir's national president to participate in public protests organised by the postal workers' trade union. The movement's leadership also spoke out against McSharry's proposals to reform the Common Agricultural Policy, against the GATT reform proposals and against the radical restructuring and downsizing imposed upon Teagasc, the Irish national agricultural development and training authority. The tendency to withdraw or curtail state-provided services, the Muintir leadership points out, undermines the ideal of "integrated" development and is incompatible with the principle of "cohesion" which was supposed to inform the movement towards a greater measure of union among the EU's member states. At the same time, this "oppositionalism" does not amount to anything like a rejection of the principle of partnership within the national organisation.

The CDCs' struggle for survival has posed a series of challenges for both individual co-ops and for the association of CDCs, Comhlachas na gComharchumann. Comhlachas was re-established in the early 1990s as an intermediary to act and lobby on behalf of the CDCs in matters of common interest. Notwithstanding their underlying financial problems, the CDCs have shown a remarkable capacity to endure. Of the 16 CDCs founded between 1966 and 1977, all but two have survived either in their original form or have been resurrected in phoenix-like fashion, though on a diminished scale. As can be seen from Table 12.the CDCs continue to be involved in a wide range of activities. The bulk of the decline in full-time employment, from 206 in 1979-83 to 79 in the late 1990s (see Table 12. is accounted for by developments in the fortunes of a small number of the CDCs. In particular, there was the mid-1980s collapse of Comharchumann Chois Fharraige and Comharchumann na nOileán, both of which had over-expanded, and a management buy-out of a CDC-initiated business in the case of Comharchumann Inis Meain.

Undercapitalisation, reflecting the weak shareholding structure of the Gaeltacht CDCs and recognised by Breathnach (1986) as one of the major internal problems these groups face, continues to be an issue (Table 12.2). The average share capital per member is still minuscule; in the latest accounts it stands at only IR£92.2 as against a mere IR£26.7 in the early 1980s. What

Name of CDC	Latest Accounts	Main activities/projects	Turnover £	Profit/ (loss) after taxation £	Profit/(Loss) carried forward £	Administration Grants £
Chorca Dhuibhne	1998	Rural development. Social employment schemes. Irish language college. Land reclamation.	504,580	20,222	7,133	33,523
Iorrais	1997	General agricultural co-op. Machinery hire	3,046,201	33,449	482,091	-
Cleire	1997	Community co-operative: Irish summer courses. Ferry service.	71,850	(13,067)	94,898	44,365
Dhuiche Sheoigheach	1997	Agricultural store; special employment schemes; Irish language classes, courses and college	557,472	35,378	(128,246)	33,000
Thorai	1997	Hall. Group water scheme, youth hostel	96,857	182	43,374	40,000
Arann/Inis Mor	1997	Community Development. Heritage centre	124,377	1,980	9,980	40,000
Caomhan	1996	General trading; airstrip; campsite; electricity scheme; handball alley; holiday homes scheme; tourism plan - cultural and heritage centre. Social employment schemes	215,905	12,249	149,038	47,497
Chois Fharraige/Shailearna	1997	Water schemes and bog development; building company (subcontracts); renovation of old school	114,372	9,542	126,351	30,250
Rath Cairn	1997	Community centre	350,58	(9,287)	32,693	33,000
Naomh Fhionain	1994	Land reclaiming; agri-contracting	992,056	17,455	62,929	19,000
Leith Triuigh	1997	Craft shop	13,763	(2,273)	3,857	4,800
Lar Thir Chonaill	1997	Sheep mart and retail stores	197,443	(35,582)	(105,864)	-
Inis Meain	1997	Electricity scheme; water scheme; air service; tourism; diving centre	145,601	3,379	96,385	13,555
Arann Mhor	1998	Agricultural goods; machinery hire. Integrated development plan.	118,050	24,776	258,142	40,000

Sources: Returns to Registrar of Friendly Societies, Udaras na Gaeltachta, Comhlachta, Comhlachas, and individual CDCs.

Note: Above table excludes Comharchumann Chonamara Thiar (1988), Comharchumann Dhun Chaochain (1997) and Ionad Dheirbhile (1997) and other small specialised co-ops (e.g. fishermen, tourism).

Table 12.2 Gaeltacht CDCs: Current main activities and projects, turnover, profit and loss, administration grants

these low figures reveal is that the financial commitment of the members does not typically go beyond their small initial investment. Members, denied any real chance of enjoying some form of "patronage refund" or exclusive benefits as shareholders, have frequently not been inclined to top up this "donation" with annual contributions (Briscoe et al., 1999). The inadequate capital structure poses liquidity problems for some CDCs. It certainly renders more difficult the raising of long-term capital from banks and other sources. What is significant, however, is that the handful of more dynamic CDCs, which have built up their members' share capital substantially by soliciting annual subscriptions, still manage to retain the enthusiasm and loyalty of their members.

What does the future hold for the Gaeltacht CDCs? The financial weakness of CDCs, and in particular their inability to finance further growth, has in some cases been critical in pushing them in the direction of privatisation. The experience has sometimes been that as businesses expand they require more attention than the CDCs, given their very limited resources and their wide range of activities, have been in a position to provide. The employee buy-out deals completed by Comhar Chumann Dhuiche Sheoigheach Teo and by Comhar Chumann Inis Meáin serve to illustrate this tendency. The view, now often encountered, that the CDCs have served a historical purpose but that their business activities can, without appreciable loss to the community, be taken over by private enterprise, indicates the absence of any ideological commitment to co-operative structures per se among some CDC activists (Neylon 1991).

The danger of privatisation, certainly in some cases, is that a private buyer of a core CDC business may decide to change location and thus deprive the locality of the jobs, income and the service that the co-op had been providing. Such a danger raises the question of what is to become of those CDCs that opt to hive off some or all of their commercial activities to private enterprise. Can they hope to sustain themselves solely on the basis of a largely non-commercial residue? What is undeniable is that many of the Irish CDCs have established a track record in satisfying local needs that are not being met by either the market or the state. The capacity they have built up of being able to provide certain services cannot conceivably be sustained without ongoing dependence on public funding.

If the ideal of current member ownership stands for little in the case of the Irish CDCs, can the same be said of the ideal of membership control? The suggestion that their democratic ideals have a better chance when co-operatives are organised on a small scale (see Hill, 1986) sits uneasily with the high levels of membership apathy among the Irish CDCs. Many of the Gaeltacht CDCs have been management rather than membership-led, at least for much of their existence. In the early days of the CDCs, it has been suggested that a lack of appropriate management and administrative skills created a problem that was often aggravated by tensions and personality clashes between managers and board members (Breathnach, 1986: 90-102). Long experience and better understanding have over time greatly eased these managerial problems. A major worry nowadays has to do with finding successors to take the place of able but ageing managers (Briscoe et al., 1999).

Foremost among the problems highlighted by Breathnach's study of the CDCs was the inadequacy of the state's support mechanisms. His conclusion here reflected the lack of comprehensive powers on the part of a single Gaeltacht authority to deal with the multi-faceted aspects of Gaeltacht preservation and development. The existence of two agencies, Roinn na Gaeltachta (Department of the Gaeltacht) and Údarás, one at central government level and the other subordinate to it and having insufficient devolved powers, generated many complexities for the CDCs (Breathnach, 1986: 102-103). As if this was not enough, the CDCs had to commit scarce administrative resources to coping and negotiating with numerous other official bodies. The functions of these other bodies ranged widely across local government and the environment, education, agriculture, social welfare, health, tourism, transport, electricity and telecommunications as well as various other infrastructural services.

After prolonged delay and much frustration, many of these difficulties have now eased, consequent on the delegation to the Údarás from Roinn na Gaeltachta of its administrative functions in relation to the CDCs, with effect from 1 January 1997. It was understandable that Comhlachas should feel uneasy in advance of this change given the trust and good relationships they had built up with the civil servants of An Roinn over many years. Most importantly, the CDCs felt assured that the administrative grants, however inadequate, would continue indefinitely as long as responsibility for the CDCs remained with An Roinn. Under the new regime, substantial increases in the administration and management grants have been agreed by the Údarás in the past two years. In addition, arrangements have been put in place whereby representatives of the Údarás and Comhlachas can now meet to discuss issues relating to CDC-based development efforts in the Gaeltacht on a regular basis.

Under the community development competition (later known as An Pobal Beo (The Living Community)) run by Údarás for several years, many of the CDCs got involved in the preparation of multi-annual plans. As a result, they became more focused in their projects and activities. An unfortunate consequence of this well-intended competition was that tensions could arise between the CDCs and the less well-endowed coistí pobail (parish councils) who also saw themselves as representative community bodies. Such rivalry discouraged CDCs and other local groups from disclosing and co-ordinating their plans and projects with potential competitors lest they "steal their clothes". For their part, the voluntary coisti pobail felt that they had little chance of winning awards in competition with the more high-powered CDCs employing full-time staff (Ó Cearbhaill and Varley, 1993: 148).

More recently, Údarás has adopted a new policy towards community development. As outlined in its document, Forbairt Phobail Buanú Gaeilge (1996), community development is seen as having an important role to play in securing the Gaeltacht's language and heritage. The new policy has committed itself to offering more generous incentives and prizes that are elements in a support system in which co-ops and community groups are encouraged to aspire to improve their performance by preparing integrated multi-annual plans. This subtler and more sophisticated planning regime has been welcomed by Comhlachas. Its hope is that it will be more positive in its outcome than was its predecessor (see Scéim Fhorbartha Pobail. An Ghaeltacht Bheo, 1998).

Conclusion

Among CCs the identification with Muintir is often but tenuous, and the attractiveness of affiliation has if anything diminished with the collapse of the cheap insurance cover scheme which the national organisation had once to offer. Many of national Muintir's problems relate to its inability to assert itself as a force that individual CCs might be prepared to identify with. The view the national leadership now takes is that the movement as a whole will be at a crippling disadvantage in the servicing of existing CCs, and in the organising of new ones, until some external sources of funding can be tapped that allow paid community workers to be employed. With the notable exception of the Community Alert scheme, the effective absence of any market for the sort of services Muintir can provide has proved to be an especially difficult problem for the organisation to overcome.

The importance Muintir has attached in recent times to Community Alert may make sense in terms of its desire to demonstrate effectiveness and to gain a new lease of life. The Community Alert groups, however, are not CCs (in Esman and Uphoff's typology, they would be found among the ranks of the interest associations). It is therefore difficult to see how adding to the number of Community Alert groups can contribute to the advancement of the CC-based model of community development that has been so critical historically to Muintir's distinctive identity and approach to "community development".

Similarly, the community development responsibilities of the CDCs clearly serve to differentiate them from the conventionally organised capitalist firm. The Gaeltacht CDCs have played an important role in maintaining the position of economically weak areas, though the benefits that sometimes accrue are not always spread evenly across local populations. In their early days, the CDCs made a crucial contribution to providing services (such as electricity supply on off-shore islands) which the market or the state had failed to provide. Nowadays, with improved state or market provision, the need for CDCs to supply many of these services has either disappeared or diminished. The multipurpose CDCs, at least when seen through official eyes, have shared with the CCs the same worrying tendency of trying to do too much with too few resources. Based on such a view, there was something of an official consensus by the mid-1980s that the CDCs should abandon their multipurpose pretensions and restructure themselves as enterprise groups.

The CDCs present us with an interesting case. On the one hand, they have substantially owed their organisational form as co-ops to the state's administration and management grant and have remained critically dependent on state support for their ongoing survival. Yet, they have been prepared on occasion to use oppositional tactics against a section of the state, in this case Údarás na Gaeltachta. The protest they organised against the lack of a comprehensive policy to resource the local co-operatives in the 1980s went so far as cause many of them to boycott the community development awards scheme run by Údarás (Ó Conghaile and Ó Cinnéide, 1991: 221). The state, of course, can be accused of pursuing a policy in relation to the CDCs of keeping them barely alive. One major consequence of the state's historical failure to provide the CDCs with enough money or an adequate career structure is that they have experienced a persisting problem in retaining high quality managers. As long as they can count on the annual administration and management grants, however, the CDCs find themselves in an infinitely better position as regards funding than is Muintir.

It can be argued that alliances such as those presented by Muintir's national organisation and Comhlachas, if they are to maintain their position over time, have to be adept at re-inventing themselves. In the distant past, Muintir's self-image stemmed from a legitimating belief that it had a real contribution to make in transcending class warfare and civil war divisiveness in rural Ireland. The issues that dominated public life in the 1930s have now been left behind (at least in their original form and intensity) and Muintir has found itself scrambling to find a new self-image and mission for itself. This it has done, up to a point, by highlighting the issues of rural decline and social exclusion (the plight of the old in particular). Lingering on in present-day Muintir are identifiable vestiges of Fr. Hayes's views that patriotism must start at the local level, and that local communities should empower themselves at the expense of national society via collective action organised from below. In sharp contrast to the urgent sense of mission of the early years, however, Muintir's recent history has been marked by much uncertainty among its national-level activists concerning their organisation's identity and sense of future direction.

Muintir's decision to engage the services of a consultancy firm in the mid-1990s to devise a strategic plan for the organisation's near-term development, reflects a conviction that expert help was needed to get to grips with the crisis conditions that had obtained over much of the previous decade. The most striking feature of the analyses and recommendations contained in the strategic plan, however, is that they entirely ignore history. They are, incredibly, presented without any mention or analysis of the difficulties that have historically dogged the efforts of both the national movement and its affiliated CCs.

The embattled positions of the Irish-speaking Gaeltacht areas and of the Irish language more generally, have provided Comhlachas with elements out of which it has shaped a sharp self-image. In comparison, the crisis that Muintir at national level is grappling with is much more diffuse, something that has contributed to the difficulties that national organisation has experienced with its own self-image. As far as aims are concerned, both the Muintir CCs and the CDCs have tended to become more specialised in what they have attempted to do. There is also a certain convergence at the level of tactics in so far as in both cases we find increasing use being made of the notion of "partnership" to develop new relationships with the state. A critical issue is obviously whether these "community" partners can participate on equal terms with their statutory counterparts or whether, alternatively, their position of weakness means that they are merely used and manipulated by the state as a means to its own ends. The evidence, if we are to go by the regular consultation process that has been initiated between Údarás and Comhlachas, is that the immediate prospects for partnership appear brighter in the case of the CDCs.

Notes

[1] The Gaeltacht refers to the officially designated Irish-speaking areas of Ireland. "Muintir na Tíre" can be translated as "People of the Land".

[2] For a contemporary discussion of the issues raised by these social encyclicals, see O'Boyle (1996).

[3] The term "community development" did not come into general usage in Muintir circles until the early 1960s.

[4] Basically, electors can either choose from a list of candidates or they can write in their preferences on an empty ballot paper.

[5] A severe blow to Muintir's ability to convince CCs to remain affiliated, or to attract new ones to the fold, was struck by the collapse of the group insurance scheme that

had acted as a powerful incentive to affiliation.

[6] Direct competition with politicians is likely only when CCs make representations on behalf of individuals (as in housing or planning permission application cases), an eventuality many of them try to avoid.

References

Allen, R. and T. Jones. 1990. *Guests of the Nation: The People of Ireland versus the Multinationals*. London: Earthscan Publications.

Breathnach, P. 1986. Structural and Functional Problems in Community Cooperatives in the Irish Gaeltacht. In D. Ó Cearbhaill (ed.), *New Approaches to the Development of Marginal Regions: The Organisation and Development of Local Initiative, Vol. 2*. Galway: 8th International Seminar on Marginal Regions in Association with University College, Galway.

Briscoe, R., D. McCarthy and M. Ward. 1999. Serving the Periphery: Community Co-operatives in Western Ireland. *Review of International Co-operation* 92 (1).

Commins, P. 1973. Some Sociological Aspects of Agricultural Co-operation. In J. F. Heavey, B. Kearney, and S. J. Sheehy (eds.), *Agricultural Economics Society of Ireland Proceedings 1973*. Dublin: Agricultural Economics Society of Ireland.

Commins, P. 1978. Co-operatives in a Modern Commercial Environment. In *People and their Co-operatives*. Dublin: Irish Agricultural Organisation Society.

Commins, P., J. P. Frawley and M. H. Igoe. 1981. *Community Co-operatives in Disadvantaged Areas*. Dublin: An Foras Talentais.

Crickley, A. and M. Devlin. 1990. Community Work in the Eighties---An Overview. In *Community Work in Ireland: Trends in the 80s, Options for the 90s*. Dublin: Combat Poverty Agency.

D'arcy, D. P. 1990. *Cooperating Communities? A Study of the Inishmaan Community Cooperative*. Unpublished M. A. thesis, Department of Political Science and Sociology, University College, Galway.

Esman, M. J. and N. T. Uphoff. 1984. *Local Organizations: Intermediaries in Rural Development*. Ithaca: Cornell University Press.

Hill, S. 1986. *Competition and Control at Work*. London: Heinemann,

Lucey, D. I. F. 1990. A review of cooperative principles and their application to today's business environment. Paper presented to the Society for Cooperative Studies in Ireland, Dublin, 12 December.

Neylon, M. 1991. *The Co-operative Firm or the Capitalist Firm? A Choice in Rural/Community Development Strategy.* Unpublished MRD thesis, Department of Economics, University College Galway.

O'Boyle, E. J. (ed.). 1996. *Social Economics: Premises, Findings and Policies.* London: Routledge.

Ó Cearbhaill, D. and T. Varley. 1988. Community Group/State Relationships: The Case of West of Ireland Community Councils. In R. Byron (ed.), *Public Policy and the Periphery: Problems and Prospects in Marginal Regions.* Halifax: The Queen's Printer for the International Society for the Study of Marginal Regions.

Ó Cearbhaill, D. and T. Varley. 1993. Gaeltacht and Galltacht Community Councils in Ireland. In T. Flognfeldt, J. C. Hansen, R. Nordgreen and J. M. Rohr (eds.), *Conditions for Development in Marginal Regions.* Lillehammer, Norway: Oppland Community College for the International Society for the Study of Marginal Regions.

Ó Conghaile, M. and M. Ó Cinnéide. 1991. Competition as a Means of Promoting Local Development: An Assessment of a Community Development Scheme in the Irish Gaeltacht. In T. Varley, T. A. Boylan and M. P. Cuddy (eds.), *Rural Crisis: Perspectives on Irish Rural Development.* Galway: Centre for Development Studies, University College, Galway.

O'Donohue, K. 1982. How Do People Help Themselves? In P. Berwick and M. Burns (eds.), *Conference on Poverty 1981.* Dublin: Council for Social Welfare.

Roche, D. 1982. *Local Government in Ireland.* Dublin: Institute of Public Administration.

Stettner, L. 1986. Community Cooperatives in Great Britain and Ireland. In Y. Levi and H. Litwin (eds.), *Community and Cooperatives in Participatory Development.* Aldershot: Gower.

Údarás na Gaeltachta. 1996. *Forbairt Phobail Buan£ Gaeilge.* Na Forbacha: Údarás na Gaeltachta.

Údarás na Gaeltachta. 1998. *Scéim Fhorbartha Pobail. An Ghaeltacht Bheo.* Na Forbacha: Údarás na Gaeltachta.

PART IV
COMPARATIVE PERSPECTIVES
ON MARGINALITY AND REGIONALITY

13 Continuity and Change in the Rural Economy: Flexibility as a Tradition

HÅVARD TEIGEN

This is a brief history of the municipalities of Lom and Skjåk over 100 to 125 years.[1] I will ask the following question: In the contemporary economic and social life of these rural communities, what has historical roots and what is fundamentally new? I will also raise the further question: Will a completely new rural economy take shape in the coming 10 to 15 years? It is a truism to state that the recording or documenting of all history is merely the interpretation of history. This means that it is possible to tell completely different stories about historical development same rural economy. In brief: Our heavenly Father can perhaps change the present and the future, but only the historian can change the past!

A common understanding of our not too distant future is that society changes at a steadily increasing and accelerating tempo. In the last 100 years we have been witness to greater changes than in the previous 1,000 years and in the next 10 years there will be even greater changes than in the last 100. I will critically question this conception. There are theoretical schools of thought which point to the large changes we believe are taking place and argue that in a fundamental sense they are superficial. They argue that the "real" developments are connected to our geographical and cognitive maps and the way these maps support a source of internalised knowledge. These theories individually and in combination provide a "path-dependent" perspective on development.[2] In the last 100 years we have also built up a material infrastructure in the form of housing, factories and so on, which provide competitive advantages in relation to the building of new structures.[3] Such geographical and material structures make it easy to understand the significance of natural resource-based production in patterns of development, but a large Norwegian study of industrial development concluded that the most certain thing we can say of the long-term dynamic is that Norwegian districts continue to produce what they have always produced. In other words, there are theoretical arguments to support both the hypothesis that the rural economy shows signs of continuity and the opposite hypothesis: that we are witnessing a new rural community and structure.

Theories Accounting for the Dynamics of Development

Even though the recording of history is basically empirical in nature, more or less explicit theories will determine what the historian chooses to emphasise. To begin with, I will give a short presentation of the theories and hypotheses.

In period of the transition from the old society, based upon production for subsistence, and the new market economy it is probably the case that society was divided between the old and the new. This dual economy theory has been used in different ways.[4] Lewis describes dualism as a dichotomy between the traditional agricultural sector and the modern, market-based industrial sector. The economic dynamic was understood in terms of how highly productive industry attracted labour from an over-populated agricultural sector. This meant that industrial production and modern enterprises could be a source of growth without a reduction in the level of total production in the traditional sector. The reason for this was that the productivity limit was negative or zero in agriculture, the sector's only contribution to economic growth was as a source of cheap labour for industry and the other modern enterprises.

Inspired by others such as Chayanov (1966) some Norwegian researchers have found that there was and is a dual economy between subsistence-oriented production and market-based production, but that this dual economy is rooted in the farmer's household. It is accepted that the market-based, export enterprises which modernised and "industrialised" Norway were timber, fish and shipping. But recent and older research shows that it was also---to a great extent---the farmer's household which was a source of labour for these export sectors. The farmer's household lived with one foot in agriculture and one foot in the market-based economy. The household-based dual economy theory regards the household as a flexible system of production able to accommodate different solutions, for example flexible specialisation or flexible adjustment to economic or natural-resource booms and slumps.

The distance is not great between these two different dual theories and the distinction between the "Fordist production regime" and flexible forms of production. Lewis's dual theory points in the direction of specialised mass production (Fordism) in the agricultural and industrial sectors after the transition from agriculture to industry has taken place. In this case, agriculture will then be integrated in the market. Another theoretical tradition[5] has emphasised endogenous and exogenous forces in accounting for regional developments. Global change-local response can stand for the explanatory paradigm where exogenous forces play a decisive role in development while the local level can only make adjustments or accommodations.

An example of adjustments to exogenous or global forces is found in the theory of international trade and the division of labour between regions based upon competitive comparative advantages. The theory predicts that from the perspective of global competition, marginal agricultural areas in Norway and other regions in the northern hemisphere will cease production while the regions with a greater fertility and cheaper labour will take over and that these marginal areas must simply make the necessary adjustments. Large sections of the traditional industrial sector will suffer the same fate. Norway is a country with high wage levels and long distances to markets and therefore industrial production will globally move to lower-cost countries. The affected regions in wealthy countries must simply make the necessary adjustments outlined by the exogenous-oriented theories. Exogenous forces in the regions of a rich country such as Norway, in accordance with the Clark-Fischer hypothesis, will lead to a reduction in employment in commodity-producing enterprises (primary and secondary sector) and a rise in employment in third sector service-based enterprises. The endogenous theories, on the other hand, emphasise how local actors can exert an influence on development and break from the apparent global trends. Actors seen to be relevant in this connection are politicians, entrepreneurs, organisations and institutions. In the endogenous tradition one of the main questions has been whether regional development is a top-down or a bottom-up process. If municipal actors have had the most important role in the development phase then we can talk of bottom-up processes. If the actors have been national actors, or actors on the EU level, then we can talk of a top-down steering of local development (Stöhr and Taylor, 1981; Taylor, 1996).

In the endogenous tradition an important point involves identifying which actor plays the leading role. Some emphasise companies, entrepreneurs and "economic man", as the driving forces, as in the traditional neoclassical paradigm. They are the driving forces.[6] Alternatively the emphasis is placed upon the institutions. In North's (1990) institutional theory, institutions are allocated a position where they more or less define "the rules of the game". In this theory the political-juridical system is more important than the entrepreneurs and firms. Or simply put, if the rules are favourable, then entrepreneurs and companies will always turn up. In other institutional theories there a more diffuse distinction is made between organizations and institutions. Organisations become institutions, i.e. institutions can be direct actors; they do not just establish the preconditions and boundaries for actors.

Phases of Development

1850-1900: Market Integration, Emigration and Mountain Tourism

As in many European nations, Norway experienced strong population growth in the first half of the 19th century. Evidence of this is found in the two municipalities we are looking at. The population in Lom and Skjåk increased from 3,401 in 1801 to 5,990 in 1865. The traditional explanation suggested by Norwegian economic historians has been built upon the so-called "stagnation theory", i.e. that agricultural production was characterised by equilibrium in terms of methods of production and productivity. Stagnant technology, the reduction in soil fertility and the stronger growth in population relative to lower growth in the outputs of cultivation combined to create a local economy on its way to extinction. Such a pattern of development formed the basis for Lewis's dual theory and Malthus's theory that development will lead to large-scale famine.

Recent research shows that this was in no way the case. There was no stagnation in technology or the development of agriculture during this period. There was in actual fact a growth in productivity which meant that the largest farmers became rich and could employ farm labourers and servants. There was also a large and growing group of men and women who were developing special skills in hand- and craft-work. Rural communities with many wealthy farmers created an internal market for their work and rural communities with good transport connections specialised and exported their wares (Seierstad, 1995, 1996). In such cases hand- and craft-work took on the form of mass production, existing as a type of transition to industrial production. In Lom and Skjåk a large part of the adult population were partly or completely employed in the hand and craft work area, but because the communities were isolated due to the long distances and poor communication, growth in craft work was limited to the local and regional market.

Even though export and also import to the region was limited because of the high freight costs, the region was not self-sufficient when it came to other commodities. Export was therefore necessary to finance these imports. Traditionally two commodities were the source of export income: the sale of grain (barley) and timber. Horses transported the grain and it was sold to among others, the workers at Norway's first industrial company, Røros Kobberverk (Røros Copper Company). The timber was floated down the rivers, to towns in the east of Norway and to the coast. From the middle of the 19th century transport improved. The railway was extended gradually in stages from Oslo to Trondheim although it never actually reached the two municipalities. The transport revolution was never more than an evolution in the period 1850-1900, but the roads for horse transport were steadily improved and the railway meant that the distance that had to be travelled by horse from Oslo to Lom and Skjåk was reduced from 400 km in 1850, to 200 km in 1860 and finally to 70 km.

Nevertheless, the market and money economy experienced a breakthrough in this period. Many small shops as well as the local insurance company and the local savings bank were founded. In total, it was the number of new organisations and the new institutions which played a decisive role in the modernisation of the old agricultural society. With local commodity production, trading companies, insurance and banking, the local community had the key functions typical of a modern economy. In hindsight we are able to see how important these new institutions were for the rural community. However, until the turn of this century they developed slowly and with difficulty. The bank and insurance company struggled to survive, as were unable to find a key function in the life of the local community and shops came and went like days of fine weather. The profits of trading were low.

Migration from the rural communities left more of a mark. From the 1860s many strong young adult men---and after a while women as well---left the communities. A stream of migrants went from Lom and Skjåk to the modern enterprises in Norwegian society, to the industrial sector and to the building and construction sector. The level of population was at its height in 1865 with a sparse 6000 inhabitants. In the next 50 years 3762 immigrated to countries outside of Europe, the majority to America.[7] There were also many that travelled to America and returned home after a few years. A large proportion of the population born between 1860 and 1900 had therefore been to U.S.A. for shorter or longer periods of time. This emigration reduced the population pressure somewhat, but it also forced agriculture to introduce less labour intensive forms of production. New technology that could rationalise work processes was a solution, but it did not have a significant breakthrough.

There was not merely a migration of people away from the rural communities. From the 1850s there was also the opposite tendency with a influx of people into the rural communities. This was the start of mountain tourism. The rural communities of Lom and Skjåk are located in the centre of Jotunheimen, the highest mountain range in Northern Europe and the English upper class, researchers and their students discovered the opportunities for hiking, hunting and fishing. The first tourist cabins and hotels were built in late 1880s and the seed for a new and modern sector was planted. However, as with other agents of modernisation, it was, at this time, only a small seed providing more incentives and experiences (for the locals as well as the tourists) than income.

1900-1940: Modernisation with the Arrival of the Car

In the period between 1900 and 1940 the transportation revolution came to the mountain communities of Lom and Skjåk and the car became the saviour. Although the first petrol-driven transport appeared around the summer 1910 the two rural communities were still dependent on horse transport during the winter until sometime between the wars. With the car as a source of transport and as an alternative to the steam machine, the processing of agricultural products and timber was revolutionised. Telecommunications also arrived during this period. Beginning in the 1890s, two local telephone companies gradually began to lay lines throughout the rural communities.

Alongside the car, the development of electricity was also an important precondition for the general development of the area. The first water-based electrical power station was built in 1918 and created the foundation for the modernisation of the farms, the sawmill and the agricultural processing industry.

- There were numerous small creameries and dairies throughout the region. Within a short period of time these were turned into two large companies which mass produced butter and cheese.

- The same thing happened to the area's many small mills. Within a short amount of time they were closed and replaced by three large grain refinement mills.

- In the timber industry the many small sawmills were re-organised into two-three large industrial sawmills with long production seasons.

- Motor vehicle transport was an enterprise in itself. Three companies were formed to cater to the growing needs of transportation connected with the local population, tourism, transport and other products.

- In retail trade the consumer co-operative was introduced and organised most of the trade taking place in the rural communities. One large trading company in the centre of the municipality and four or five smaller co-operatives were established.

During this period nearly all the "modern" elements were established in the rural community. There was a new infrastructure with roads, telephones and electricity, and further processing of agricultural produce and forest resources. Above all, the companies that had been established in the 19th century were the source of expansive development. The insurance company, the bank and the traders were responsible for raising and were now in turn one of the forces in the modernisation process. The old society based upon self-subsistence was now replaced by one based upon specialised production.

1940-1980: State-led and Corporate Modernisation

The period between 1940 and 1980 was characterised by a strong structural change in agriculture and forestry. In agriculture they began to replace the horse; by the end of the period there was hardly a work horse to be seen. Servants and hired help more or less disappeared completely from the farms and the farms became family enterprises in the sense that they used almost exclusively the labour power of family members.

Better designed and more specialised modern production buildings and barns were built to replace the old subsistence form of farming which had many different buildings including one for each form of livestock. Specialised cowsheds were built and with the introduction of new techniques (the milking machine and milk collection in tankers rather than churns) many switched from milk production to less capital-intensive production: pigs, sheep and just corn production. In forestry rationalisation took place even more quickly. The forest tractor replaced the horse and floating timber on the river lost out to road transport. Most significant to the revolution was the motor-saw which meant that the need for lumberjacks was greatly reduced.

The need for labour power in farming was greatly reduced causing significant flight from the rural community was significant. Nevertheless, the level of population remained the same and in 1970 a new period of growth even began. Three factors account for why rationalisation in the primary sector didn't lead to a corresponding reduction in the population:

- The old agriculture and forest-based industry changed from seasonal employment year round employment. This actually resulted in a slight rise in the number of jobs in the old industry.

- New forms of industrial activity arrived. The most important was the manufacturing of furniture which created about 100 new jobs. In addition a mechanical workshop (offshore industry) was established along with some smaller varied industrial enterprises.

- Tourism and other forms of private service provisions increased as a result of growing personal spending power and more leisure time. New hotels, motels and camping sites were built and traders benefited from the tourists. At the end of this period there was an increase in the level of interest in "mountain activity tourism": summer skiing, river paddling, etc.

- Last but not least, the welfare state employed greater numbers. Women entered the labour force, often employed by the municipality in care-giving occupations. This part of the public sector also provided work for the steadily increasing portion of the population with higher education.

In this period the (national) state played a leading role as an actor in both the business sector the welfare state by acting with and organising different interests. The corporate connections between the central authorities and national organisations were a powerful driving force in Norway (Pekkarinen, 1992; Slagstad, 1998).

In the agricultural sector there was an organised co-operation between the state and farmers' associations, which worked towards the "industrialisation of agriculture". The state was an important driving force with an extensive administration and increasing economic subsidies directed towards a future-oriented agriculture which could provide an income for the farmer's entire family. The state was also active in modern sectors such as industry and tourism. State banking services were established to cater to growth and changes in the private sectors and regional policy gained its own development fund. National standards in welfare policy led to a more equal standard of living between people and regions than was the case in other comparable countries.

1980-2000: Neo-Fordism and New Elements

In the course of the 1970s many long-term trends changed. A large amount of offshore oil was discovered in the Norwegian North Sea. The new wealth in oil has made it possible for the state to greatly increase subsidies awarded to different groups and regions. On the other hand, many of the state's goals and interests have changed. In agriculture, income increased significantly through state subsidies in the 1970s, but as in many other countries, this resulted in over-production. In the 1980s this was a closed sector, where the most important product, milk, was regulated by quotas. After a while the state abandoned the goal of income equality between farmers and industrial workers. Optimism in these agricultural communities gradually turned into pessimism.

The state also gradually abdicated its role in regional policy. State subsidies were reduced and more power and responsibility was delegated and decentralised to the county and local municipality (Teigen, 1999). State ambitions in regional policy were reduced and instead economic and business policy was directed towards the realisation of economic growth. This developmental trend was especially visible in the 1990s. The Regional Development Fund responsible for regional policy was merged---in a subordinate position---with a business development policy agency. In this period no new elements made their entry into the business life of these rural communities.

- Industry has gone through a number of crises in this period, but the companies and jobs have been saved.

- The tourist branch has experienced some growth and renewed itself with a greater emphasis on activity, knowledge and culture-based tourism.

- The numbers employed in agriculture is still decreasing, but in an impressive manner it has managed to consolidate its position.

- As a whole employment in the public sector has continued as a growth area during this period, the "caring municipality" has been further developed.

This stabilisation of "business enterprises", measured in terms of the number employed and the number of companies, disguises two large and important changes in employment and economic life:

The first change is the entry of women into the labour market. This started in earnest in the 1970s, but in the course of the 1980s and 1990s it became normal for women to have paid work outside of the farm and the home. This put a pressure on the local labour market. Before, it was enough for the male spouse to find work in the rural community, but now both spouses wanted employment. This made it more difficult to recruit new households to the rural community. The second large structural process of change was connected with the absorption of locally-owned companies by national concerns. The local insurance company merged with what is now Norway's second largest financial corporation. The dairy processing plant was merged into a co-operative for the whole of the eastern region of Norway thus losing its local management. The agricultural co-operative has merged several times resulting in a steadily more distant management. These trends in development over the last 20-30 years are by no means restricted to these two mountain communities. Several of the companies have retained their independent economic status, more than in other places. Most notably the bank and the consumer credit union have retained their local management.

The 100-year Perspective: Change and Continuity

The historical facts highlighted in this brief presentation can be interpreted in different ways by the historian.

The Emphasis upon Change

- The rural community is unrecognisable if we compare 1870 with 1999. In 1870 the settlement pattern in the municipality was characterised by dispersal whereas today a large part of the local population live in the municipal centre.

- In 1870, 10-15 people lived and worked on each farm in contrast with today where only one or two people live and work on a farm.

- In 1870, the majority of the population earned their living from the soil as farmers, crofters, tenants and wage labourers. In 1999, only 20-30 per cent of the population list agriculture as their main occupation.

- In 1870, nobody was employed by the municipality. Today the

253

municipality is the largest employer in the local community.

- In 1870, 80-90 per cent of the production in the agricultural sector was consumed in the rural community. Today 80-90 per cent is exported out of the local community.

- In 1870, the majority of the people had little contact with the urban society and abroad. Today the local community is connected to Norway and the world through the Internet and the most modern forms of telecommunication.

- In 1870, it took two days to travel to the nearest town and a day to travel from north to south in the municipality. Today local inhabitants can travel to the U.S.A. in the course of a day.

The list could be extended to provide further evidence of the enormous changes that have taken place in the last 125 years.

The Emphasis on Continuity

- In 1870, even though the travelling time was longer, the "mental distance" between the U.S.A. and the communities of Lom and Skjåk, was shorter. A greater number of people from Lom and Skjåk had been to and worked in the U.S.A. than is the case today. In short: the labour market was more globalised at the turn of the century than today.

- Even though a greater number of people were dependent upon the soil a 100 years ago, there is today, surprisingly, just as many independent farms as in 1870.

- One hundred years ago it was rarely the case that the only form of income on the individual farm was the cultivation of the soil. Money was earned in the forests, through transport, as craftsmen, etc. In short we are talking about a multi-activity use of time and closer study shows that this is still the case today. It is only on a small minority of the that crops and/or livestock are the main source of income. Both spouses often work outside of the farm.

- One hundred years ago women had the main responsibility for raising families with a larger number of children than is common today and they also took care of the elderly. Today women are employed as wage labourers although the majority of these jobs are still involved with care of children and elderly.

Take-off

We have seen that over a 125-year period there are factors of continuity and of course significant changes. Are there periods where the changes have been especially quick, or have the changes accelerated with each decade?

I would highlight the period between 1900 and 1940 as especially important. Car-transport changed the location of business activity and there were significant investments. The companies established in this period are today still among the most important in the rural communities. The car companies, the co-operatives, the dairy plant, the power station and the saw mill were all established in the space of a few years, between the end of the First World War and the start of the depression in the 1920s. All these enterprises had local owners. It was the organisations from the second half of the nineteenth century that were in a position economically and from an organisational point of view to help the new enterprises. The savings bank, the insurance company, the local municipality and the joint stock company were important in this respect. This indicates how the enterprises established in the 19th century played an important role, but they were not able to change the rural economy in the short-term. They first had to accumulate capital before they could help others.

It was during this period that the rural communities were modernised and exemplified the normal characteristics of the industrial revolution: large companies mechanised production, specialisation and a large export and import of commodities. In agriculture the largest revolution came after the Second World War; in the space of a few years, from 1947 to around 1960, all the farms changed from using horses to using the tractor. At the same time the old farm buildings, and there were many of them on each farm, were replaced with large buildings where all the functions could be concentrated on one site.

The developments since 1960 represent a further lengthening of the structures first established around 1900. After 1960 the large, visible changes in the business sector have been connected with the growth of the "service-society". The growing wealth and prosperity after 1960 has been used to purchase services. Private and public providers of services have been dominant in terms of the number employed. The pattern of development is in this sense totally in agreement with the Clark-Fischer theory about the transition from commodity production to service provision.

What is New, What is Old? Flexibility in New Ways

In my opinion the most important factor in this 125-year period is what we can call "flexibility as a tradition".[8] The only explanation for there being so many

255

farms today compared to a century ago is that they have always been based upon flexible combinations with other activities. The farmer has combined work on the farm with income derived from activities in the primary sector (forestry, fishing), in building and construction and in craft work. He was a forester-farmer, a fisherman-farmer, a carpenter-farmer and so on.

Today it is the "service-farmer" who dominates. And today it is a pluriactive family: both the man and the woman is active outside the farm. The most common combinations are farmer and tourist host, farmer and teacher, and bureaucrat-farmer although the carpenter-farmer is not unusual. Today only a small minority of farmers have an education in agriculture, more and more have a university education. This is also true of the women. Before it was almost always the case that it was the men who worked outside the farm, now it is more and more the case that the women have good qualifications and can gain employment outside the farm. But the sociological phenomenon that "children from the same background marry" is still just as valid. When one of the spouses has a university education, this is usually true of the other spouse. They both tend therefore to work outside the farm, running the farm as a secondary business or with the use of hired help.

In other words, the dual economy still exists, but in a modern form. Agriculture is still practised to preserve an element of self-subsistence, but primarily as a source of flexibility above all things. When other markets are prosperous, the effort devoted to farming is reduced. In bad times, or when the family's need to consume and source of labour is large, it is farming which occupies a dominant role.[9]

Resource-based Renewal

The second factor of continuity is that enterprises are still today fundamentally dependent on natural resources. If we in accordance with economic base theory make a distinction between basic industries and derived industries, then most of the basic enterprises are directly or indirectly connected with our natural resources. This is of course the case with agriculture and agriculture based industry and forestry and the timber-based industry. I would also argue that the furniture industry is indirectly based upon local natural resources. The entire industry is based upon pine as the raw material because we have pine forests. Today this industry could just as easily import pine for the manufacture of furniture, and does in fact do this to some limited extent, but there exists a reservoir of accumulated knowledge founded on these natural resources.

There are industries which clearly are not based upon the local availability of natural resources. One manufacturing company, with about 40 employees, imports its raw material for environmental filters from the U.S.A. This company has a virtual monopoly in Norway and exports to other European countries. A second industrial company produces for the offshore sector and is completely based upon their competence in welding.

Agriculture is the largest basic sector while industry and tourism with equal sectors come in second. Tourism is also fundamentally based upon natural resources. Most hotels survive by selling the natural scenery around them and they organise activities with nature as a production factor. A special success story is the Norwegian master chef Arne Brimi who is the head chef at the largest hotel in Lom which employs some 10-15 chefs. They travel around the world offering their services as cooks and have their "base camp" in Lom. Brimi's famous kitchen, called "Nature's Kitchen", is based upon the use of local raw foodstuff combined with inspiration from French cuisine in the preparation of the dishes. Another successful company is the "Lom Stone Centre". This company produces stone jewellery, has a trading outlet and in addition runs a stone museum which is a large tourist attraction. The company is in many ways super-modern, but natural resources are the starting point for its skills and raw materials.

The third factor of continuity is connected to the type of entrepreneurs in the local economy. Most companies are either family enterprises or companies under collective ownership, i.e. co-operatives or a corresponding form of collective ownership. I have earlier chosen to call them "third sector companies". These companies are traditionally neither private nor public. On the other hand, the tradition the rural communities lack is the "Schumpeterian" form of entrepreneur. Two to three of the larger companies were founded by typical entrepreneurs, but in these rural communities they represent the exception more than the rule.

From Endogenous Control to Management from Afar

The modernisation process in rural Norway took place from the bottom upwards. The telephone company, the insurance company, the bank, the electricity company, the dairy and the consumer co-operative were all local in origin. They had local owners and produced for a local market.

From this common starting point they have developed in different ways. The bank, co-operative and electricity company are still locally owned and locally managed. But most of the enterprises have been taken over by national companies with their strategic head offices in the capital. The national telephone company has now merged with the Swedish telephone company and has its head office in Stockholm. Viewed from the perspective of the rural community, the economic development of the business sector has for a long time moved from endogenous management towards exogenous leadership. If we look at the public sector the picture is the same. The rural community has on the one hand, become more and more dependent on state subsidies and grants, especially in agriculture while on the other hand, the state has intervened and stopped the local community earning income from its natural resources. Twice in the past 30 years the municipalities have had applications for the development of water resources into electric power refused. It is now the case that nearly all the area's waterfalls are governed by conservation orders. This is also true of large areas of mountain terrain where different forms of environmental restriction make their economic exploitation difficult. In the last decade the preservation of wildlife, such as the lynx, wolverine and bear, have made it more and more difficult to raise livestock. This is particularly the case with the rearing of sheep because they graze in the forests and mountains.

Globalisation?

A commonly accepted view is that all economies, large or small, peripheral and in the districts are more and more strongly integrated into the world economy. All can highlight the influence of globalisation, but often with a level of precision which makes it difficult to measure if we have really entered the turbo-capitalist phase, where labour power, capital, commodities, culture and so on regard the world society as their own back yard or "home venue" (Bairoch, 1996). Globalisation can be both a threat and an opportunity. A common market for food is without doubt the greatest threat faced by rural communities in Norway. Many are of the opinion that the threat is real and that it will be felt as Norway through the WTO agreement is forced to reduce trade restrictions on food commodities. However, the rate of reduction is so slow that there is no need for anxiety in the next 10 years.

If we compare rural communities today with those from a 100 years ago we find that a larger portion of the population was more directly dependent upon on the world market and its prices then than is the case today. I would argue that never has such a large section of the population had its employment in protected sectors. Both those in public employment and a significant number of those engaged in the private service sector are in the short run little influenced by fluctuations in the international economy. Norway is a society with a significant dependency upon oil and its price. It is this which has the strongest influence on the rest of the rural economy, but it is nonetheless an indirect influence.

The labour market, as we have argued in this article, is less globalised than 100 years ago when emigration to the U.S.A. was a viable alternative for the new generation. The greatest change in today's labour market has nothing to do with the state of globalisation, instead it is related to the ongoing educational and feminist revolution. What is new in the rural economy is that the labour market must try to satisfy the ambitions of women and a highly educated labour force. The market for capital, on the other hand is nationalised and globalised. While the rural population previously invested locally, they now invest for the most part in shares quoted on the Oslo stock exchange. This means that their investment capital becomes part of a national company which operates globally, and is invested in international shares and funds. This marks the latest shift in the rural economy, one we have seen developed during the last five years. Before investment capital went from the centre to the districts, now it is the opposite.

Despite different tendencies in a number of directions: local orientation via the regional to the national and the global, in my opinion there is a clear main tendency identifiable over the last 30 years which is that the national level has become more important for the local community. Most of the private companies located in the Lom and Skjåk municipalities have their head offices in the capital, Oslo. The state, especially through local government (the municipality) has been more important as a place of work, a site for the welfare state and as a regulative regime. Within the regulating regime there is also evidence of internationalisation. A special agreement means that Norway now comes under the EU's rules for competition. It is more often the case that we in the local community are directly affected by a decision made in Brussels through, for example international agreements, meaning that Norway must think in terms of the global management of wildlife---something which rural communities in central Norway are particularly affected by. There is, in other words, evidence of tendencies towards internationalisation and globalisation, but it is the national that sets the framework: change from the bottom up, with management from the top down and the national state on the "top".

Notes

[1] This essay is based upon my book, *Banken som bygdeutviklar: Lom and Skjîk Sparebank gjennom 125 år* (Tano Aschoug Forlag) (The Bank Developing Local Communities: Lom and Skjåk Savings Bank in the last 125 years).

[2] "Path dependence": see Arthur, 1989, 1994; Krugman, 1991; Storper, 1992.

[3] See the "sunk cost" literature, e.g. Hayter, 1997.

[4] The dual economy theory has its strongest origins in the work of Lewis, 1954. Most well-known is perhaps North, 1981. This model has been used in Norway by Hodne,

Flexibility as a Tradition

1973; Teigen, 1976; and Wicken, 1997.

[5] Fischer, 1935, 1939; and Clark, 1940 have both received the honour of having first developed the theory, having done so independently.

[6] Schumpeter, 1983.

[7] Hosar, 1998.

[8] "Chayanov's Rule".

[9] But the co-operative movement is, of course, international (Birchall, 1997)

References

Arthur, W. B. 1989. Competing technologies, increasing returns, and lock-ins by historical events, *Economic Journal* 99: 116-131.

Arthur, W. B. 1994. *Increasing Returns and Path Dependence in the Economy.* Ann Arbor: University of Michigan Press.

Bairoch, P. 1996. Globalization myths and realities: One century of external trade and foreign investment. In Boyer and Frache (eds.), *States Against Markets.* London: Routledge.

Birchall, J. 1997. *The International Co-operative Movement.* Manchester: Manchester University Press.

Chayanov, A. V. 1966. *The Theory of Peasant Economy* (D. Thorner, B. Kerblay and R. E. F. Smith (eds.). Manchester: Manchester University Press.

Clark, C. 1940. *The Conditions of Economic Progress.* London: Macmillan.

Fischer, A. G. 1935. *The Clash of Progress and Security.* London: Macmillan.

Fischer, A. G. 1939. Primary, secondary tertiary production. *Economic Record,* June.

Hayter, R. 1997. *The Dynamics of Industrial Location.* Toronto: John Wiley and Sons.

Hodne, F. 1973. *Growth in a Dual Economy: The Norwegian Experience 1814-1914.* Economy and History.

Hosar, H. 1998. *Reginal Økonomi og Politikk.* Oslo: Universitetsforlaget.

Krugman, P. 1991. History and industry location: the case of the manufacturing belt. *American Economic Review* 81: 80-83.

Lewis, A. W. 1954. Economic development with unlimited supplies of labour. *The*

Manchester School 22.

North, D. C. 1981. *Structure and Change in Economic History.* New York: W. W. Norton.

North, D. C. 1990. *Institutions, Institutional Change and Economic Performance.* Cambridge: Cambridge University Press.

Pekkarinen, J. 1992. Corporatism and economic performance in Sweden, Norway, and Finland, in J. Pekkarinen, M. Pohjola, and B. Rowthorn (eds.), *Social Corporatism: A Superior Economic System?* Oxford: Clarendon Press.

Schumpeter, J. A. 1983. *The Theory of Economic Development.* Transaction Books.

Scott, A. J. and M. Storper. 1992. Regional development reconsidered, in H. Ernste and V. Meier (eds.), *Regional Development and Contemporary Industrial Response: Extending Flexible Specialisation.* Belhaven Press.

Seierstad, S. 1995. Bedrifter i nisjer og nettverk: Et streiftog i teori og emperi om regional næringsutvikling. AFIs rapportserie nr. 1/95, Bodø.

Seierstad, S. 1996. Regioner i oppbrudd. Regional næringsomstilling belyst med teori og eksempelstudier. AFIs rapportserie nr. 7/96, Bodø.

Slagstad, R. 1998). De nasjonale strateger. Pax Forlag A/S, Oslo.

Stöhr, W. B. and D. R. Taylor. 1981. Development from Above or Below? The Dialectics of Regional Planning in Developing Countries. Chichester: Wiley.

Storper, M. 1989. The transition to flexible specialization in the U.S. film industry: external economies, the division of labour and the crossing of industrial divides. *Cambridge Journal of Economics* 13: 273-305.

Storper, M. 1992. The limits to globalization: technology districts and international trade. *Economic Geography* 68, 1: 60-93.

Taylor, M. 1996. Good government: on hierarchy, social capital, and the limitation of rational choice theory. *Journal of Political Philosophy* 4: 1-28.

Teigen, H. 1976. Økonomisk utvikling i Nord Gudbrandsdalen og på Toten ca 1870-1910. Hovudoppgåve Bergen/NHH.

Teigen, H. 1976. Poteta og Folkeveksten i Noreg 1815-1865. *Historisk Tidskrift* 4.

Teigen, H. 1997. Distriktspolitikken ved ein Korveg, in K. Aasbrenn (ed.), *Opp og Stå: Gamle Norge.* Landbruksforlaget.

Teigen, H. 1999. *Banken som bygdeutviklar: Lom og Skjåk Sparebank 1873-1998.* Tano Aschoug.

14 Appropriating the Margins, Creating a Centre: The Group of Seven and the Construction of Canadian National Identity

RICHARD APOSTLE

Because landscape is the most important product of both power and imagination, it is the major cultural product of our time.

Zukin, 1991: 268

Introduction

One of the recurring problems in Canadian social science has been our inability to articulate a clear vision of what Canada is, as a moral landscape, in North America. Since John Porter's seminal work in *The Vertical Mosaic* (1965) established the intellectual foundations of Canadian sociology, Canadian academics have struggled with the question of isolating a unique set of cultural elements around which a distinctive Canadian national identity might coalesce. We have usually looked south, with some envy, at the direct, if simplistic, ways in which the United States has defined core values which are effectively enforced with assimilationist policies. We also look east, usually with disdain, at the more traditional and unified European cultural heritages we have tried to abandon or escape. But neither envy or disdain help me to evade the fact that Canada has, at best, a tenuous hold on an identity it may call its own.

The Group of Seven, both through its work, and their eventual institutional encapsulation in major art galleries and holdings, has been as influential as any of the various artistic endeavours in providing a strong Canadian identity. This paper is predicated on the assumption, to be examined below, that the social and aesthetic dimensions of art are inextricably connected.[1] This paper will first attempt to describe the Group's activities from a social science point of view, and then assess the strengths and weaknesses of their work.

The Group of Seven as a Cultural Project

There are many ways of understanding or interpreting the work of individual artists or groups of them. Over time, the painters collectively known as "The Group of Seven", have been the subjects of art collections devoted to their commonalities (Blodgett, Bice, Wiston and Martin, 1989; Hill, 1995; Mellen, 1970; Newlands, 1995), or expository works (Harris, 1964; Housser, 1926; Hunkin, 1976). Additionally, there have been individual collections, particularly about the more important figures in the Group (Duval, 1978; Murray and Fulford, 1982; C. Varley, 1981; P. Varley, 1983). There has also been a minor amount of autobiographical work (Harris, 1964; and especially Jackson, 1958), a biography of Lismer (McLeish, 1973), a memoir on Jackson (Firestone, 1979), as well as Harris's intellectual defence (1954) of abstract expressionism, towards which he personally drifted in the later stages of his career.

To date, little of this writing has treated the social elements of their activities explicitly (e.g. Hill, 1995: 15-16) and, when such issues are addressed, they are normally dismissive. This paper, by contrast, takes the position that the artistic work of the Group of Seven is eminently social and political. Further, it seems clear that the social sciences have much to add to a fuller appreciation of the contributions, aesthetic and otherwise, of these painters.

There are a number of aspects of the Group's life and impact which can only be appreciated through the social sciences. First, there is the issue of group composition. The cardinal presence, but early mysterious death (in 1917) of Tom Thomson, has frequently led commentators to regard Thomson as an integral component of the Group. If this is the case, the Group may have eight members, or it may be known as the "Group of Seven and Tom Thomson" (Newlands, 1995). Alternatively, one may propose, as Charles Hill (1995: 17) does, that the Group is better regarded as the "Group of Five", given that Frank (Franz) Johnston was only briefly connected with the Group, and Frank Carmichael, as a full-time commercial artist, was only a marginal participant in the Group.[2]

There is an associated social question about group cohesion. The usual characterization of the Group recognizes Lawren Harris and J. E. H. MacDonald, or perhaps MacDonald alone, as providing the intellectual leadership.[3] A. Y. Jackson and Arthur Lismer, while still core members of the group, were somewhat later associates of Harris and MacDonald, and were regard as constituting the more public face of the Group. Fred Varley, also a full-fledged member, was partially marginalized by occupational circumstances, as well as some interesting lifestyle choices, which undermined his marriage and personal stability. Even with this set of hierarchical connections, the "Group" represented a loose set of affiliations, as joint presentation of artistic work[4] was very much a voluntary undertaking, and other common endeavours like sketching trips[5] were only partially coordinated. Hill (1995: 16) rightly maintains that it is generally "far too easy to emphasize the word 'Group' in speaking of this collaboration". As we will try to establish below, both hierarchy and loose connections affected the Group's activities and accomplishments.

One of the tangible ways in which Group structure was created, and proved influential, was through the key institutional settings around which its work revolved. The issue here concerns the social and physical environment necessary to produce any art work. Howard Becker emphasizes the social dimension when he refers to an "art world" as "the network of people whose cooperative activity, organized via their joint knowledge of conventional means of doing things, produces the kind of art that art world is noted for" (Becker, 1982). Alternatively, Goffman emphasizes the physical "setting" in developing his dramaturgical perspective. He defines a "setting" as "involving furniture, decor, physical layout and other background items which supply the scenery and stage props of human action played out before, within, or upon it" (Goffman, 1959: 22).

The first important pair of settings---the Grip Company and Rous and Mann---were two Toronto firms which specialized in commercial art work, and through which most of the members were employed and recruited. The Group of Seven is quite distinctive in its origins in the commercial art endeavours of Toronto in the early twentieth century; J. E. H. MacDonald, as the earliest employee at the Grip Company,[6] was influential in persuading many of the Group to take up paid employment at the Grip (Thomson in 1907, Carmichael and Lismer in 1911 and Jackson in 1912). Carmichael, Thomson and Johnston followed the company's art director, Albert H. Robson, to Rous and Mann in 1912, and they were probably joined by Varley (on Lismer's encouragement, through connections to Sheffield and the Académie Royal des Beaux-Arts in Antwerp). The work at these two firms had multiple consequences. It facilitated communications and the initial efforts at joint painting ventures, as well as discussion of novel artistic endeavours. Also, while the employment had the salutary effect of providing living incomes, it also limited the amount of time they could dedicate to independent activities. In fact, MacDonald himself chose, in early 1911, (Duval 1978: 24) not to join Rous and Mann, but tried, for a period, to work freelance to increase his own time for painting. Work as commercial artists left a clear imprint on the artistic endeavours of the Group members. In particular, design was an abiding concern in the Group's painting (Stacey and Bishop, 1996). In part, this imposed a constraint on the efforts to break with realist traditions in Canadian landscape painting, but it was a constraint which meshed with the expectations of the external audience. As Arthur Robson put it, the "most modern of our Canadian landscape painters have retained a sanity of viewpoint and a sincerity of purpose that entirely precludes them from the accusation of 'Modernists' in the Continental sense" (1932: 12).

The second crucial setting for the Group was the Studio Building in 1913, at 25 Severn Street in Toronto's Rosedale Ravine, near Bloor and Yonge. The building was largely funded by Harris (Murray and Fulford, 1982: 11), with some support from an acerbic, but important supporter, Dr James MacCallum, who many of them met through an important ancillary Toronto organization, the Arts and Letters Club.[7] The Studio Building gave the Group an important physical base during its formative years, as well as some modest legitimacy in the world of serious culture.[8] The Studio Building also serves as the basis for the serious exchange of ideas and encouragement. Thomson, for example, as one of the individuals with less formal schooling and training, received news about important new trends in French art, both impressionist and post-impressionist, from Jackson. In particular, Thomson benefited from discussions of controlled brush work, more striking use of colours, and the effectiveness of flatter picture planes (Murray, 1998: 75-76).

The Group of Seven as an Aesthetic Project[9]

The Group's artistic work is usually regarded an experiment in Anglo-Canadian cultural nationalism which emphasizes the centrality of the rugged, unpopulated "north" in defining Canadian identity. While it must be acknowledged that the group subsequently expanded its ambit from British Columbia to Atlantic Canada, the initial curiosity about the Group's approach is the plasticity of its conceptions of "north". The first ventures were primarily to places close to Toronto. Whether it is Thomson's journeys to Algonquin Park, group excursions to Georgian Bay or more extended journeys into the area of Algoma, the original efforts were based on rural areas in reasonable proximity to Toronto. While it is true that these places, given the transportation and amenities available in the first four decades of the century, were indeed adventures in challenging, frequently unpopulated terrain, they were also modest expansions of geographic boundaries in a northerly direction.[10] Many of the best works by Group members involve venues which are easily within reach today. What this pattern suggests is the prospect that the "true north" becomes more northerly, but only gradually, and in such modest ways, that one must recognize a mythological dimension to the Group's bleak, challenging portrayal of Canadian nature. As Rob Shields puts it, in a more general context, what is at stake here is a "southern image of the north".[11]

A second spatial dimension in the Group's aesthetic project is the deliberate way in which it went about expanding its boundaries in both easterly and westerly directions. The recruitment of A. Y. Jackson was intended, in part, to bring Montreal and Quebec into the fold. The later addition of Edwin Holgate was meant to add to this strength, and LeMoine Fitzgerald's induction was partially guided by a desire to include like-minded work from western Canada. Further, members of the Group, both during the 1920s and after, expanded their own travels to further the image of an inclusive project. Both the First World War and separate trips associated with personal commitments, added the Maritimes to the Group's focus by the 1920s, and later travel by Harris, MacDonald and Varley added northwestern Ontario, the Rockies and British Columbia to frequently-treated subjects in their collective work. In all instances, the additions were intended to emphasize both spatial expression on an east-west axis, as well as the more unifying theme concerned with the portrayal of Canada's fundamentally northern heritage.

At the same time, it should be recognized that the Group, as were many Canadians early in the century, were uniformly committed to an integrated federal experiment. For example, Duval (1978: 143) describes MacDonald as a passionate believer in a united Canada, an individual for whom any idea of separatism would have been abhorrent, as it would have been to any other member of the Group of Seven. The Group's members, several experienced war painters among them, were neither naive nor sentimental. Rather, they reflected the optimistic mood of the times, a mood we now judge more harshly than they would appreciate.[12]

There remains considerable uncertainty about properly characterizing the aesthetic allegiances and qualities of the Group. There is some consensus about the "modernist" credentials which much infuriated their traditional (and semi-colonial) rivals and critics, particularly in Montreal.[13] However, the problem of a more precise definition is difficult, both due to the range of the Group's works and the obscurity of historical linkages. While aware of European impressionist, post-impressionist and expressionist developments, as well as Scandinavian landscape work of the period, the fairest characterization of their innovative adaptations of external influences may be to suggest that they represent a delayed, embattled introduction of some impressionist principles[14] to Canadian culture. Given the unrelenting hostility of established and establishment-oriented painters, primarily in Montreal, as well as unschooled (and probably anti-intellectual) newspaper criticism, the Group was effectively limited to modest experiments in light, colour and non-figurative art.[15] Robson states, "The 'Modern' Canadian painting might be analysed as having a strong decorative tendency, a desire to summarize and eliminate detail, and a search for the elemental facts and underlying truths of characterization. This single formula cannot by any stretch of the imagination be considered 'extreme'"(1932: 12-13).[16]

Further, there was some tension within the Group, even at the height of its activities in the 1920s, regarding the desirability of making a clearer transition to abstract painting. Johnston left the Group in 1924, in part due to his disagreements with even the mild impressionistic experiments represented by the Group's work. On the other side, Varley, and especially Harris, were already providing indications of moving towards a stronger expressionist stance. Carmichael, Jackson, Lismer and MacDonald remained in the centre, even in the post-Group phases of their efforts.[17] MacDonald posed the dilemma well in a 1929 talk. While firmly committed to what he referred to as a "poetic feeling" as the fulcrum between visual perception and "painterly sensibility", he also spoke disapprovingly of "the modern tendency [in painting] . . . to shun all poetic feeling, in a search for a cold geometry of pattern, a leaden quality of volume, and a mystery of significant form" (Whiteman, 1995: 13).

Figure 14.1   A. Y. Jackson, *The Edge of the Maple Wood*, 1910.   By permission of the National Gallery of Canada

We may examine the general progression of the Group's work through a series of paintings that are reasonably representative of their aesthetic and geographic scope. The first picture, A. Y. Jackson's *The Edge of the Maple Wood* (1910), served as a catalyst for Group efforts. Group members, on discovering the work of a then-unknown Montreal painter in an Ontario exhibition (the Ontario Society of Artists in 1911), regarded it simultaneously as confirmation of their fledgling efforts, and as the basis for a broader communication network. Murray (1998: 47) comments that the springtime frame "has the feel of a real Canadian season . . . . The landscape was wet and sodden, and sap pails hung on the maple trees. The final effort, they felt, was natural, simple and unpretentious. It suited their own unvarnished personalities and preferences, both in art and life". MacDonald, on behalf of Harris, contacted Jackson to find out if Jackson was prepared to sell the painting (first shown in Toronto in 1912 at the Ontario Society of Artists Exhibition), to Harris. The exchange around the painting, which is a fine example of the impressionist influences then operating in Jackson's life, created a link which later helped facilitate the formal creation of the Group.[18]

Figure 14.2   J. E. H. MacDonald, *Tracks and Traffic*, 1912.   By permission of the Art Gallery of Ontario

The second painting, J. E. H. MacDonald's *Tracks and Traffic* (1912) is, according to Mellen (1970: 28), his first and most significant "Impressionist canvas". In keeping with the obvious parallels to Turner and Monet, MacDonald employs a Toronto industrial site (one of the relatively few the Group did) to compose a careful, successful integration of different shades of light emanating respectively from gas storage tanks, railway tracks and snow. Both this painting, and the preceding one, give evidence of the significance of new European influences in Canadian painting, and of the prospect that these changes might stimulate a distinctive new school of Canadian landscape painting.

The third painting, MacDonald's *The Tangled Garden* (1916), joined the public battle over the acceptability of these new artistic trends at the Ontario Society of Arts Exhibition that year. The painting, not unlike some of Monet's own garden compositions, provides a lush portrayal of the sunflowers and trees which populated MacDonald's backyard. However, the painting's public presentation earned the ire of the important, but unsympathetic Saturday Night

Figure 14.3   J. E. H. MacDonald, *The Tangled Garden*, 1916.   By permission of the National Gallery of Canada

critic, Hector Charlesworth. Charlesworth condemned the painting for the "crudity of its colours"; MacDonald responded in spirited defence that this, and other, similar paintings were intended to demonstrate "the spirit of our native land" (Newlands, 1995: 34).[19]

The next canvas, one of Tom Thomson's---*The West Wind* (1917)---is one of the classic Canadian paintings. As the "portrait" of a pine tree, it has become, as Town (Town and Silcox, 1977: 174) describes it, "our emblem tree, our token tree". In typical Canadian fashion, it uses muted colours to suggest the human accessibility of our natural surroundings. Ours may be a rough, frequently harsh environment, something Thomson's vigorous brushwork emphasizes, but it is ultimately one we can come to terms with.[20] At a technical level, Thomson's innovative post-impressionist use of complementary colours, especially green and red, creates work which, according to Murray (1998: 79), has a "hallucinatory quality".

Figure 14.4   Tom Thomson, *The West Wind,* 1917.   By permission of the Art Gallery of Ontario

Fred Varley's stunning *For What?* (1918) is one of the great paintings to emerge from the First World War. Working as a memorial painter for the Canadian government in Europe, Varley, who viewed himself more as a portrait than a landscape painter, nevertheless managed to capture "the mood . . . of hopelessness and despair" which pervaded the European theatre at the end of the first period of slaughter (C. Varley, 1981: 44). This painting, which employs some of the general Group approaches to composition, is one of a set he did which clearly belies any efforts to romanticize the Group's aims or activities. As Christopher Varley puts it, in decidedly modernist terms, the sky above the soldier from the burial detail "literally weeps" (181: 44).

Arthur Lismer's *A September Gale, Georgian Bay* (1921) is typical of the early postwar efforts from the Group's members. Using methods similar to Thomson's, Lismer brings the viewer close to the waterline to experience the storm's impact. However, unlike Thomson, Lismer captures the force of the wind and storm through more careful delineation of the waves, trees and rocks. The power nature is capable of unleashing on the unwary is a constant feature of our existence.

Figure 14.5   Fred Varley, *For What?*, 1918.   By permission of the Canadian War Museum

Figure 14.6 **Arthur Lismer, *A September Gale, Georgian Bay,* 1921. By permission of the National Gallery of Canada**

The geographic range and aesthetic ambitions of the Group are best represented in two of Lawren Harris's works. His well-known *North Shore, Lake Superior* (1926) takes the Group further into northwestern Ontario, and it portrays the rugged landscape of the area in ways which are designed to impress one with the grandeur of the setting. It also raises the prospect that even such challenging surroundings can be integrated into the larger cosmos, as the pine stump reaches for the sun and the heavens. Sydney Key, a curator of one of Harris's exhibitions, argues that Harris "went further in applying the new rules with unyielding discipline and in rejecting the disturbing humanitarianism of the eastern pictures, in favour of detailed, firm statements of law and order" (Art Gallery of Toronto, 1948: 31).[21] Harris's ventures to the Rockies, however, were even more central to his philosophical goals, and *Maligne Lake, Jasper Park* (1924) demonstrates some of the parallels in Harris's techniques and perspectives. The plainness of the drawing, the

Figure 14.7   Lawren Harris, *North Shore, Lake Superior,* c. 1926.   By permission of the National Gallery of Canada

stillness of the lake, give evidence of the way Harris's reverence for nature shaped his painting of it. Larisey comments, "Only totally still water will mirror its surroundings so perfectly. The contours and surface of the mountains have been simplified and smoothed out, achieving a monumentality of proportion . . ." (1993: 101).[22]

Two of A. Y. Jackson's paintings from the later 1920s---*Barns* (1926) and *The Beothic at Bache Post, Ellesmere Island* (1927) extend the Group's interests and coverage eastwards and northwards. *Barns* (1926) is typical of the work which predominates in Jackson's overall collection, work done largely in rural Quebec.[23] *The Beothic* (1927), although not his best (Mellen, 1970: 174), does provide evidence of the optimistic, exploration-oriented attitudes which pervaded the Group at this point in Canadian history.[24] Jackson maintained an ongoing concern for the further reaches of Canadian dominion, echoing the nationalistic themes of his early years in his

Figure 14.8   Lawren Harris, *Maligne Lake, Jasper Park*, c. 1924-25. By permission of the National Gallery of Canada

autobiographical assertion that if "a Canadian wishes to visit the Canadian Arctic, he has to get permission from Washington" (1958: 111).

There remains, nevertheless, uncertainty about sources of inspiration, and other influences. For example, Duval is quite certain that MacDonald had the opportunity to study Turner's work in London, but the prospect of having seen the French impressionists is left in doubt (Duval 1978: 31). This particular question has salience, like others, because one of MacDonald's paintings discussed above, *Trucks and Traffic* (1912), bears a striking resemblance to Monet's masterpiece of the Gare St Lazare, Paris.[25]

Discussion

The Group of Seven continues to occupy an important position in debates

275

about Canadian cultural identity. A good part of their continuing relevance is based on their ability to draw visions of marginal areas into an attempt to establish links to an evanescent Canadian centre. In the process of undertaking this project, the Group's key members also, and perhaps unintentionally, demonstrated the malleable conceptions of northerliness which inhere in their work, and provide some evidence of the regionally-variable approaches to integration. As Shield points out, we may be able to define "the north" in reasonably unambiguous terms; nevertheless "the north" is less a real region than it is a cultural context with "historically-variable, socially-defined content" (1991: 194). Further, the Group's work draws attention to the fact that the great majority of Canada's population is clustered in urban centres along narrow geographic band close the U.S. border. We remain fascinated with our northerly extensions, and occasionally visit them, but home remains firmly in the south.

Figure 14.9   A. Y. Jackson, *Barns*, c. 1926.   By Permission of the Art Gallery of Ontario

276

Figure 14.10   A. Y. Jackson, *The "Beothic" at Bache Post, Ellesmere Island,* 1929. By permission of the National Gallery of Canada

There are a number of criticisms, more and less defensible, of the Group's work.   It is true that the primary focus on unexploited natural areas can generate an unduly romantic view of our interests in more northerly areas (Whiteman, 1995: 8).   We are every bit as concerned to derive economic benefit from the natural resources of northern regions as we are in the economic conditions in our southern cities.   Indeed, it is possible the "unspoiled nature" of the Group's painting is simply the mirror image of "industrial despoliation" which is rationalized by the very separateness of nature from humanity (Bermingham, 1986: 155).

However, we must also put the Group's work in historical context.   As early-century optimists, the Group's members may well have objected to some of the more exploitative uses to which we have put northern resources and the many aboriginal peoples who live there.   Certainly, in the context of these times, Harris's paintings in Cape Breton leave little room to doubt his disapproval of the social depredation of industrial exploitation in this area. Hill describes Harris's painting *Miners' Houses, Glace Bay* as "a social tract done in paint" (1995: 198).[26] On the other hand, one cannot ignore the extent to which Group members overlooked the clear evidence of industrial re-configuration of the rural landscapes they so admired. In a detailed analysis of the Group's activities in the Algoma region of Ontario from 1918 to 1920, Fletcher (1989) demonstrates that the area was a major new site of industrial development for mining and smelting, pulp and paper, and energy projects. Harris, Jackson, Johnston and MacDonald, all of whom worked in the region, passed by many of these sites in their "boxcar" trips, and chose for various reasons, to concentrate on landscape painting.

Figure 14.11   The Group of Seven at the Arts and Letters Club, Toronto, c. 1920. By permission of the McMichael Canadian Art Collection

An associated problem with the Group's work is its urban bias. These landscapes are very much perspectives from the larger cities, particularly Toronto. This difficulty manifested itself in a willingness to overlook the ways in which lumbering companies were reshaping, often for the worse, the relatively pristine milieux in which they chose to sketch (Tippett, 1998: 23, 67, 72, 78, 167). There is also a class dimension to this urban bias (Cole, 1978). Middle and upper class residents from urban areas like Toronto were more likely to have the resources necessary to explore rural areas, and to establish summer residences away from the rougher dimensions of urban occupations and life.

More to the point, there is little doubt that the Group's work was, with a few, notable exceptions, a resolute celebration of masculine virility, and the requirement of manly strength to cope with the rigours of northerly climates. The Group's most formidable critic, Hector Charlesworth, correctly identified a (masculine) tendency to overemphasize "the most sinister aspects of the Canadian wilds", at the expense of the more poetic approach Charlesworth favoured (Walton,1992: 98).[27] Speaking more directly to social themes, Joan Murray comments that the Group was "essentially a grown-up boys' club. The boyish atmosphere extended to the kind of paintings the Group produced. They are full of boys'-story searches for a site, in a manner less like Monet's constant quest for motif, than like the Hardy boys' adventures" (Murray, 1993: 7).[28] While one can again note the Group's members were typical of their generation, as part of a tradition that thrived for at least another forty years, their work is definitely limited in contemporary terms.

Finally, we need to appreciate the extent to which the Group's landscape is a part of the "political and ideological processes" of the day. At the same time the Group was valiantly, and successfully, elaborating a viable conception of Canadian independence, it did so in a social context limited by social, ethnic and financial boundaries which placed firm limits on the degree of aesthetic innovation or radicalism they could present. If we follow Zukin's felicitous notion of "landscapes of power" (1995: 16), the Group was indeed affected by the way powerful institutions inscribe their fundamental ideas about gender, social class and ethnicity in their depictions of landscape.

And, as discussed above, there is a temporal dimension to the architecture of power. We know power constellations shift, new ones energizing, old ones declining. These broader societal changes also have various, complex relations to the worlds of art. In our case, as Canada moves towards a new century, there is a clearer conception that the hold of the centre is slipping. Canada's self-proclaimed "national" newspaper, the Toronto *Globe and Mail*, a paper firmly committed to projects of economic integration with the United States, now challenges the Group's contributions. In a recent article header on a retrospective for A. J. Casson, who replaced Frank Johnston in the original

279

Group, the *Globe and Mail* claims, "When it comes to Canadian icons, the Group of Seven painters are right up there with hockey and maple syrup. But they weren't very innovative and hardly anyone outside Canada knows them". Blake Goprik, the paper's visual arts critic continues, in the same article: "In the international scheme of things, these painters weren't original or innovative outside of Canada, they're plain unknown . . . the Group didn't reflect Canadian identity: it built a nationalistic, restrictive myth about it" (November 21, 1998, C5). While the most immediate evidence come to us in political and economic forms, we also recognize that the cultural projects suited to the new context will be more diversified, and will be organized on a more decentralized basis.

We have much to learn from the Group of Seven, precisely because they were a courageous, progressive force with enduring accomplishments. However, the challenges and tasks are new; so must the cultural projects be.

Notes

[1] Janet Wolff neatly connects aesthetic concerns with the social sciences when she observes: ". . . the fact that it is an historically contingent matter that we have a separate aesthetic sphere or discourse of art in no way negates that sphere. The importance of the sociology of art, however, consists in its critique of the ideology of timelessness and value-freedom which characterizes art theory and art history in the modern world. It enables us to see that art always encodes values and ideology and that art criticism itself, though operating within a relatively autonomous discourse, is never innocent of the political and ideological processes in which that discourse has been constituted" (1981: 43).

[2] In 1926, A. J. Casson became a "new" seventh member of the Group; Edwin Holgate was accepted in 1929 and LeMoine Fitzgerald in 1932 (Hill, 1995: 195, 256, 270). Roger Buford Mason provides an interesting new defence of Johnston's 1924 departure, emphasizing Johnston's principled commitment to a "more traditional way" of painting, as well as his ongoing friendships with the Group's members (1998: 54, 68).

[3] Harris's independent wealth complicates the analysis. His financial resources were certainly crucial to the Group's material well-being. However, it may be argued that MacDonald was a source of earlier, more enduring creative guidance for the group.

[4] There were eight joint Canadian Exhibitions in May, 1920; May, 1921; May, 1922; January, 1925; May, 1926; February, 1928; April, 1930 and December, 1931, as well as the crucial April, 1924 British Empire Exhibition in Wembley, which ironically established their Canadian reputation (Hill, 199: 89, 96, 105, 142, 155, 179, 208, 261,

280

268). The Group effectively ceased operation in 1933 when its members merged into a broader "Canadian Group of Painters" (Hill, 1995: 281).

[5] Duval reports (1978: 85) two important "boxcar" trips to Algoma in September, 1918 and September, 1919. In both instances, Harris financed the expeditions. McLeish (1973: 71) lists five separate trips, extending to 1925.

[6] McLeish states that Grip "obtained its curious name from the pseudonym of a well-known Toronto cartoonist, named Bengough" (1973: 24).

[7] The creation of the Studio building and the collective move to Rous and Mann (for commercial reasons) "decimated" the Grip operation (McLeish, 1973: 27-28).

[8] Generating income was a perennial problem for all members of the Group save Harris. There was no credible market for the Group's work, even its key paintings, until the 1950s (Hill, 1995: 224). Hill estimates that MacDonald sold "barely 30" of his works over a twenty-five year period (Hill, 1995: 289).

[9] T. J. Clark (1973: 11) makes this point forcefully:". . . it is actually a strength of social art history that it makes its analogies specific and overt . . . . [F]lirting with hidden analogies is worse than working openly with inelegant ones, precisely because the latter can be criticized directly".

[10] The Group's interest in utilizing nature and the north as a focus, received a powerful impetus when Harris and MacDonald, as the Group's informal leaders, found impressive parallels to their work and interests in a 1913 exhibition of Scandinavian painting, much of its landscape painting, in Buffalo, New York (Duval, 1978: 47).

[11] It is true that Harris, and especially Jackson, took trips much further north to Baffin Island in the 1930s, and made several notable contributions which augment our conception of "northerliness". Nevertheless, this work comes late in the Group's existence, or after it.

[12] Even the most ethereal of the Group, Lawren Harris, who was much taken with theosophy and other spiritual matters (Lacombe, 1982), enlisted during the First World War, and had a brother killed in the war. Hill (1995: 15) comments, "In the 1920s, in praising T. S. Eliot' s *The Wasteland*, Harris recognized the 'disillusioned, fearless and penetrating vision of the true modern . . .'".

[13] With the significant qualification that their works leaned to the more conservative end of the modernist spectrum.

[14] Robson makes an important qualification when he states: "The ultimate in design becomes pattern and the general tendency in the work of the Group is a movement in the direction of the simplification of masses and a careful organization of these forms into a decorative arrangement . . . It is obvious that this viewpoint carries them definitely away from the subtle atmospheric efforts of the Impressionists . . ." (1932:

160).

¹⁵ Tippett (1998: 123) comments, "Though considered too modern by some commentators, they were conservative compared to the European avant-garde who did not feel compelled to communicate with the general public or to maintain contact in their work with the visible world". Tippett (1990: 83-85) elaborates this point in some of her earlier writing.

¹⁶ Thom also notes, in a volume on Lismer's fine cartoons: "Lismer was not the Goya or Daumier who would provide a needed 'national cleansing'; his spirit was too gentle for that. Indeed, he doubted that 'Canadians could take' such satire" (1985: 16).

¹⁷ Thomson represented the intense cutting edge of the Group's simultaneous commitment to design and experimentation.

¹⁸ Lismer reports his reaction to this painting: "I can remember this one canvas. It stood out among the usual pictorial array of collie dogs, peonies and official portraits like a glowing flame with potential energy and loveliness. I can remember looking at it with MacDonald, Thomson and Harris, and talking enthusiastically about its quality" (McLeish, 1973: 44).

¹⁹ McLeish describes the "uproar" as "producing a stream of abusive attack . . . MacDonald could be almost as vivid and facile with the pen as with the brush, and he traded blow for blow in an extended debate that used up columns of space in the Toronto Star, the Globe, and the Mail and Empire . . ." (1973: 70).

²⁰ I have chosen to include Thomson in this discussion because his work was directly connected to Group development in this, the last year of his life.

²¹ One of the ironies about the Group's work in northwestern Ontario is the fact that its bleakness was "enhanced" by prior human habitation, and associated forestry activities, including fire (Art Gallery of Ontario, 1945: 10; Larisey, 1993: 89).

²² Robson adds, "[T]his interest in spatial relationships, this freer use of imaginative form, and the stressing of rhythmic order, is pushing his work further and further from realism" (1932: 154).

²³ Graves (1968: 42) states, "More than any other single Canadian artist during the quarter-century from 1920 on, it has been A. Y. Jackson who has created the image of rural winter-time Quebec".

²⁴ Graves (1968: 2) acknowledges Jackson's role in pushing actual northern boundaries furthest: "the Bache Peninsula is on the Akane Basin Coast of Ellesmere Island, Canada's most northerly territory, westward from the top of Greenland". The canvas which was based on the drawing "seems to have been reproduced more often than any other work" by Jackson.

[25] In his later work, Harris (1954) moved beyond "non-objective" to "non-representational" art, endorsing the basic principles of abstract expressionism. Town also claims that, had he survived, Thomson would have moved into some form of "non-figurative" art, like abstract expressionism (Town and Siliox, 1977: 30).

[26] Rick Kardonne, in an article on social realism in nineteenth-century Dutch painting, also notes that "only one artist anywhere outside Holland dealt unambiguously with social-economic issues in the early 20th century: the Canadian Lawren Harris. His *Black Court Halifax* (1921) was probably the very first visual portrayal anywhere of the misery of an Afro-North American slum ghetto" (*National Post*, November 4, 1998, B6-B7).

[27] Charlesworth's own modest credentials as a journalist made him as underqualified as most media critics in the fine arts. Charlesworth's more fanciful associations of the Group of Seven members with Futurism, as an art movement, and with political radicalism in Ontario, clearly missed the mark. His own attachment to prewar agrarian mythology and a gentler form of modernism, were both decidedly ideological. Walton (1990) more accurately identifies an "extractionist myth" which motivated the Group's work. "In contrast to agrarianism, it celebrated the wilderness areas of North America as a limitless treasure house of raw materials that had previously been inaccessible. Now they could be discovered and violently extracted from the land by means of modern science and technology without significant damage to a vast and supposedly desolate environment" (Walton, 1990: 175).

[28] Murray addresses the sexual connotations of the Group's work even more directly, focusing somewhat surprisingly on Thomson and Harris (Murray, 1993: 14, 21).

References

Adamson, Jeremy. 1978. *Lawren S. Harris: Urban Scenes and Wilderness Landscapes*. Toronto: Art Gallery of Ontario.

Art Gallery of Toronto. 1948. *Lawren Harris: Paintings 1910-1948*. Ottawa: National Gallery of Canada.

Becker, Howard. 1982. *Art Worlds*. Berkeley: University of California Press.

Bermingham, Ann. 1986. *Landscapes and Ideology: The English Rustic Tradition, 1740-1860*. Berkeley: University of California Press.

Bice, Megan. 1990. *Light and Shadow: The Work of Franklin Carmichael*. Toronto: McMichael Canadian Art Collection.

Blodgett, Jean, Megan Bice, David Wiston and Lee-Ann Martin. 1989. *The*

McMichael Canadian Art Collection. Toronto: McGraw-Hill Ryerson.

Clark, T. J. 1973. *Image of the People: Gustave Courbet and the Second French Republic 1848-1851*. Greenwich, Connecticut: New York Graphic Society.

_____. 1984. *The Painting of Modern Life: Paris in the Art of Manet and His Followers*. New York: Knopf.

Cole, Douglas. 1978. Artists, Patrons and Public: An Enquiry into the Success of the Group of Seven. *Journal of Canadian Studies* 13: 69-78.

Davies, Blodwen. 1967. *Tom Thomson: The Story of a Man Who Looked for Beauty and Truth in the Wilderness*. Revised memorial edition. Vancouver: Mitchell.

Davis, Anne. 1974. *An Apprehended Vision: The Philosophy of The Group of Seven*. Unpublished Ph.D. thesis. Toronto: History Department. York University.

Duval, Paul. 1951. *Alfred Joseph Casson. President. Royal Canadian Academy*. Toronto: Ryerson.

_____. 1978. *The Tangled Garden: The Art of J. E. H. MacDonald*. Scarborough, Ontario: Cerebrus.

Firestone, O. J. 1979. *The Other A. Y. Jackson: A Memoir*. Toronto: McClelland and Stewart.

Fletcher, Allan. 1989. *Industrial Algoma and the Myth of Wilderness: Algoma Landscapes and the Emergence of the Group of Seven, 1918-1920*. Unpublished M. A. thesis. Vancouver: University of British Columbia.

Goffman, Erving. 1959. *The Presentation of Self in Everyday Life*. Garden City, New York: Doubleday Anchor.

Groves, Naomi Jackson. 1968. *A. Y.'s Canada: Drawings by A. Y. Jackson*. Toronto and Vancouver: Clarke, Irwin.

_____. 1988. *One Summer in Quebec. A. Y. Jackson in 1925: A Family View*. Kapuskasing, Ontario: Penumbra.

Harris, Bess, and R. G. P. Colgrove (eds.). 1969. *Lawren Harris*. Toronto: MacMillan.

Harris, Lawren. 1950. *Arthur Lismer: Paintings 1913-1949*. Toronto: The Art Gallery of Toronto.

_____. 1954. *A Disquisition on Abstract Painting*. Toronto: Rous and Mann.

_____. 1964. *The Story of the Group of Seven*. Toronto: Rous and Mann.

The Group of Seven

Harrison, Charles. 1997. *Modernism.* Cambridge: Cambridge University Press.

Hauser, Arnold. 1957. *The Social History of Art.* Volume Four: Naturalism, Impressionism, The Film Age. New York: Vintage.

Hill, Charles C. 1995. *The Group of Seven: Art for a Nation.* Toronto: National Gallery of Canada.

Housser, F. B. 1926. *A Canadian Art Movement: The Story of the Group of Seven.* Toronto: Macmillan.

Hunkin, Harry. 1976. *A Story of the Group of Seven.* Toronto: McGraw-Hill Ryerson.

Jackson, A. Y. 1958. *A Painter's Country: The Autobiography of A. Y. Jackson.* Toronto: Clark, Irwin.

Kelly, Gemey. 1982. *Arthur Lismer: Nova Scotia 1916-1919.* Halifax, Nova Scotia: Dalhousie Art Gallery, Dalhousie University.

Lacombe, Michele. 1982. Theosophy and the Canadian Idealist Tradition: A Preliminary Exploration. *Journal of Canadian Studies* 17: 100-118.

Larisey, Peter. 1993. *Light for a Cold Land. Lawren Harris's Work and Life: An Interpretation.* Toronto: Dundurn.

MacDonald, Thoreau. 1972. *The Group of Seven.* Toronto: McGraw-Hill Ryerson.

Martinsen, Hanna. 1984. The Scandinavian Impact on the Group of Seven's Vision of the Canadian Landscape. *Konsthistorisk Tidskrift* 13: 1-17.

Mason, Roger Burford. 1998. *A Grand Eye for Glory: A Life of Franz Johnston.* Toronto. Dundurn.

McGregor, Gaile. 1985. *The Wacousta Syndrome: Explorations in the Canadian Langscape.* Toronto: The University of Toronto Press.

McLeish, John A. B. 1973. *September Gale: A Study of Arthur Lismer and the Group of Seven.* Toronto: J. M. Dent.

Mellen, Peter. 1970. *The Group of Seven.* Toronto: McClelland and Stewart.

Murray, Joan. 1971. *The Art of Tom Thomson.* Toronto: Art Gallery of Ontario.

_____. 1973. *Impressionism in Canada 1895-1935.* Toronto: Art Gallery of Ontario.

_____. 1993. *The Best of the Group of Seven.* Toronto: McClelland and Stewart.

_____. 1998. *Tom Thomson: Design for a Canadian Hero.* Toronto:

Dundern.

Murray, Joan, and Robert Fulford. 1982. *The Beginning of Vision: Lawren S. Harris.* Toronto: Douglas and McIntyre.

National Film Board of Canada. 1995. *The Group of Seven. In Celebration; The Work of Group of Seven Artists A. Y. Jackson, Arthur Lismer and Frederick Varley.* Montreal.

Newlands, Anne. 1995. *The Group of Seven and Tom Thomson:An Introduction.* Willowdale, Ontario: Firefly.

Porter, John. 1965. *The Vertical Mosaic.* Toronto: University of Toronto Press.

Reid, Dennis. 1970. *Le Groupe des Sept/The Group of Seven.* Ottawa: The National Art Gallery of Canada.

_____. 1976. *Edwin H. Holgate.* Ottawa: The National Gallery of Canada.

_____. 1985. *Canadian Jungle: The Later Work of Arthur Lismer.* Toronto: Art Gallery of Ontario.

Rewald, John. 1973. *The History of Impressionism.* New York: The Museum of Modern Art.

Robson, Albert H. 1932. *Canadian Landscape Painters.* Toronto: The Ryerson Press.

_____. 1938. *A. Y. Jackson.* Toronto: The Ryerson Press.

_____. 1973. *J .E .H. MacDonald.* Toronto: The Ryerson Press.

Shields, Rob. 1991. *Places on the Margin: Alternative Geographies of Modernity.* London: Routledge.

Stacey, Robert and Hunter Bishop. 1996. *J. E. H. MacDonald---Designer: An Anthology of Graphic Design, Illustration and Lettering.* Guelph: Archives of Canadian Art.

Thom, Ian. 1985. *The Cartoons of Arthur Lismer: A New Angle on Canadian Art.* Toronto: Irwin.

Tippett, Maria. 1990. *Making Culture: English-Canadian Institutions and the Arts Before the Massey Commission.* Toronto: University of Toronto Press.

_____. 1998. *Stormy Weather: F.H. Varley, A Biography.* Toronto: McClelland and Stewart.

Town, Harold and David Silcox. 1977. *Tom Thomson: The Silence and the Storm.* Toronto: McClelland and Stewart.

Varley, Christopher. 1981. *F. H. Varley.* Edmonton: The Edmonton Art Gallery.

Varley, Peter. 1983. *Frederick H. Varley.* Toronto: Key Porter.

Walton, Paul H. 1990. The Group of Seven and Northern Development. *RACAR (Revue d'Art Canadienne/Canadian Art Review)* 17: 171-179.

_____. 1992. Beauty my Mistress: Hector Charlesworth as Art Critic. *The Journal of Canadian Art History* 15: 84-107.

Watson, Scott. 1991. Disfigured Nature: The Origins of the Modern Canadian Landscape. In Daina Augaistes and Helga Pakasaar (eds.), *Eye of Nature.* Banff, Alberta: Walter Phillips Gallery.

Whiteman, Bruce. 1995. *J. E. H. MacDonald.* Kingston: Quarry Press.

Wolff, Janet. 1981. *The Social Production of Art.* New York: St Martin's Press.

Zukin, Sharon. 1995. *Landscapes of Power: From Detroit to Disney World.* Berkeley: University of California Press.

287

CONCLUSION

15 New Directions in Community Development

REGINALD BYRON AND JOHN HUTSON

Rural livelihoods based upon the exploitation of natural resources---and the the settlement patterns that they sustain---have come under intense, continuing pressure in recent years. Environmental concerns, conservation measures, the reform of price supports, and other economic and demographic factors have combined to provoke questions about how these activities and communities can survive. Earlier volumes in the *North Atlantic Margin* series have explored a variety of issues in contemporary social and economic development. This volume, the fourth in the current series, has taken community development at its theme. These contributions attempt to understand the conditions which have adversely affected rural livelihoods, and the emerging alternatives to traditional forms of making a living in profoundly rural places. We evaluate the economic and social dynamics of farming, forestry, fishing and other kinds of self-employment and small-scale enterprise in the context of their contemporary economic and policy environments; and we analyse the efforts of individuals, community groups, private- and public-sector agencies and national- and supra-national institutions to maintain and develop economic opportunities for the people who live in these regions.

The Characteristics of Peripherality on the North Atlantic Margin

Limited Natural Resources

Characteristically, these regions have, or produce, few things that business enterprises located in the urban centres cannot obtain on the world market as cheaply or more cheaply: foodstuffs, timber, and minerals. The people who live in these regions are employed principally in primary activities: agriculture, fishing, and forestry; fewer are employed in processing, and fewer yet in services. The carrying capacity of the local economy in terms of the number of people these resources and activities can support is very limited; these are characteristically low value-added and low-return economic activities which support relatively few people.

Limited Human Resources

Because of the limited natural resources, the human population in these regions tends to be low in density, dispersed, static or declining in numbers, and ageing or disproportionately aged. Either there is a high rate of emigration or a standard of living that is low compared with metropolitan areas. A demand for higher levels of education for which no local opportunities requiring the appropriate skills exist will further erode the numbers of people remaining in the periphery, and may draw off the most talented of the younger generation.

Limited or Poor-quality Infrastructure

Characteristically, these regions suffer from a lack of infrastructural provision. Given a population of low density, there is little economic justification for investment in capital-intensive improvements such as roads, bridges, and hospitals. The lack of services, amenities and communications traps remote localities in a situation which impedes their development: initiatives requiring a certain level of infrastructure will not be attracted to areas which lack their requirements; but investment in infrastructural improvements is unlikely to happen unless development has already occurred.

Distance from Markets

Generally, the more remote the region, the more it is handicapped by its distance from the markets for its products. The higher transport costs involved in getting products to market may cancel out any advantage in labour costs or land values, if, like potatoes or wool, there is nothing special about the product. Specialised equipment and any commodities that cannot be produced locally, which may include nearly everything except potatoes and wool, needs to be imported at a transport premium, adding further to the marginal costs of production and depreciating the value of human labour to household incomes.

Unfavourable Weather

In northwest Europe and maritime Canada, cold and wet weather, frequent and unpredictable gales, and very short growing seasons set limits on many economic activities.

Lack of Political Leverage

In proportion to their geographical size, peripheral areas have small electorates. Typically, the national agenda in economic and social matters is dominated by issues relating only, or mainly, to urban regions. As territorially-expansive units with different kinds of problems, rural regions on the geographical margins have little political leverage when compared with metropolitan areas, unless special recognition is given to them.

Approaches to Rural Development

Since the Second World War, the countries on the North Atlantic margin have attempted to manage the economies of their peripheries in various ways. Four main strategies can be identified:

Central Direction

The national government defines certain regions or sectors as a problem to be solved or as a potential source of value to be harnessed to the national interest, and creates central agencies which it empowers to direct developments. A planned, comprehensive management strategy is characteristic. With varying degrees of public consultation (from a great deal to none at all), the state, through its agencies, decides upon the appropriate responses and implements them administratively. Through such mechanisms as planning permissions and financial incentives, private companies and entrepreneurs are encouraged to locate, to extract or process certain natural resources, to provide employment and contribute to the maintenance or growth of the local or regional economy; the state may also direct the establishment or relocation of public enterprises in designated growth centres providing both direct employment and trickle-down effects.

Selective or Indirect Universalism

The state and its agencies seek to foster regional balance, social equity and economic growth through a more-or-less ad hoc assemblage of piecemeal measures rather than through a planned, comprehensive strategy. Kick-start programmes of one kind or another are designed to provide the initial stimulus to developments which it is hoped will have beneficial effects, as are differential taxation rates or relocation allowances. Benefits are in principle available to any applicant who meets the objective criteria. Also common are enhanced national welfare provision and special treatment of certain classes of people, such as small farmers and fishers, by production and operating subsidies, income guarantees and cheap loans for housing and capital equipment. Infrastructural improvements to energy supplies, water and sanitation, transport, education and health may be provided on the grounds of regional equity where their economic cost cannot be justified. Frequently these programmes are administered by a variety of agencies at different levels of government: supra-national, national, regional, and municipal. The involvement of local people in consultative forums and feedback processes is variable, but generally sporadic and low. The degree of coordination between these agencies, and the overlaps, gaps, and contradictory requirements between their programmes is often a source of difficulty, leading to inter-agency friction and sometimes inhibiting the success of the programmes. From the rural resident's point of view, red tape, repeated form-filling and poor targeting of resources may be the dominant impression of this approach to regional development.

Negotiated Targeting

The characteristic structural form of this approach is the regional development agency which responds to the requests of client localities or individual entrepreneurs for especially-tailored advice, assistance or brokerage. This strategy allows for the fact that clients' circumstances and goals can differ greatly in different sectors, regions and localities. Thus the agency's style of operation is market-driven, but it is also interested creating a market for its services and engaging support for its charter objectives such as enhancing technical and organisational efficiency and supporting business start-up and expansion schemes which will lead to sustainable gains in economic growth. Resources are drawn in and focused upon particular problems. The measures are often selective forms of financial support linked to continuing practical assistance.

Community Initiatives

A variety of means of "empowering" local people to take charge of the economic development of their own communities have been attempted. A common form is the "integrated development programme" which assists local people to set their own agenda and cooperatively to pool their resources in pursuit of enhanced economic security. The underlying philosophy is that a community which has developed the organisational capacity actively to plan ahead has empowered itself, and is better able to cope with unforeseen circumstances as they arise. In some places, these schemes have been very successful where they have been sensitively introduced with appropriate monitoring and effective back-up by the sponsoring agency. But this approach has its limitations. Appropriate decision-making or leadership capacities may not exist: simply throwing the weight of responsibility for their own salvation onto a "community" which has no significant corporate institutions and upon people without the requisite technical skills and political leverage may achieve little, and risks leaving the locality worse off than before.

Current Trends

Most of the countries mentioned in this book have applied most of these strategies in a roughly sequential order, but the earlier policies and agencies have not necessarily been swept away as new fashions have come in; they may have simply been added. Postwar reconstruction in Europe tended to have strong state direction; many of the policies and agencies set up in the immediate aftermath of the war lasted into the 1980s and some continue into the present. The general trend since the 1970s has gradually moved away from the command and universalistic approaches to more focused strategies and to community-based initiatives.

The Papers in this Book

For over thirty years the International Seminar on Marginal Regions has discussed at its biannual meetings a wide range of theoretical and practical issues concerning the problems of, and appropriate strategies for the economic and social development of regions on the North Atlantic margin. It has promoted inter-disciplinary perspectives on problems across many sectors, and has emphasised the need for inter-regional and inter-temporal analyses, fine-grained local field studies, and participative planning and development strategies that are attuned to local conditions.

This book is organised around four themes: the first set of papers explores new perspectives on community development; the second set considers the changing fortunes of farming and fishing and other natural resource-based industries in the economies of marginal regions; the third set examines the resources and constraints in community development; and the final set addresses comparative perspectives on marginality and regionality.

Current Perspectives on Community Development

In Part One, two papers discuss new ways of seeing community development in marginal regions. In the first paper, Tim Jenkins and Nicholas Parrott outline some of the features characterising rural areas in Europe today---they are subject to forces of external control; they have a growing diversity of population, economies and lifestyles; and they themselves are increasingly packaged as consumable commodities. At the same time, rural development models have changed direction from narrow economic objectives to broader "holistic" concerns encouraging the participation of local people and institutions. Against this setting, the authors discuss the Welsh findings from an inter-disciplinary project which focused on the production and consumption of certain "quality products and services" (QPS) in 12 marginal regions in six countries. Drawing on a number of theoretical approaches, including actor-network theory, they show how patterns of production and consumption may be conceptualised as the outcomes of intersecting networks of particular producers, agencies, institutions and consumers. They argue that producers in marginal areas are able to target niche markets with quality products and services which maximise images of locality, tradition and authenticity. Despite being subject to international and national regulatory contexts as well as to the powers of multiple retailers, there are opportunities for local producers to meet the demands of increasingly discriminating and knowledgeable consumers. As they say, "Local processes are embedded in, and feed back into, global processes in a continual cycle of interaction".

In the second paper, Paul Olav Berg focuses on the vulnerability of peripheral regions to the effects of the reorganisation of the public sector that is currently taking place in Norway as well as in other OECD countries under policies of so-called New Public Management (NPM). These policies aim to make the public sector more cost-efficient by adopting private sector models of market competition on the assumption that more local autonomy will lead to greater efficiency. However, as increasing emphasis is put on short-term strategic gains, it looks as though democratic control and direction have been weakened. In the Post Office, remote rural services were subsidised from more profitable areas. Now this cross-subsidisation cannot occur and grants must be sought to support rural services. As telephone charges and petrol prices show, price cuts tend to be in central markets where competition is fiercest rather than in peripheral regions. This restructuring of the public sector may have serious negative consequences for peripheral regions and local communities. Political authorities must ensure that consideration of social and societal considerations is maintained.

The Changing Fortunes of Natural Resource-based Industries in the economies of Marginal Regions

In Part Two, four papers take a historical perspective on the responses of local producers and community members to the changing fortunes and policies of natural resource-based industries. In the first paper, Reginald Byron reflects with hindsight on the causes and effects of the 1967 crash in the Swedish herring fishery. He outlines the traditional form of joint patrimony by which fisher households accumulated capital gradually over the generations to renew equipment and boats. During the boom years, this system had been replaced by the purchase of brand-new boats through bank loans which were, however, secured by other fishermen with their boats. When catches fell, interest payments could not be met, the banks foreclosed and the productive base of the fishing industry collapsed like a house of cards. Before the government could intervene, two thirds of the Swedish North Sea fleet had gone. While some 3,000 men lost their livelihoods as fishermen, the fortuitous development of new industry and improved local transport infrastructure gave them access to new jobs, but resulted in a steady decline of coastal villages as sites of production. The stabilisation of the fishing industry was also begun with a strict licensing scheme and state loans available to finance smaller boats which employed as many men as the large trawlers but took fewer fish. A clear division has developed between the big herring fishermen and the rest whose fate hangs in the balance as they have to struggle with finance, increasing bureaucratic controls and lower fish stocks. Byron argues that the fishing crash completed the process of national modernisation, but while the socially anomalous fishermen have been turned into mainstream citizens, a unique culture associated with a traditional production-system which had developed over two centuries has been lost.

In the second paper, Jens Christian Hansen takes an actor-centred approach to look at not only how "actors with power" are involved in restructuring of communities, but how "actors without power", especially young people, influence the structure and future of their communities by the choices they make about education, jobs and lifestyle. He takes a historical perspective on five communities with natural resource-based economies in peripheral parts of Norway---three based on hydro-electric power and two on fishing. He outlines their histories of restructuring and looks at young people's decisions to stay or leave. By their choices at the intersections of paths of opportunity in education, work and lifestyle young actors without power also change the communities in which they grow up. Each community and each generation makes choices within local infrastructures, current policies and contemporary perceptions and evaluations of life at home and abroad.

A similar theme is addressed in the two papers on farming which both look at the choices made by farm families since the end of intensive agriculture began with the introduction of quotas on production in 1984. In the first, John Hutson looks at the effects of changing agricultural policies on the viability and forms of family farms over nearly almost twenty years in southwest Wales. He focuses on the way the form and content of family relationships are linked to relations of production and market forces in particular cultural and social settings. In the early 1980s agriculture was doing well and multigenerational families farmed expanding holdings. By the late 1990s over

297

half the farms were still run by the same families, but these were actively involved in a number of strategies to survive the farm crisis. Both economic growth and recession have differing economic impacts on farm businesses according to local infrastructure opportunities, the size of holding, type of farming, stage of farm and family cycles as well as individual life chances.

Alison McCleery focuses on ten French farm households in Normandy, which she has observed over ten years, as examples of how farming can adapt and survive. All are now pluriactive households combining two or more jobs, but they range along a "continuum from total disengagement from agriculture at one end, through partial disengagement, to agricultural specialisation and development at the other"; from retired couples to expanding farm businesses. The author discusses the personal pressures attached to different strategies of diversification and argues that "The development of a farm business represents a negotiated and evolving path carved out between the constraints imposed by structural-level policy change on the one hand and individual-level opportunities within a given farm household on the other".

Resources and Constraints in Community Development

In Part Three, six papers discuss resources and constraints in community development. In the first paper, Peter Sjøholt writes about the effects on employment of the practice of outsourcing where public authorities and large corporations purchase services from private providers. Drawing on a range of examples mainly from northwestern Europe, the author discusses theoretical issues of the reorganisation of production and shows that the effects are multifaceted and may be both positive and negative. The impact on overall employment in an area varies according to the structure, size and location of the local economy as well as the social environment. Small, one-company towns are most vulnerable to losses in overall employment as most outsourced jobs leak out into more centralised places. In more differentiated industries, outsourcing can mean more work to new local companies taking on the provision of services. Losses may also be greater where outsourcing affects higher level advanced services rather than those such as maintenance, cleaning and refuse collection.

In their paper on crafts producers on the Celtic fringe, Anne-Marie Sherwood, Nicholas Parrott and Tim Jenkins summarise the results of research on quality craft production in northwest Ireland and west Wales. They argue that with the increasing policy emphasis on diversification of the rural economy in a post-agricultural era, craft production may have a significant role to play in future development strategies in marginal areas. Crafts not only make a significant direct economic contribution, but foster local identity and cultural heritage. "Crafts producers are often in-migrants in search of more authentic and sustainable lifestyles in which quality of life and product tend to predominate." They tend to be small-scale, prepared to work for relatively low returns, do not seek to expand their businesses beyond a certain point and prefer to be home-based. "Crafts people are generally in sympathy with a small-business economy in which pools of local employment are created and local resources used for the clear benefit of local communities." Thus they do not fit the ideal supported by development agencies of large-scale or high-growth entrepreneurial enterprises which promise to deliver new waged or salaried jobs. This raises serious issues about the type of development appropriate to marginal regions and the role of non-economic factors in businesses, development and communities which need to be confronted by policy makers and developmental institutions.

In his paper on the economic impact of Welsh National Nature Reserves (NNRs), Michael Christie demonstrates that while they are designated to preserve and maintain wildlife and landscape, they also provide a significant source of income-generation in peripheral regions because they attract large numbers of visitors to remote and relatively deprived areas where they will spend money. Studying three reserves in Wales, he used multiplier analysis to measure the overall effects of such an "injection" of expenditure into local economies. Rounding up the findings to Wales as a whole, research suggests that a total income of £27 million and 5,000 FTE jobs are created in Wales as a result of NNR designations. Traditionally only considered in terms of their environmental benefits, NNR can clearly generate substantial income and employment benefits in remote rural areas.

In the next paper Jørgen Amdam discusses the history of planning in the rural commune and small town of Volda where there is still farmland near the centre ideal for building development, but where there is also reluctance to force land owners to sell. Most new development, therefore, has occurred on land on the valley sides. The author looks at a series of development plans and outlines the factors playing a part in their implementation or non-implementation. He concludes that overall plans work best on land on the periphery of the built up area while the in-filling of existing built-up areas is characterised by chance and piecemeal development since many parties have conflicting interests. The way forward is a strategy of negotiation and communication to find some compromise and common vision between these interests.

Susan Hutson and Stuart Jones report on a two-year evaluation of a self-build scheme in Wales run by a children's charity in which vulnerable young people built six two-bedroomed houses. The aim was for the young people, who were all disadvantaged socially in terms of education or lack of family support and employment, to build houses which they could rent, while learning significant skills and gaining qualifications in the process. In the event, the scheme overran significantly in terms of both time and money. Few of the builders obtained any formal qualifications and only three ever took up tenancies in the houses. The authors account for the apparent failures of the scheme in terms of a lack of fit between housing and labour markets, between mainstream training structures and the welfare system as well as the rather different agendas of housing, training and support agencies. These structural failures carry much more of the blame than do the young people whose attendance, behaviour and commitment tended to be blamed. It is easier to measure failure in material terms of time, cost, product, and diplomas; it is much harder to measure the social success of the project in terms of improving the self-esteem of the young self-builders and the positive ways in which the scheme changed the lives of many of the young people.

In the final paper in this section, Diarmuid Ó Cearbhaill and Tony Varley compare two Irish community development movements, one a community council movement dating from the 1930s and the other a community development co-operative dating from the 1960s. Their paper describes the varied factors which have lead to both these agencies facing problems of effectiveness and representativeness while struggling to survive despite the acceleration of community development activity in Ireland over the last decade. "In both cases increasing use is being made of the notion of partnership to develop new relationships with the state, but it remains to be seen whether these agencies can participate on equal terms with their statutory counterparts or whether they will be used and manipulated by the state as a means to its own ends."

Comparative Perspectives on Marginality and Regionality

In the final section, two papers take a historical view of rural change and the construction of national identity. The first paper is by Håvard Teigen, who evaluates continuity and change in two Norwegian municipalities over the last 100 years. Identifying four periods of social and economic transformation in rural Norway between 1850 and 2000, the author shows how while in many ways the communities have changed beyond recognition and there is greater dependence on world markets and on external institutional control, there are also significant continuities. Teigen stresses the tradition of "flexibility" which still dominates patterns of production and lifestyle in the economic dependence on natural resources, the globalised labour market, the pluriactivity of the same number of farm enterprises and women's continuing domestic and child care responsibilities.

In the final paper in the book, Richard Apostle considers the contribution of a set of painters, collectively know as the "Group of Seven", towards the construction of a distinctive Canadian national identity---something always rather vague in contrast to the US with its much more clearly defined core values. Early members of the Group worked as designers and commercial artists in Toronto and their "bleak, challenging portrayal of Canadian nature" painted in the surrounding regions represented a mythical image of "the north" for the vast majority of Canadians who lived in urban centres along the US border. The author discusses ten paintings and shows how while they are very much products of the social and political concerns and prejudices of their time, their contribution and continuing relevance today is their ability to bring home images of marginal regions to the Canadian centre. For most Canadians there is a continuing fascination with the wild north "but home remains firmly in the south".

Future Directions in Community Development

Richard Apostle's contribution, the last paper in this volume, points to something that is a crucial issue in community development: that is, how communities, and the livelihoods of people within them, are perceived from within and without and how these perceptions may change over time. What constitutes an image of the community, or "a problem" or an issue in community development depends on *where* the viewpoint is located among a range of possible viewpoints, and *when* the problem is perceived to occur and how it is related to broader societal, economic and cultural shifts. Most of the contributions to this book have taken a long view of community development, and have demonstrated the way in which longitudinal studies over periods of ten, twenty, thirty, or a hundred years can help us to understand the nature of the problem, and what its essential attributes are. The contextualisation of perspective, which is as much tied up with cultural and social differences as it is with insider and outsider perspectives, and with individual, local, regional, and global economic scales, reveals another set of the attributes of commmunity development problems that needs to be understood if policies intended to ameliorate them are to have reasonable prospects of succeeding.

An assessment of the future directions of community development would have to start with the observation that there has been too much stress on macroeconomic modelling, which in turn is driven by changing political fashions. "New Public Management" approaches, and outsourcing, among the recent trends in political economy mentioned in this book, together with the perennial temptation of governments to seek quick fixes that can show results (such as new private-sector industrial jobs) within the lifetime of a political party's hold on power while in office may produce headline success stories for the government's (or the agency's) spin doctors, but may be at the expense of the local communities these measures were ostensibly meant to help, if their

301

net effect is to make these communities the clients of governmental agencies and their politically-driven programmes, rather than genuinely empowering these communities to help themselves.

A prime example of this is the general lack of interest by development agencies in very small, part-time, and low-growth or no-growth enterprises, perhaps on a domestic scale, which may be significant strands in the pluriactive livelihoods of many people in peripheral places, and are far more important to the long-term health of local communities than a here-today-gone-tomorrow branch plant of a footloose international corporation. The predominant official approaches to rural development seem often to be guided by macroeconomic theory, and the idea that maintaining or creating livelihoods is the same thing as generating or sustaining "employment", and that "employment" consists of discrete, quantifiable waged or salaried jobs. The small-scale self-employed, particularly those whose main interest is to provide only for themselves and their families, are generally given short shrift by the agency, if this kind of economic activity figures in the agency's ethos at all. The domestic-scale operator is frequently either turned away, or discovers that the development agency is unwilling or unable to supply helpful business advice. This disinterest impairs the capacity of rural families to develop or maintain the means to sustain themselves through productive labour and to reproduce economic opportunities within the community to provide for the well-being of the next generation, a strategy which has guided the management of livelihoods in peripheral communities for centuries, but which does not appear to figure in the conventional, narrowly economic thinking that informs the approaches of most rural development agencies.

Genuinely new directions in community development, as the papers in this book have suggested, need to turn away from textbook theories and focus instead on the household and its interlinked social, cultural and economic attributes as the site of human agency, rather than hypostatised, reified, and de-personalised "communities" and "sectors". Households are about provisioning, and making ends meet; they are also, in rural places, of central importance in the passing on of viable, do-it-yourself ways of supporting a family to the next generation. While having some undoubted benefits, pressing industrial models of employment upon rural people has exposed them to greater risks and insecurities than urban people. In urban milieux, there is a greater range of alternative sources of employment. In the peripheral places, the failure of a single production system, upon which families have become wholly reliant, may not be capable of being compensated through their engagement in locally-available alternative production systems. Welfare dependency and out-migration have the potential to accelerate at a rate that is greater than would have been the case in a regime where households had the capacity to shift freely between a variety of types and combinations of part-time productive activity.

The contributions to this book have emphasized the need for local participation in development policy and strategy. Too often, however, local people are merely asked to "buy into" policies and programmes devised elsewhere by "experts" who have little knowledge of the locality or of rural livelihoods, on the basis of the latest fashions in political economy. What is presented as participation, frequently, is in reality merely a marketing exercise that sets out to persuade people that whatever has already been decided is good for them. If the initiative fails, there is a greater likelihood that the local people will be blamed than the authors or administrators of the development initiative. As the contributions also emphasize, the people in these places are not just economic agents pursuing purely material satisfactions, but are also social and cultural actors who have all sorts of attachments and aspirations which purely economic models cannot quantify: for complex personal reasons people may prefer to work at home, and to combine two or more unstable sources of part-time income rather than have a nine-to-five waged job even where such jobs are readily available, and young people do not always leave home and migrate to the cities because there are no jobs but because they want to fulfil themselves emotionally, socially, or culturally. The field of human activity in which community development efforts are located is a complex interaction of many forces which defy heavy-handed responses, politically-expedient short-cuts, sound-bite "solutions", and quick fixes. Effective community development efforts will demand research from a variety of disciplinary perspectives, nuanced understandings, and imaginative approaches, as the papers in this book have attempted to demonstrate.